Unskilled Labor for Development

A World Bank Research Publication

UNSKILLED LABOR
FOR DEVELOPMENT
Its Economic Cost

Orville John McDiarmid

PUBLISHED FOR THE WORLD BANK

THE JOHNS HOPKINS UNIVERSITY PRESS

BALTIMORE AND LONDON

Library of Congress Cataloging in Publication Data

McDiarmid, Orville John, 1909–
  Unskilled labor for development.
  Bibliography: p. 201.
  1. Underdeveloped areas—Wages. 2. Wages—Asia.
3. Unskilled labor. I. International Bank for Reconstruction
and Development. II. Title.
HD4967.M3   331.7'98'091724   76-47398
ISBN 0-8018-1938-5
ISBN 0-8018-1949-0 pbk.

Contents

Figures

Tables

Statistical Appendix B. Indonesia and Philippines

Currency Equivalents

Republic of China (Taiwan) new Taiwan dollar
1970: NT$40.10 = US$1
June 1974: NT$38.10 = US$1

1970: W316 = US$1
June 1974: W339 = US$1

Philippine peso
1967: ₱3.93 = US$1
1970: ₱6.48 = US$1
June 1974: ₱6.78 = US$1

Indonesian rupiah (major export rate)
1967: Rp176 = US$1[1]
1970: Rp340 = US$1[2]
June 1974: Rp374 = US$1[2]

1. Major import rate about one-third lower in dollar terms. □
2. Major import rate about 11 percent lower in dollar terms. □

Acknowledgments

This book uses empirical data to estimate the social costs, or, as I prefer to designate them, the economic costs to the economies of selected Far Eastern countries of using unskilled agricultural labor for purposes of economic development. Therefore my principal acknowledgments are to the authors who have formulated theoretical frameworks applicable to the economic appraisal of development projects. These authors are principally Ian M. D. Little and James A. Mirrlees who presented one approach and Partha Dasgupta, Amartya Sen, and Stephen Marglin who have viewed the problem in a related but formally distinct manner. Their works are cited in appropriate places. I am of course also indebted to the many other authors cited in the bibliography and text who have addressed problems related to the economic pricing of labor.

This study does not purport to be a manual for the economic analysis of projects. The recent publication by the World Bank of *Economic Analysis of Projects* by Lyn Squire and Herman G. van der Tak (Johns Hopkins University Press, 1975) deals with that broader problem. That book was not available when my own work was undertaken, but I have noted some of the main points of difference between the Squire–van der Tak approach and the one I have used. I am also indebted to Lyn Squire for helpful comments on an early draft of this book.

Although the field work I was able to devote to this study was limited, I received a great deal of assistance from the Ministry of Labor, the Census Bureau, and the Planning Board in each of the four countries I visited: Korea, the Republic of China (referred to in the text as Taiwan), the Philippines, and Indonesia. I also received assistance from officials of enterprises and institutions in the private sectors of those countries. My field survey was done in early 1973. Significant changes have occurred since then in the absolute values, but perhaps not in the relative values used in this book.

I am particularly grateful to two anonymous readers of my original draft for the many insights I obtained from their comments. John W. Sifton edited the final manuscript. Any errors of fact or in application of methodology are, of course, my responsibility.

Orville John McDiarmid

Unskilled Labor for Development

Introduction

THIS BOOK IS AN ATTEMPT to use empirical data, officially available or calculated by me, to estimate the shadow price (or, as I call it, the economic price) of unskilled agricultural labor in selected Far Eastern countries. It also explores certain other related problems and issues having to do with the labor markets in developing countries. The methodology used was suggested by the major works mentioned in the Acknowledgments above, but limited and modified by the data available. At the end of this introduction I summarize my findings and indicate the value which I place on this exercise.

What is the Economic Price of Labor?

The short but perhaps not too meaningful answer to this question is that the economic price of a particular worker is the total measurable impact on the economy, of which the worker is a part, of his employment in a particular occupation. This may but probably will not be accurately reflected in the money wage paid for his services. If his wage is not a true reflection of the cost to the economy of his employment, it is necessary to delve rather thoroughly into the circumstances surrounding his employment to arrive at a measure that will more accurately gauge his economic cost and therefore the way and the extent to which he and his fellows should be used in the development process. It may be that, as in this book, rather than measuring a worker's economic price in absolute terms, it is easier and more meaningful and accurate to determine the ratio between the economic price of the class of labor in question and other labor which is of similar skill but employed in a more competitive labor market. In such a market it may be concluded that the wage is a reasonably good reflection of the economic price.

Some broader applications of economic pricing as distinct from market pricing or valuation have been familiar in economic literature for quite some time. For example, some of the staunchest free-market economists of the neoclassical school explicitly recognized that a particular economic activity could result in a significant difference between the increment to private welfare and the increment to public or social welfare. A. C. Pigou illustrated the idea clearly.[1] One of Pigou's simpler examples was the divergence between the gain to a manufacturer and the gain to society as a whole when his production process belches noxious fumes on the adjacent community. If no tax or other penalty is charged the manufacturer for this environmental contamination, the net gain to the producer would clearly be greater than the net gain to the economy as a whole from the output involved. In economic terms the marginal social net product is less than its private counterpart, a point that is the economic underpinning of so much ecological concern these days.

Cases that present the opposite side of the coin, namely, where social values are greater than private ones, are rather less readily visualized. For example, no one has yet devised a factory emitting rain-making smoke in an arid region. But the whole assemblage of social and economic by-products such as skills, unpatented technological advances, and economies of scale for satellite or ancillary industries—labeled by economists positive externalities—yield net social or economic benefits that exceed the private marginal product obtained by the primary or initial producer.

The distinction between social and private advantage, now well understood in the commodity field, applies in a selective and not identical fashion to the rewards and costs of the factors of production, notably unskilled labor and investment capital. The main difference is that commodities usually involve only one production process, whereas with a factor such as unskilled labor alternative ways of employment must be considered. The main purpose of this book is to try to estimate the ratio of economic (or social) wages to market (or private) wages for unskilled agricultural labor in two developing countries, Taiwan and the Philippines, and to discuss the general conditions in the labor markets in those countries as well as in Korea and Indonesia.[2] I hope, of course, that the methodology may have wider application. The worker, unlike Pigou's factory, does not emit noxious fumes (unless he smokes cigarettes and this annoys his abstemious fellows). If the labor market is functioning with reasonable efficiency, the worker's wage should approximate his worth (private marginal product) to his employer; but it will not necessarily reflect the worker's worth to the society to which he belongs when that worth is measured by the effect on social welfare of his withdrawal from his present employment.

1. A. C. Pigou, *Economics of Welfare* (London: MacMillan Co., 1960), p. 184.□
2. Throughout this book the Republic of China is referred to as Taiwan; the Republic of Korea, or in popular usage South Korea, is referred to as Korea.□

In determining the major factors in the economic price of labor, opportunity cost, however ascertained, is a principal component. Two other factors to be considered are the effect of fresh employment on consumption compared with savings and investment, and the general economic consequences of the redistribution of income resulting from increased employment. It will of course be appreciated that the consequences of income redistribution can occur only if rather large numbers of workers are employed at higher incomes than they previously received.

As a concept in respectable economic literature, the opportunity cost of goods and services has now reached its eightieth birthday. It is therefore appropriate that it receive attention in economic planning and project appraisal. In the 1935 edition of the *Encyclopaedia of Social Science* (vol. 4) Jacob Viner defined the opportunity cost of producing commodity A as the amount of commodity B that might have been produced with the same expenditure of resources.[3] With respect to the factors of production, the opportunity cost of a particular type and grade of labor (applied to the production of some economic good or service) should be measured by what is forgone because it is not being applied to the best alternative use. But, having defined the concept (as it is still generally understood), Viner dismissed it rather summarily, stating that the usefulness of the idea in economic analysis depended on an assumption of homogeneity (in respect to marginal productivity) of the factors of production working in identical combinations in different industries. This condition is seldom encountered under real life conditions. Since the same assumption applies to any accurate comparison of the true productivity of factors, however valued, Viner's conclusion seems somewhat harsh. More to the point would be an observation that despite its conceptual clarity the quantification of the opportunity cost of a particular good or service must in large measure rely on subjective or nonmarket factors, and therefore different observers might come to widely differing conclusions.

The determination of the economic price of a particular good or service is to a great extent an art or at least a case for value judgment rather than precise statistical inference or calculation. At bottom it consists of taking observed market values or combinations of such values and adjusting them in the direction common sense indicates to reflect more nearly their significance to the economy rather than to the individual. It is not altogether surprising that these adjustments can be done in a number of different ways, using a number of different formulas to arrive at the same goal.

The other components of the economic price of labor will be discussed

---

3. The doctrine of opportunity cost appears to have been first given that name in an article by David I. Green, "Pain Cost and Opportunity Cost," *Quarterly Journal of Economics*, vol. 8 (1893–94), pp. 218–29. □

later in this introduction. At this point it is enough to say that the factors and circumstances that may make for differences between the private and public return from a particular production process apply in a similar but not identical manner to the difference between the private and public price of labor.

The Need for Economic Pricing of Labor

A generally acknowledged rule of economic development, irrespective of the socioeconomic system, is that the national objective should be to derive maximum economic welfare from the disposition of the scarce resources available. Unskilled agricultural labor is a most abundant resource in developing countries, and most development projects will draw upon this resource for both construction and operational purposes. Usually, however, the project designer has considerable leeway as to the proportions of labor, land, and capital to be used, and there is of course a wide range of choice among different projects serving the same economic objectives. In the presence of such choices it follows that the impact on the cost of using any factor of production can be measured either in straightforward financial terms by the prevailing wage or by the effect of such use on the economy as a whole. If the labor market is working efficiently, and particularly if labor is both fairly mobile and fully employed, the money wage is a preferable measure. The lack of these conditions, however, prompts the rather difficult task of estimating the economic wage. One of the main objectives in undertaking this study was to ascertain if there exists any compelling need to put an economic price on labor in Korea, Taiwan, and the Philippines.[4] The prospects for a useful study of the question in Indonesia, the fourth Far Eastern country considered here, were less favorable for reasons that will become apparent in chapter 6.

This somewhat skeptical point of view reflects certain reservations regarding the accuracy possible in the socioeconomic pricing process. A closer examination of the facts in two of the countries studied led to the conclusion that it would be worthwhile to attempt to put an economic val-

---

4. The selection of the term "economic" rather than "accounting" or the much used "shadow" as the word for the social (as distinct from the market) price of labor is esthetic rather than substantive. I use the familiar letters SWR (shadow wage rate) for economic price of labor, largely because their meaning is widely recognized. In the title and text I have eschewed "accounting" and "shadow," since neither seems to express the essence of the matter, namely, the economic cost to society of a unit of a certain kind of factor of production. "Social" also seems to miss the mark.□

uation on unskilled agricultural labor in relation to market wages of labor in other sectors. As the formal analysis will make clear, the ratio between the economic and the market prices of labor may be more easily ascertained than the numerator of the ratio alone.

Stated simply the reason for seeking the economic price rather than accepting the prices thrown up by market forces is that there is some doubt that the latter perform the allocative function of a proper pricing mechanism. That is, market prices do not assure that each factor of production is employed at its maximum with reasonably uniform marginal productivity in its alternative uses. The arguments against economic pricing should also be considered, however, as well as the level (national, regional, or project) at which economic pricing should be undertaken. Consideration of the practical problems and difficulties of the task of economic pricing will be deferred until chapter 2.

What, then, are the arguments against economic pricing, particularly the economic pricing of common labor? The estimation of the ratio of economic price to market price is clearly not relevant to day-to-day decisions on private (or, for the most part, public) financial operations. The ordinary person concerned with his own affairs may go through life quite well without any knowledge of his true economic value to society. Similarly, the private entrepreneur need not look beyond income and cash flow statements.

The serious critics of economic pricing fall into three overlapping categories. The first group, with which I admit some sympathy, holds that economic price, particularly because of the time dimensions required, is too abstract and "shadowy" a concept to occupy serious economists. It is at this group that this book is particularly aimed. The second group, with which I am less sympathetic, would argue that if a government wants to enforce a minimum wage measure or to subsidize an interest rate, its judgment should be respected and the price of labor or capital that it establishes should be used in economic project analysis.[5] The difficulty with this is that it simply will not work if the developing countries are to get the most out of their all too slender productive resources. The result will probably be the underutilization of some of the scarce factors of production and the overutilization of others. I have, of course, every sympathy with those who hold that the scarcest of all resources are good planners, whose efforts should not be burdened with unnecessary concentration on economic pricing. I will try to show that this need not occur.

5. Some government decisions, as will be seen in chapters 2 and 3, are necessary in computing economic wages and prices.□

The third group of critics feels that if, for purposes of project preparation and appraisal, a factor of production is given a valuation different from that determined by market forces, the project is likely to require extensive monetary subsidies because the market wage, not the economic wage, would be paid in the actual construction or production process. This is certainly correct. Economic pricing does not change unit labor costs normally incurred. The response to this point is that the object is to minimize social, not monetary, costs.

Another question might properly be, why choose unskilled agricultural labor as the subject? The short answer is that its proper economic valuation is more important than other productive resources in most developing countries—and this despite the intricate relationship between the economic valuation of labor and of capital, even in the simple two-factor, two-sector model that underlies this analysis. Most important, in the countries studied, the supply of unskilled agricultural labor is the main human resource from which other components of the labor force are drawn or evolve.

When there is abundant evidence of a substantial discrepancy between the market price and the economic price of labor, there are good reasons for attempting to quantify this discrepancy. Such quantification should produce meaningful economic costs that provide a sounder basis for project appraisal than straightforward financial analysis. Whether projects are selected on the basis of cost-benefit analysis or the internal rate of return, the use of the economic price of labor should improve the design of the projects. The designs should reflect the combination of factors having the lowest economic cost when flexibility in the combination of such factors is technically feasible.

External evidence of the discrepancy between the market price and the economic price of labor is usually not too difficult to detect. Extensive unemployment or underemployment in a given sector, accompanied by economic or social barriers to the mobility of labor, is the first strong indication that employed labor in that sector may be overpaid. Discrepancy is also likely in the presence of effective private or public measures to defend the market wage rate at a particular level. Strong labor union activity and minimum wage laws are the most common of these. One of my critics blames the entire spread between economic and money wages on these artificial constraints on the supply side of the labor market. My disagreement with this view is explained in chapter 2.

The timing of economic pricing in relation to the life cycle of the project also needs some discussion. The improvement of the mix of factors, one of the purposes of economic pricing, will probably be more feasible at the construction than at the production stage of commodity-producing projects. Once the planning of the construction stage is completed, combinations of the factors, including both capital and labor inputs, will necessarily be contained within rather narrow limits. In such a commodity-producing project, the designers must strive to minimize economic costs that have been discounted to their present values for both the construction and production phases. The quality of labor involved and thus its economic cost may differ substantially between these two phases of the project's economic life.[6]

There are some limitations to the efficacy of economic pricing of factors, particularly unskilled agricultural labor. As de Wilde has pointed out with respect to African agriculture, even placing the economic cost of labor at or near zero "is a long way from regarding the creation of additional opportunities for employment as a positive benefit."[7] No one, so far as I know, has suggested using a negative economic value for labor, though this might sometimes be necessary to accomplish the objective of rapid labor absorption in backward areas. A specific economic wage should apply to a limited geographical area. This is partly because of the lack of mobility of labor and partly because the seasonal demand for labor will tend to vary substantially between regions, depending on such phenomena as crop cycles. De Wilde observes that, unless the economic wage (for project purposes) is more or less tailor-made for a particular region, it may well result in the neglect of comparatively poor and yet populous agricultural regions and thus it may aggravate the pressure toward urban migration and urban unemployment.

This raises the next issue, namely the physical area to which a particular ratio of economic price to money wage should apply.

Oriented to Country, Region, or Project?

The real question here is whether the ratio of economic price to money wage is meaningful on a national basis for specific project analysis. Furthermore, are regional or project area data likely to be available for such a

6. It may be contended that this inability to see very well into the future is a grave handicap in trying to place an economic evaluation on labor or any other factor of production. In my estimates it is assumed that financial costs of capital will not change over the life of the project. Nor will the rate of savings and the premium on income redistribution. The same problem will be present whether economic or straight financial cost estimates are made. Therefore it is better to start with an economically correct evaluation of factors, even though some error is unavoidable.□

7. John C. de Wilde, "Manpower and Employment Aspects of Selected Experiences in Agricultural Development in Tropical Africa," *International Labour Review*, vol. 104, no. 5 (November 1971), pp. 367–85.□

determination? My answer to the first question is a qualified yes (depending on the country selected) and to the second a rather less qualified no. It is true that with most development projects that are local or regional, unit labor costs (financial or economic) will depend on local as well as national circumstances, even in relatively small economies. But, as subsequent analysis makes clear, the relation of economic and financial values of a fairly homogeneous resource, such as unskilled agricultural labor, should be a valuable guide and at least a starting point for ratios to be employed for individual projects.

Adjustments will of course need to be made to reflect the difference between the national average and the supply and demand conditions in regional labor markets. I am convinced, however, that the national ratio will be much more stable than the local ratio over any extended time and that adjustments of the national ratio for local conditions should be done sparingly if at all in small- to medium-sized economies. Since labor allocation is a long-term decision for most projects, the mobility of unskilled labor will have adequate time to iron out differences among local labor markets—unless of course such differences are based on fairly permanent barriers to mobility (such as religious differences) which transcend economic considerations. If such impediments exist, they will obviously reduce the value of national ratios and increase the importance of local factors. In such cases it may be difficult to obtain the necessary data if government facilities cannot be used to collect them.

Components of the Economic Price of Labor

Although passing reference to these components has been made, the matter is so fundamental to this book that further elaboration is appropriate. In its broadest sense the economic cost of a unit of labor used for a specific purpose may be divided into three elements.[8] These are, first, an immediate cost, namely the production that would have occurred if the unit of labor had been used in the optimal available alternative employment; second, the additional consumption (in lieu of saving) that may re-

8. It has been suggested that the supply price of labor is the best indication of its economic cost. In the absence of a good (if not perfect) labor market, it seems to me difficult to obtain the supply price from empirical data. With good market conditions, labor would receive its marginal product, which might or might not be its supply price in another employment. In any case, the consumption and redistribution effects of a change in employment would not be available.□

sult from the employment of labor for the purpose contemplated;[9] and, third, a factor reflecting the redistribution effect of increasing wage incomes in the economy as a whole. A rather intimate knowledge of the consumption and savings propensities of the class of labor being costed is required before a conclusion can be reached on the magnitude of any of these elements of cost. Also, because the present value of future production, consumption, and savings is of concern, the future supply of, and demand for, investment resources must be measured in order to quantify the discount factor that is to be applied to future consumption and the production expected to flow from future savings or investment.

More precise formulations of these problems and their suggested solutions are taken up below. Simply stating the elements of the problems involved indicates their complexity, although in the country analyses some simplifying assumptions can be made.

The debt I owe to the pioneer writers in this field will become apparent. One point of difference between my method and that of other writers is that my basic measuring rod is the economic cost only to the economy and not to the worker. Therefore I have not included the relative disutility of work in different occupations (or work in relation to no work) as a component of economic cost.[10] The reasons for this exclusion are, first, the different degrees of disutility from different jobs cannot be measured in any objective fashion; more important, in most situations in developing countries the excess of the disutility of work in the new job over that of the old is very marginal, even if the old job was unemployment. If there is a greater disutility in the new job it may be more than offset by the higher wage received. In any event, my definition of economic cost seems much

---

9. There may be some strong objection to treating consumption as a cost rather than as a benefit. I find it hard to comprehend this difficulty. Consumption undeniably benefits the consumer. But the discussion here concerns costs to the economy, which may of course be benefits to the individual. Similarly, a benefit to the individual, for example, consumption, must be a cost to the economy unless the consumption is of a free good. If it reduces savings, as it usually does, a cost equal to the discounted value of future production derives from investing the wage. This is of course elementary, but the visceral reaction of some against considering consumption as a cost in the way used here seems to imply that a rose by any other name will not smell as sweet. To be quite fair, this reaction appears to stem from the basic principle that consumption is the ultimate end of economic activity. This does not seem to me to conflict at all with the equally sound principle that what is consumed now cannot, at the same time, be committed to enhancing future production.□

10. It should be understood that loss of leisure and the disutility of work are not additive, since part of the disutility of work is usually the loss of leisure. The disutility of work factor is provided for in Lyn Squire and Herman G. van der Tak, *Economic Analysis of Projects* (Baltimore: Johns Hopkins University Press, 1975).□

clearer if it is not burdened with an attempt to evaluate this factor, important as it may be in the thinking of some welfare economists.

Selection of Countries for Study

In some respects the difficulty of estimating the economic cost of labor is in direct proportion to the need for such estimates. In countries where labor and capital markets are very imperfect and future trends, including trends in the opportunity cost of capital, are difficult to predict, the proper economic pricing of labor will be most desirable. The poorer the country or region within a country, the more likely these conditions are to prevail. In measuring both the production and the consumption and savings effects of employing additional labor (or any labor if a new project is being considered), the life of the project will be important, as will the rate at which future increases in consumption are discounted. It is at once apparent that the economic cost of labor is linked with the rate at which future production-consumption becomes available.

In selecting countries for study it was therefore important to select those where forecasting of future economic change is reasonably easy or, even better, those that appear to have already reached a certain degree of stability so that features such as the future economic cost of capital and the relative value of consumption and investment may be predicted with reasonable assurance from present values. Taiwan, Korea, and, perhaps to a lesser extent, the Philippines seem to meet these criteria. Unfortunately the data at hand for Korea were insufficient to carry the analysis to its final conclusion; the study did, however, throw interesting light on the Korean labor market.

The unemployment statistics available in most developing countries grossly understate the extent of unemployment, not to mention underemployment. Nevertheless I felt that labor force and related statistics might be somewhat better in the Far Eastern countries selected than elsewhere in the developing world. The official measures for coping with the lack of full employment in the rural areas of these countries seem to make a strong case for placing a lower price on unskilled labor, particularly unskilled agricultural labor, than the going market wage for purposes of project selection, preparation, and appraisal. Then too, it seemed useful to compare the ratio of the economic price to market wage in a rapidly growing and relatively open economy, such as Taiwan, with a rather slower growing and less open economy, such as the Philippines. The countries selected also differ sufficiently in their stage of development and extent of unemployment to point up the underlying economic environment as a factor in the economic pricing of labor and to identify the importance of this environment under varying conditions.

General Approach to the Problem

It is not my intention to summarize here the complexities of this study; they will be discussed in nonmathematical terms in chapters 1 and 2 and in a formal presentation in chapter 3. Reference has already been made to the three main components of the ratio being sought: the opportunity cost, the consumption effect, and the income redistribution effect. With respect to the economic cost to the economy, the first two are very likely to be positive and the third to be negative, since it is assumed that nearly all countries would gain in welfare from a more even distribution of income. More productive use of the common labor stock should accomplish this better income distribution. The most important element in the first of these three components is the marginal productivity of agricultural labor. This also proved to be the most difficult to estimate and required a pragmatic approach, country by country. The main parameters for dealing with the consumption and redistribution effects are the ratio of labor to capital in industry, the social marginal productivity of capital, the social rate of discount for future consumption, and the respective rates of saving of the capitalists (savers) and of the populace as a whole. Although it is possible to obtain reasonable approximations of the present magnitudes of these elements in financial terms, the ability to translate these financial values into social values and forecast their change over time depends largely on previous knowledge of the countries and a fair prediction of future change. The desirability of selecting countries with a fair chance of continuing on their present course is self-evident. An operative economic development plan and a degree of sophistication in project appraisals are also necessary. The four countries selected for study here appear to qualify in these respects.

Results Obtained and Their Value

If results that agree fairly well with expectations are an indication of truth, the results of this study have some validity. It was expected that the economic price of agricultural labor would be somewhat higher in relation to nonagricultural wages in Taiwan than in the Philippines. This expectation was prompted by Taiwan's lower level of unemployment, more rapid economic growth, and greater mobility of labor. The redistribution factor was expected to be less important in Taiwan because of its much more even distribution of income. When this factor is excluded, my results indicate that the economic price of unskilled agricultural labor is about 75 percent of the money wage of industrial labor in Taiwan and about 60 percent in the Philippines. When the redistribution factor is included, the relative ratios are 71 percent for Taiwan and 50 percent for the Philippines. Data were not adequate for similar computations for Korea and Indonesia.

These conclusions confirm the need for planners (particularly those entrusted with the allocation of their country's resources) and project appraisers to be concerned with the fact that market forces do not necessarily indicate the optimal uses of productive resources. Market prices of such resources need to be adjusted as an important first step toward optimal allocation. The next step is to combine the economically priced resources in projects and programs that will produce the benefit-cost relationship most advantageous for the economy as a whole. Obviously, both benefits and costs have, at minimum, welfare and time dimensions which must also be measured in social rather than private terms. How this may be approached with respect to the cost of utilizing a particular resource is the basic problem of the following analysis.   □

{1}

Structure of Labor Markets
in Developing Countries

LABOR MARKETS IN SOME DEVELOPING COUNTRIES may be even more complex than those in more fully developed economies. The rural labor market, particularly for unskilled labor, is probably fairly homogeneous; however, it will be discussed country by country in chapters 5 and 6.

General Features of Labor Markets

Increasing attention is being given to the stratification of labor markets, particularly in the urban areas of developing countries. Such analysis tends to suggest a division of urban labor supply into two more or less disparate groups that are noncompeting, at least in the short run. These markets may be divided into informal and formal subsectors. The former consists usually of new arrivals from rural areas who, for a variety of reasons, can find no immediate employment in the commercial or industrial urban establishment. They try to eke out a living by street work, such as selling unusual merchandise, or by working in labor gangs from day to day. Many live at subsistence level for extensive periods, and of course some return periodically or permanently to their rural villages. The formal urban labor market consists of workers who have found a niche in the urban commercial, industrial, or public sector economy. A large number of subgroups may exist in each of these two broad categories, which may have varying degrees of competition within and between them. In contrast the rural labor force, though not strictly homogeneous, is probably less diversified than the economically active urban population.

Other labor economists have regarded the urban labor markets in developing countries as even more complex. They divide the formal portion of the market between entry and nonentry jobs.[1] In the short run the

1. Entry jobs provide on-the-job training, however spasmodically, for full-time employment in the organized or service sector.□

two parts operate independently of each other, but in the long run they are integrated in the sense that those on the outside gain entry and compete with those already on the inside. The main point is that these two parts of the formal sector are independent of the subsistence market or informal sector, which is made up of workers who, whether new arrivals in the city or not, lack the physical, intellectual, or other capacity to "make it" as part of the labor force in the established economic structure of the urban areas. Both the entry and postentry segments of the urban labor market may also be termed "capitalist," and presumably the subsistence group is "noncapitalist." This dichotomy might perhaps better be drawn between those who are employed—either by others or by themselves, usually to work with plant (machinery and buildings)—and those who are not "employed" in the sense that they do not look to others, either employers or customers, for regular pay. Such workers as bootblacks and petty salesmen may of course use a modicum of equipment or stock of goods in their work. There are many borderline cases, such as cottage industry labor, and the variations are infinite.

These analyses of the labor markets have important implications for the concepts of labor supply and opportunity costs. They indicate that it is too simplistic to classify labor as skilled and unskilled, with the assumption, for practical purposes, of an unlimited supply of unskilled labor at the going market price (that is, perfect elasticity of supply). Such a classification does not take account of the fact that probably a large but usually unknown fraction of this unskilled labor is incapable, for one reason or another, of participating in the organized or capitalist sector of the economy and that those categorized as members of the formal or capitalist sectors (whether in the entry or nonentry subsectors) are really a different productive resource from those in the subsistence or informal sectors. The supply of such labor (at prevailing wages) is not infinitely elastic and the economic wage is not at or near zero. Because of the mobility of labor within the formal or capitalist sectors (neither term is very satisfactory), the supply of labor should not be regarded as fixed over any significant period, even though the capitalist labor market may approximate full employment. This mobility may not, however, be as crucial as it first appears for wage determination, since exogenous factors (Arthur Lewis's term), such as trade unions and minimum wage laws, may force wages up, even in situations of much less than full employment. These factors are, however, of minor significance in most developing countries (the Philippines may be an exception).

The amount of differentiation among the different subsectors of the labor markets, in both urban and rural areas, will vary significantly, depending on many factors, notably the rate of growth of the different sectors of the economy and the economy as a whole, and the nature and efficiency of economic planning. It is important to recognize the interdependence of the labor markets and the economic (particularly the industrial) structure. The supply curve facing the employer will of course depend greatly on the degree of monopsony of the industry or group of industries in the labor market. Miller points out that limited knowledge about job opportunities among the different segments of the labor market tends to make the supply of labor much less elastic than otherwise.[2] He says that in Latin America factory employment absorbed fewer employees during the 1960s than it had in the previous decade, despite a 6 percent rate of growth of output. Of course the structure of industrial growth, as well as factors in the labor market, would have to be examined before definitely attributing this rate of labor absorption to market conditions.

Wages paid by foreign-owned or partly foreign-owned firms are usually higher than those of domestic firms because social welfare legislation tends to be much more strictly enforced against such firms. These measures have the greatest effect on wages in the entry subsector of the labor market. Enforcement of these measures will also increase the incentive of such firms to substitute capital for labor to the extent politically and economically possible. The economic price of labor should bear on decisions of this sort.

Legal restrictions on work force adjustment, such as those in Indonesia, are also calculated to bring about a substitution of capital for labor in new enterprises, because entrepreneurs are reluctant to take on a large work force if they cannot reduce it later in response to altered business conditions. This reluctance may offset the job-maintenance effects of the regulations limiting discharge of employees.

Industrialization may increase the participation ratio for young females, depending on the nature of industrial growth. In Taiwan, for example, there was growth in the manufacture of electronics, which involves detailed and precise physical tasks thought to be particularly suitable for females. Industrial growth of this kind may not reduce unemployment among those previously in the labor force.

As a way out of the growth-unemployment dilemma, Miller recommends increasing growth in agriculture, which is labor intensive, and growth in the subsistence sector of industry. He does not define the latter, but presumably he is referring to sweatshop industry. He also mentions construction as a labor-absorbing sector, but this may not be labor intensive.

2. Richard U. Miller, "The Relevance of Surplus Labour Theory to the Urban Labour Markets of Latin America," *International Institute of Labour Studies Bulletin*, no. 8 (1971), pp. 220–45.□

Reconciliation with the Two-Sector Model

The problems raised by the obvious lack of homogeneity of the urban labor market may be cited as an argument against the two-sector model used in this book. As mentioned above, however, agricultural labor is more homogeneous than urban labor. Once a national ratio has been established between the economic price for unskilled agricultural labor and the market price of other unskilled labor, factors may be applied to adapt the average economic wage to local conditions and different employments.

It may be asked what connection exists between the differentiation of urban labor markets and the ratio between the economic price of agricultural labor and the market wage in other sectors, which is estimated in chapters 5 and 6. It seems to me that there is very little connection. In the calculations of SWR/W that are given later, the W's are the wages paid in the formal nonagricultural labor markets, since these data are officially available. It may be argued that the alternative opportunity for unskilled agricultural labor is to enter the informal urban sector. If this were true the SWR/W ratios derived below would be too low. Admittedly, this point has some validity in a surplus labor economy. Its relevance for project analysis is doubtful, however, because the market wage in the formal sectors would presumably be paid on development projects as a matter of public policy. Possible exceptions are make-work projects to which normal economic considerations would not apply in any case.

The Lewis Model of the Labor Market

The most familiar model constructed to reflect the labor market situation in most developing countries is probably that postulated by G. Arthur Lewis in his classic articles of 1954 and 1958.[3] L. G. Reynolds tested this model in Puerto Rico and found that, in general, the Lewis model reflected labor market conditions there.[4]

3. W. Arthur Lewis, "Economic Development with Unlimited Supplies of Labour," *Manchester School of Economic and Social Studies*, vol. 22, no. 2 (May 1954), pp. 139–91. Also "Unlimited Labour—Further Notes," *Manchester School*, vol. 26, no. 1 (1958), pp. 1 ff.□

4. One purpose of Reynold's study was to test the validity of the Lewis model, which assumes an unlimited supply of labor in the noncapitalist sector of the economy. A striking feature in Puerto Rico was that, despite a rapid growth in per capita GNP, rates of unemployment declined from 15.3 percent for men in 1951 to only 14.1 percent in 1963. The decline of unemployed women in the labor force was much sharper, from 15.6 percent in 1951 to 8.9 percent in 1963. This, however, may have been the result of female needleworkers withdrawing in large numbers from the labor force during this period, in part because under the Puerto Rico minimum wage laws wage rates rose above those in countries at similar stages of development. The rise in incomes among male workers may have caused the reduction in the

(*Note continues.*)

The Lewis model is dealt with in some detail because the assumptions that underlie it are consistent with but not necessary for the analysis used in this book. These assumptions concern the homogeneity of the nonagricultural labor force and the sharp distinction between workers and nonworkers with respect to savings and consumption. This model also assumes a chronic surplus of labor in rural areas.

Puerto Rico is similar to many developing countries in that it began its period of rapid development with a surplus of agricultural labor. It differs in several respects; the openness of the Puerto Rican economy in relation to the U.S. market, the pressure of labor unions there to raise wages toward U.S. standards, and the associated freedom of migration—as well as the substantial investment of U.S. capital and capital-intensive technology in Puerto Rico. A sharp drop in agricultural employment occurred, while agricultural output rose in real terms from $70 million in 1949–50 to $130 million in 1960–61. There was, in fact, a reduction of labor requirements throughout the economy per unit of production during a period of rapid growth, the result of much improved management, more capital-intensive technology, and the important role played by the minimum wage, the last not a typical factor in developing countries. Reynolds concluded that, despite the variations noted above, Puerto Rico illustrates the classical model of a labor surplus economy, with an infinitely elastic labor supply curve at prevailing levels of employment, even though it was moved upward by the minimum wage. The marginal product of labor was progressively moved to the right along a supply curve for labor that was rising with adjustments in the minimum wage.

Lewis's model assumes a surplus of labor in rural areas and in the informal urban sectors as well. Therefore, the marginal productivity of labor is low or zero, and its supply is infinitely elastic within the relevant range of demand. If a person is employed, his productivity at the margin will determine his wage. If unemployed, he may receive an income from past savings, from the state, or from relatives.

Figure 1 illustrates my conception of such a labor market. Producers' (capitalists') income is N_1Q_1W at the first stage. After savings of producers materialize in larger investment, the labor productivity curve moves to the right (N_2Q_2). The supply curve for labor will be infinitely elastic until nearly everyone willing and able to work is employed. Then the labor supply curve SS will turn up sharply to meet the WS_1 line, which also will turn sharply upward at the point S_1 and beyond. Lewis points out that the end of labor surplus in Western economies resulted from industrialization

female labor force in the cottage needleworking industry, although Reynolds did not indicate this. See L. G. Reynolds, "Wages and Employment in the Labor Surplus Economy," *American Economic Review*, vol. 55, no. 1 (March 1965), pp. 19–39.□

Figure 1. Wage Determination with Surplus Labor

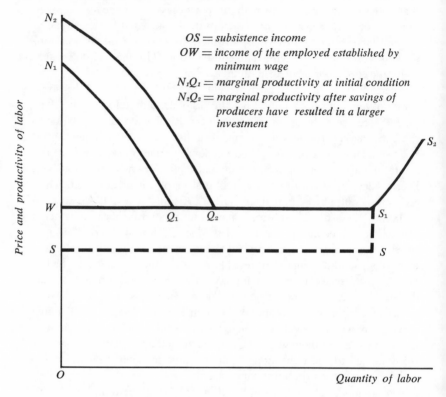

$OS = subsistence\ income$
$OW = income\ of\ the\ employed\ established\ by$
$minimum\ wage$
$N_1Q_1 = marginal\ productivity\ at\ initial\ condition$
$N_2Q_2 = marginal\ productivity\ after\ savings\ of$
$producers\ have\ resulted\ in\ a\ larger$
$investment$

Price and productivity of labor

Quantity of labor

and that this shifted the interest of economists away from economies with infinite labor elasticity. The Keynesian model, which assumes unlimited capital as well as labor, and the neoclassical model do not usually apply to developing countries. Lewis's basic point is that in most of the developing countries the conditions resemble those assumed by the classical economists, and unlimited supplies of unskilled labor in relation to demand do prevail. Lewis would agree that this assumption does not apply to the market for male skilled labor in developing countries.

The labor situation in developing countries cannot be explained entirely in economic terms. Wages, particularly in the subsistence sector, are in part determined by noneconomic considerations. Many persons are employed who have little or no marginal productivity—for example, unskilled public employees in countries such as Kuwait. Also, the transfer of women's work from inside to outside the household is one of the striking features of economic development—a phenomenon that makes a term such as "full employment" rather difficult to define in developing countries.

In the capitalist sector, in which classical or neoclassical motivations prevail, capital will be applied to labor only up to the point at which the marginal product of labor equals the current wage. Outside the capitalist sector, labor will earn what it can in the subsistence economy, but the marginal-productivity analysis hardly applies to this group. A mixture of philanthropic and sociopolitical factors will influence wages and therefore income distribution. Statistically, however, people in the subsistence economy are considered part of the employed labor force, and thus a low rate of unemployment appears to prevail in most developing countries. Lewis estimates a gap (WS in figure 1) of 30 percent or more between wages paid by capitalists and the subsistence wage. The difference in real wages may be less than the difference in money wages because workers in the capitalist sector normally work where costs of living are higher.

In the Lewis model a question arises as to why the employers do not hire additional laborers until their marginal productivity is reduced to the level of the subsistence wage (OS). This would seem to conform to the theory of Ricardo that labor's long-term equilibrium wage is its cost of subsistence. In the case of Puerto Rico the answer appears to be that, unlike the situation in many developing countries, the minimum wage law is enforced. Lewis suggests a number of other explanations, such as transfer costs and the difference between trained and untrained workers. These considerations seem to depart from the view implied in his presentation that there is a permanent difference between the wage level in the subsistence and capitalist sectors. But the sharp distinction he draws between the capitalist and subsistence sectors may not be warranted.

In his 1954 article, Lewis treats technical progress and capital accumulation as the same with respect to their effect on the marginal productivity of labor. Technical progress may reduce labor in a firm, however, and may also change the shape of the productivity curve, usually causing it to rise. For the purpose of this book it is not necessary to pursue in detail the general theory of economic development expressed or implied in the Lewis model, although its general outline is relevant to labor market conditions in developing countries.[5] Since labor in the capitalist sector

5. In the Keynesian model the existence of surplus labor is assumed because consumer goods and investment goods can be increased simultaneously. In his discussion of credit expansion and other factors, Lewis proposes a somewhat similar model in which investment, savings, and profits expand and the supply of productive capital is buttressed by an unlimited supply of surplus labor. If capitalists' real income rises in proportion to total output, inflation is avoided by increased investment and production. Labor is without bargaining power in this

(Note continues.)

is assumed to receive its marginal product, and all labor offered is absorbed in that sector, a divergence between economic and money wages would not seem to arise outside of agriculture. This is the assumption on which the estimates in chapters 5 and 6 are based.

Basic to this type of analysis of the labor market is the fact that when workers move out of the subsistence sector (whether from unemployment or from jobs with very low marginal productivity) they go to employment with higher marginal productivity, in which the wage is equal to the marginal product. No account is taken of workers who are attracted to urban areas in excess of what the labor market there can absorb and who may therefore have a lower marginal product in their new location than in their old. The Lewis thesis is summed up by the remark that "the average product of a worker in the capitalist sector exceeds that of a worker outside this sector because he produces his wages plus a surplus."[6]

Lewis attributes nearly all savings to profits and rents. He also assumes that profit earners have a much higher propensity to save than do receivers of rents. If the marginal productivity of capital in agriculture is no lower than that in industry, the justification for this assumption is not clear. A last point relevant to this analysis is that in Lewis's classification the subsistence sector is not coterminous with the underemployed sector. The subsistence sector consists of peasants producing food and the capitalist sector is everything else.

To sum up Lewis's view of the course of economic development, as long as unlimited labor is available at a fixed wage, the share of profits in

---

model. Lewis seems to rely mainly on stability in money supply to avoid inflation, but how this is consistent with capital formation by credit creation is not well explained. He also seems to have great confidence that increased production will eventually lower prices. He notes that "No Government should consider deficit financing without assuring itself that a large part of increases in money income will automatically come back to itself" ("Economic Development with Unlimited Supplies of Labour," p. 168). Sales taxes would be most effective in this respect. He further comments, "If labor is abundant but physical resources scarce, the primary effect on output is exactly the same, whether the government creates capital out of taxation or out of credit creation—the output of consumer goods is unchanged but is redistributed . . . Anything which raises the productivity of the subsistence sector will raise real wages in the capitalist sector" (ibid., p. 171). This seems to consider only the "goods" side. If the increase in money wages in the subsistence sector is proportionate to the increase in real wages, why should the real wages in the capitalist sector increase?□

6. This tenet is different from the physiocratic doctrine that agriculture is the source of economic surpluses; it bears a resemblance to the Marxist theory of surplus value. Eli Ginzberg observes: "In the controlled economies of Eastern Europe the policy has long been to extract as much 'surplus value' as possible from the farmer in order to encourage capital accumulation and, in the process, force a redistribution of the labor force in favor of the industrial sector. Only if the farmer is encouraged to grow more food and increase his income will there be a demand for the products of new local manufacturing; only thus will urban wages be kept from rising too steeply." *Manpower for Development* (New York: Praeger, 1971), p. 14.□

national income will increase because the capitalist sector will increase, but the return on capital will fall if wages increase faster than technical progress occurs. The vital point is that the constraint on employment is the supply of capital, and anything that reduces capitalists' income will curtail investment and employment. (This conclusion is very close to that of Ricardo and his followers.) Lewis does not think that the reduction of labor in the farm household will reduce farm consumption and increase savings, since those remaining will consume more. His stages of development are the following: First, with unlimited labor at a fixed wage, the share of profits in national income will increase and the capitalist sector will grow relative to the rest of the economy. Second, profits may fall subsequently if wages rise in relation to national income or the terms of trade become adverse to the capitalist sector. This is likely to happen when the supply of labor becomes inelastic.

As in most models, some rather rigid assumptions are built into the Lewis model that do not conform to reality. Other things remaining the same, wages would fall if the labor market wage reflected declining marginal productivity. Thus, the assumption of unlimited labor at a fixed wage is not realistic. His model also assumes that neither the wage earner nor the government is capable of accumulating savings; this assumption is clearly invalid, even in poor countries.

Lewis's conclusions seem at odds with a considerable body of current thinking about economic development. In his model progress in developing countries would depend not on raising the incomes of the poor but on raising the share of profits in national income, a share which he says is low. He observes that there may be a valid argument for tariff protection in countries with surplus labor because of the costlessness of labor in the subsistence sectors.

The Lewis thesis leads to the conclusion that a more equitable distribution of national income will increase the demand for wage goods, increase consumption, and, given a limited capital stock, reduce the production of capital goods and savings and reduce the capacity to produce wage goods. In these circumstances, the use of economic pricing of labor would increase the labor component of projects and have two somewhat contrary effects: First, it would increase demand for wage goods and thus have the effects referred to above; and second, it would reduce the demand for capital goods by substituting labor for capital. The basic question is, can employment be increased without capital accumulation except by technical change (which normally is biased in the direction of increasing the capital intensity of production)? If excess capacity exists in the capital equipment of the economy for the production of wage goods, the answer seems to be affirmative. If not, there would have to be a tradeoff between economic growth and equity in income distribution. Political authorities would have to determine the course, but such decisions should be made on rational grounds, with full awareness of the magnitude of the trade-offs involved.

Contrary to the entire Lewis approach, it has recently become popular among development economists to downgrade economic growth and upgrade distributional improvements that result in a national product smaller than its potential. In short, rather than strive for a larger pie, it is considered better to cut a smaller one into more pieces. This approach may seem to contribute to optimum welfare, particularly in countries where the very poor predominate, but it may be self-defeating in the longer run. To develop fully the pros and cons of this question, however, is beyond the scope of this book. Perhaps no generally applicable conclusion can be given, considering the variations in affluence, intensity of use of capital stock, institutions, motivations, and reactions that exist within and between countries of the developing world. All schools of thought would agree, however, that productive factors should be used to their best economic advantage.

The Urban-Rural Labor Problem

The relation between unemployment and the market price of labor in urban as compared with rural areas contains an enigma that cannot be exorcised by the rules that are supposed to govern in a free labor market. Considering the various limitations on market forces—some, the relics of a not too distant feudal past—that are to be expected in rural areas, it might be supposed that the impact of surplus labor on market wages would be greater in urban localities than in rural. This appears not to be the case. Wage discrepancies in favor of urban labor seem little affected by the movement of rural labor into towns, even though the number of people may be three or four times the emergent job opportunities. The lure of the bright (or at least brighter) lights in towns and cities is partially noneconomic, and people seem to prefer taking a chance on employment in the large cities and capitals, even where the chances for quick employment are rather slim. But these social and psychological factors do not explain the widening discrepancies between rural and urban wages, especially when employment statistics reveal much higher ratios for urban than rural unemployment.

It is not surprising that, even though food prices are lower in rural areas, the lower real rural wages create a cityward movement of labor; but it does seem strange that this movement is not accompanied by a narrowing of the urban-rural wage gap. This question will be examined in the country discussions below. Commenting on imperfections in the labor markets, Bruton points out that urban wages in many countries are rising in the face of mounting unemployment in urban areas.[7] This is the case in the Phillipines. In Africa it has been estimated that urban wages for government employees are two or three times higher than agricultural wages for similar skills.[8] This imbalance is economically wasteful, because the cost of maintaining the unemployed (including the cost of maintaining public order) is higher in cities. To help remedy the situation rural life should be made more attractive by land reform and rural industrialization, and the average real urban wage should not exceed the average real rural wage for comparable skills. Also, measures that tend to turn the terms of trade in favor of urban areas, such as import controls, only exacerbate the problem.

The statistics and the definitions of terms, such as unemployment, that underlie them are notoriously incomplete and inexact, but the repetition of the same observations in nearly all developing countries is impressive. This widespread occurrence of urban-rural differences seems to imply that it would take a substantial redistribution of income in favor of low-income persons in rural areas to halt or even appreciably slow down this movement of people that has given rise to acute political and social as well as economic problems.[9] Of course, in such fast-growing economies as Korea and Taiwan the problem is much less serious; in Taiwan it seems scarcely to exist. In these countries a major segment of the economic expansion has been in the industrial sector, which is located primarily in the larger cities. Even in Korea, however, steps are in train to make rural or semi-rural life more attractive, both socially and economically.

If present trends continue, and they seem likely to do so for the foreseeable future, two major adverse developments may occur: The labor force in most developing countries will grow more than twice as fast as em-

7. Henry J. Bruton, "Economic Development and Labor Use: A Review," World Development, vol. 1, no. 12 (1973), pp. 50–55. □

8. Carl Eicher (ed.), Employment Generation in African Agriculture (East Lansing: Michigan State University, July 1970), p. 9. □

9. It is possible to formulate a rather simple mathematical model showing the relationship between the factors that prompt movement of labor from rural to urban areas. Todaro has proposed such a model. It incorporates wages in rural and urban areas, the probability of securing urban employment, and the cost of moving from country to town. The laborer will move if the probability of employment in town, times the urban wage, minus the rural wage summed over relevant periods (presumably determined by the time his urban relatives will support him), exceeds his moving expenses. This model can also be used to determine the elasticity of supply of labor in the urban area and the rate at which urban unemployment may be increasing. See Michael P. Todaro, "A Model of Labor Migration and Urban Unemployment in Less Developed Countries," American Economic Review, vol. 59, no. 1 (March 1969), pp. 138–48. □

ployment opportunities (perhaps in the ratio of two or three to one during the decade of the 1970s), and the proportion of urban dwellers to the total population will continue to increase.[10]

Frederick H. Harbison has made an appraisal of the employment problem facing the developing countries if reliance is placed on industrialization.[11] He postulated an urban labor force of 10 percent of the total labor force with the total labor force increasing at 3 percent a year. If all the increase in the labor force has to be absorbed in the urban sector, employment there must increase by 30 percent a year. If the ratio of increase in output to increase in employment (labor costs) is unity or higher, output in the urban sector would likewise have to increase by 30 percent or more to absorb the full increment to the labor force. This is obviously highly unlikely. More realistically, Harbison says that the urban rate of population increase is usually three times that of a country generally. This would mean a 9 percent rate of increase of the urban labor force, and perhaps a rate of growth of urban output of 12 to 15 percent. This increase is not unreasonable in a relatively affluent economy such as Malaysia or Taiwan, but it is high where industrial investment is a real constraint, as in most developing countries. In the event of such growth in the urban labor force and output, employment in the rural areas would have to increase by 2.3 percent a year.[12] If the incremental output-labor ratio were two to one in the rural areas because of technological progress such as the green revolution, agricultural output would have to grow only by 4.6 percent a year to absorb available labor that is not absorbed in the cities. If

10. Despite the fact that in Asia and Africa agriculture provides 60 percent of total employment, of the new workers coming into the labor force up to 1980, the ILO has estimated that the rural sector in Asia will absorb only 30 percent (in Africa, 35 percent) of additional potential workers. The industrial sector is expected to provide 30 percent with jobs in Asia, compared with 25 percent in Africa. In Asia this leaves 40 percent to be absorbed by the service sector or unemployed. At present the service sector probably absorbs about 30 to 40 percent of the labor force in Asia's developing countries. See John A. Lacarte, "Aspects of International Trade and Assistance Relating to the Expansion of Employment in the Developing Countries," *Journal of Development Planning*, vol. 1, no. 5 (1973), p. 60.□

11. Harbison actually postulated an incremental output-labor ration of three to one in urban areas. In the absence of rapid technical change this seems far too high. See Frederick H. Harbison, "Possible Solutions to the Problems of Unemployment in Newly Developed Countries," *Manpower and Employment in Lower Income Countries* (Washington, D.C.: Agency for International Development, February 1971), pp. 67–72.□

12. Derived as follows: Increase in the urban labor force is 10 percent (the percentage of the labor force classified as urban) times its annual rate of growth, or 9 percent. This gives 0.9 percent of the total labor force. Since it is assumed that the total labor force is increasing by 3 percent a year, the rural labor force would have to increase by 2.1 percent of the total or 2.3 percent of the rural labor force to absorb the total increase in the labor force.□

rural output grows faster than this (as it did in a number of developing countries during the green revolution), the wage discrepancy between rural and urban areas should narrow in favor of the former. In any case, a reasonably rapid increase in agricultural output along with measures to increase the attractiveness of rural life are essential—if the growing labor force in the developing world is to be absorbed, regardless of the long-run efficiency of population control programs. A number of measures can be suggested to this end, the most important being:

1. land tenure reform policy, aimed at more intensive labor use
2. removal of impediments to labor mobility
3. change of public policy which subsidizes the use of capital in preference to labor
4. transfer of labor-intensive technology, principally among developing countries
5. improvement of the labor market, perhaps by developing better communications as well as instituting more formal labor market arrangements.

The 1973 report of the chairman of the Development Assistance Committee (DAC) devotes considerable attention to urban-rural labor and employment problems in developing countries. The report states that the urban component of the population of developing countries in Asia increased from 6 percent in 1920 to 19 percent in 1970, and is projected to increase to 31 percent by the year 2000. Probably in most developing countries (Korea and Taiwan may be exceptions), urban development will not be able to keep pace with the influx of population from rural areas, and even narrowing the income discrepancy in favor of rural areas may not be very effective in preventing labor surpluses from accumulating in the cities. Dislike of the manual labor involved in rural living, lack of access to utilities, and the drabness of rural existence operate on the negative side; access to better educational facilities and the attraction of government jobs (even at the lowest levels) in the cities work on the positive side to stimulate this urban influx. These factors may be as important or more important than higher urban incomes. The best course to pursue in the poorer developing countries would therefore seem to be one of executing programs to provide village electrification, to improve facilities for primary education, and to upgrade medical and entertainment facilities at the village level, as well as to introduce controlled mechanization to take some of the drudgery out of agriculture without displacing too much labor. At the same time, the urban shift of population probably cannot and need not be curbed in the faster growing and more affluent economies of East Asia. The DAC report points out that industrialization need not necessarily be linked as closely as heretofore with urbanization but concludes that there is little chance of checking the movement of the agriculture population into urban areas.[13] This may be an overly pessimistic view.

Extent of Unemployment

As the preceding discussion has shown, it is a difficult task to say just what constitutes unemployment and define its extent. When the situation in Korea, Taiwan, the Philippines, and Indonesia is reviewed, it will be noted that the official rates of unemployment recorded are usually very low by standards of developed countries in nonrecession times. This is particularly true of rural areas. The problem, of course, is one of definition and measurement. Perhaps the most difficult case is India, where in a 1971 report to the Planning Commission a committee of experts concluded that unemployment and underemployment are not measurable by statistical tests, such as the National Sample Surveys (NSS). Instead, an income or consumption test was recommended, under which anyone unable to spend more than a certain amount a year on consumption needs would be categorized as underemployed. Private investigators had previously arrived at a similar conclusion.

Other studies have shown, however, the difficulty of using the income test to define underemployment, or at least of using the same minimum amount of spending over a broad geographical area in which consumption needs may differ radically. It has been suggested that, with reasonable refinement, statistics on employment could be meaningful even in rural India. Raj Krishna makes the point that, while there may not be any single measure of unemployment, there are a number of factors which, taken together, throw light on the extent of the problem.[14] In his view, in order to meet the unemployment test a worker must be idle, poor, and willing to work. Those characterized by combinations of these factors (idle and poor; idle and willing; poor and willing; idle, poor, and willing) may then be quantified. The percentage of the work force meeting all three of the tests will probably be relatively substantial at any particular time. The NSS data give only the number that are idle and willing to work, not their degree of poverty. Using only the criteria of idle and willingness, which Krishna thinks are reasonably adequate, the NSS data have indicated that 9.1 percent of the national labor force of India is unemployed (9.7 percent in rural and 5.8 percent in urban areas). This

13. Annual Report of the Chairman, Development Assistance Committee (Paris: OECD, 1973), pp. 96, 107.□

14. Raj Krishna, "Unemployment in India," Economic and Political Weekly (March 3, 1973), pp. 475–77.□

amounts to 21.5 million unemployed (19.3 million rural and 2.2 million urban). Probably these figures are still much too low and certainly they do not measure underemployment. As will be seen, in the Philippines more refined methods are used, though much is still left to subjective factors, for example, whether the person wants to be registered as unemployed. It is no consolation, but worth noting, that even the United Kingdom and the United States measure different conditions to arrive at unemployment statistics.[15]

When dealing with the subject of economic wages, it should be noted that certain intellectual difficulties exist if unemployment is measured by the level of real income received, since real income may not reflect marginal productivity. All those with incomes below a certain level should thus not be classified as unemployed, that is, with zero marginal productivity. A person may have a very low income and yet be marginally productive, and his marginal productivity should be included in measuring the amount of his economic wage.

There is no point in further belaboring the difficulties involved in measuring the degree of utilization of the labor force in developing countries. It is worth noting, however, that the more tradition-bound the society, the more the labor force is likely to be underutilized. Where religion or social mores designate individuals or groups for particular jobs and restrict their movement into other occupations which may have a higher economic return, the productivity of the economy will suffer. The extended family may also exert influence to prevent some family members from accepting a low-paying job or one with a social stigma. Another factor affecting the utilization of labor is social pressure to keep redundant labor on the payroll. This pressure is found even in such developed and efficient countries as Japan, and it is certainly a potent force in thinly disguising unemployment in Indonesia and elsewhere in the developing world.

Factors in the Supply of Labor

In developing countries the major emphasis has been on reducing the supply of unskilled labor and increasing the demand for it.[16] Notable exceptions, of course, are the very fast-growing countries. Although the problem has been well identified, there is little agreement on its solution. Population control is regarded by many as the ultimate solution, though

---

15. The United Kingdom uses labor exchange data, whereas U.S. estimates are based on sample surveys that purport to measure the labor force and those in it seeking employment.□

16. As for skilled labor (but not necessarily professionals) the emphasis has been the reverse.□

only for the next generation, rather than in the short term. There is also some skepticism as to whether family planning can be made economically acceptable to the rural poor. For example, in India the large family may be an economic asset to the landed rural poor because of labor needs at the peak season. Providing more of the landless with land may therefore work against the efficacy of family planning. In urban communities there are fewer opportunities for child employment, however, and family planning may enjoy some success.

Apart from population control, which can have only long-term implications, the supply of labor can be affected by adjustments in the participation ratio (ratio of labor force to working-age population) and by changing the quality of labor. Education, particularly vocational training, will have an important bearing on both of these elements in the labor supply-demand equation. The participation ratio is of course a function of income level, industrial structure, educational opportunities, and other factors. An extreme case of changes in the quality of labor is shown by a study made by Watanabe in Japan.[17] According to this study, labor's production function indicated an unexplained increment—that is, one not explained by incremental applications of capital and labor—equal to 50 percent of the increase in the postwar productivity of Japanese industry. Of course, in exercises of this kind the benefits of improved technology must be assigned quite arbitrarily. In this case, the labor supply data were adjusted with a labor quality index which, in effect, credited to labor the benefits of improved technology, a procedure followed below in estimating the marginal productivity of labor in the Philippines.

Factors in the Demand for Labor

Several useful studies and observations concern factors on the demand side of the labor market. These factors range from public policy with respect to the structure of industry and public works, through fiscal and monetary policy, to specific measures for the protection or subsidy of particular industries. In a study for the Organisation for Economic Co-operation and Development (OECD), Turnham and Jaigar made useful intercountry and interregional comparisons of participation ratios, composition of the labor force, and income distribution.[18] Some of these comparisons are appli-

17. T. Watanabe, "Improvement of Labor Quality and Economic Growth: Japan's Postwar Experience," *Economic Development and Cultural Change*, vol. 21, no. 1 (October 1972), pp. 33–53.□

18. David Turnham and Ingelis Jaigar, *The Employment Pattern in Less Developed Countries* (Paris: OECD, 1971).□

cable to the particular countries studied in subsequent chapters of this book. The authors reach the following conclusions regarding the general outlook for the developing countries: First, the labor force will grow by 2 or 3 percent a year until 1985, regardless of family planning; second, the modern sector, particularly manufacturing, can absorb only a small portion of the increments to the labor force; third, large groups of people have experienced no improvement in living standard during the 1960s; and fourth, urban unemployment is becoming more acute.

As mentioned above, a number of criticisms can be made of the alleged overemphasis on economic growth, particularly on capital intensification, that is implied in the Lewis model. Bruton observes that the standard approach to economic growth and fuller employment has been to increase capital formation. Often the possibilities both for fuller utilization of existing capacity and for substituting labor-intensive for capital-intensive techniques are overlooked. The use of capital-output and foreign exchange savings models may have impeded progress toward solving the employment problem. Even the Little-Mirrlees approach to shadow pricing of labor measures the cost of labor in terms of the savings (and therefore the increments to future consumption) that are foregone. This approach implies that employment is at the expense of capital formation and seems to overlook the demand side, which is the basis of the Keynesian analysis of unemployment. Bruton says, "a capital intensity unjustified by factor endowment will mean lower output than is technologically possible."[19] In many developing countries there is a conflict between rapid growth and lower employment arising out of the structural changes that rapid growth entails. It is sometimes felt that this conflict is greater than that experienced in Japan, Taiwan, and Israel, which have had both rapid growth and a labor shortage.

Diffusion of Employment Opportunities

Four principal areas of choice govern the diffusion of employment opportunities. These choices are as follows: First, import substitution as against export orientation; second, small-scale as against large-scale industrial and agricultural units; third, the extent to which resources are committed to avowedly make-work projects which may (not necessarily must) have a lower priority on other grounds; and, fourth, an education policy that ameliorates the employment problem or one that makes it worse. These

19. Bruton, "Economic Development and Labor Use," p. 52.□

subjects will be considered further in the country chapters, but certain general points will be covered here.

Import substitution

What can be said about the relation between employment and the choice open to some countries of whether to encourage export industries or import-substitution industries? Import-substitution policies that change production patterns distort the degree and structure of utilization of factors. Such policies may normally be expected to increase capital-labor ratios in developing countries, particularly if the import substitution is by foreign-owned enterprises. If import substitution is in wage goods and wages are held constant, real wages may fall because prices of such goods will rise. If capital-intensive technology is imported from economies with high labor costs, the lower ratios of labor cost to capital cost in developing countries may not change the factor mix sufficiently, compared with that used abroad.[20] This problem is compounded by the fiscal incentives for new investment provided by several countries in Southeast Asia. These incentives are mainly in the form of exemption from the corporate income tax for a number of years. This encourages capital intensification, since the net return on capital is raised. In Malaysia, for example, the subsidy to capital is progressive, and the length of the tax holiday varies directly with the amount of the investment for pioneer industries.

Hughes believes that as a general rule the freer the market and the entrepreneur are from constraints and controls (particularly tariffs and capital subsidies) the more labor intensive the factor mix is likely to be.[21] The relatively low real cost of labor has had less than optimal effect on the degree of labor intensity of industry because of public policies, including foreign investment policies and other exogenous factors. Governments tend to subsidize the price of fixed capital but not working capital and to provide foreign aid that is confined largely to the financing of imported capital equipment. These tendencies encourage a distortion of invest-

---

20. In some economies, such as those of the oil-producing countries, the export sector has little relation to the rest of the economy or the optimal factor mix. The tendency is to underutilize domestic factors, particularly labor, and to subsidize them out of oil income by putting them on the public payroll. It would be preferable to utilize redundant labor for productive purposes, even if this means heavy subsidies of labor-intensive domestic activities. Real GNP would increase, but of course this is of less importance than the greater social and political stability that would be achieved.□

21. Helen Hughes, "Scope of Labor-Capital Substitution in the Development Economies of Southeast and East Asia," World Bank Economic Staff Working Paper no. 140 (Washington, D.C.: January 1973).□

ment in favor of capital-intensive industry. Although the manufacturing sector has been the principal beneficiary of supports of various kinds, it is probably intrinsically more capital intensive than construction or agriculture. It should be noted, however, that the larger and less labor-intensive agricultural units tend to be the most highly subsidized units in the agricultural sector, because they are the best credit risks and are relatively free from direct taxation.

Hughes summarizes her views as follows: "The experience of Southeast Asian and East Asian countries thus bears out those theoretical insights which suggest that the policy framework in bringing together market prices with actual factor availabilities, and in determining the sectoral and product mix, is critical to the adoption of appropriate techniques of production." Probably everyone would agree that, perhaps under the auspices of the United Nations or regional banks, greater effort and resources should be expended on the development of new technologies appropriate for developing countries. But the possibility of altering techniques to fit the requirements of a factor mix with optimal social and economic costs will depend on the time frame of construction and production and the point in the process at which a decision can be taken regarding factor proportions. If the political judgment is that time is critical in proceeding with industrialization (as in India in the 1950s), those who favor adjusting techniques to permit a more rational combination of factors for the country concerned will probably be ignored.

Streeten has made some interesting observations on the plight of poor countries with respect to technology adapted to their needs.[22] He points out that there is not only a communications gap but also a "suitability" gap between the developed and the developing worlds. This gap is emphasized by the fact that "compared with the rich countries, poor countries have to provide about three times the number of jobs with about one-sixtieth of the investable resources per worker. Therefore, only about one-sixtieth of the investable resources per worker used in the rich countries is available for the creation of jobs in poor countries, if only additions to the labor force in the poor countries are to be employed."[23] This provides no margin for reducing unemployment or underemployment.

Technological advances in developed countries can best be introduced to the poor countries through foreign investment, but such countries as

---

22. Paul Streeten, "Technology Gaps between Rich and Poor Countries," *Scottish Journal of Political Economy*, vol. 19, no. 3 (November 1972), pp. 213–30; also Frances Stewart and Paul Streeten, "Conflicts between Output and Employment Objectives in Developing Countries," *Oxford Economic Papers*, vol. 23, no. 2 (July 1971), pp. 150–60.□

23. Streeten, "Technology Gaps between Rich and Poor Countries," p. 218.□

India have preferred to have the first without too much of the second. Streeten quotes an estimate that only one percent of research and development funds expended in developed countries is directed at the solution of the problems of the poor countries. This compares with the 5 percent suggested by the Pearson Commission.[24] Some skeptics have concluded that the economic development of Asian countries in the nineteenth and early twentieth centuries was in inverse proportion to their contacts with the West, citing Indonesia and India as countries with extensive contacts and Japan as a country with limited contacts. There may, however, be a spurious element in this negative correlation. The fact remains that the developing countries will probably have to look mainly to themselves for the new techniques suitable for their factor combinations. It is probable that, unlike the more affluent nations, developing countries have not adapted their indigenous science and technology for the optimal economic use of labor and capital. Social attitudes, particularly dissatisfaction with "inferior" technology, are partly responsible for this. The development of a nuclear device for peaceful purposes in India is an extreme example.

Public policy favoring one line of activity over another will have a bearing on the problem of the economic pricing of labor. As has been pointed out, autarkical policies of industrialization have tended to boost industrial money wages in relation to agricultural wages.[25] This would seem to establish a case for the economic pricing of industrial labor at lower than its market price.

Scale of productive units

It is probable that most small industries are more labor intensive than medium- or large-scale units, though there are important exceptions to this rule. The nature of the product, rather than the scale of the project, is the governing consideration. World Bank studies of India have shown that the value added per employee in 1965 was over twice as great for large-scale as for small-scale industry. The interindustry variance is, however, quite high within the small-scale sector; for a sample of 150 establishments, it ranged from 3,138 rupees of value added per worker to 24,963 rupees.

My own observations in a number of countries indicate that it is very difficult to draw general conclusions about the relative effects on employ-

24. The Commission on International Development, Lester Bowles Pearson, chairman, *Partners in Development* (Washington, D.C.: Praeger, 1969), p. 205. □

25. I. M. D. Little, Tibor Scitovsky, and M. Scott, *Industry and Trade in Some Developing Countries* (Paris: OECD, 1970), pp. 50–68. □

ment of sponsoring small-scale and large-scale industry. Many small units engaged in processing an intermediate or raw material may have a machine or a series of machines that form, stretch, or otherwise process the material, and there may be only a minimum of labor input. Although very little labor-capital substitution is possible for technical reasons, if a small firm performs the same operations as a large one, it will probably do so in a more labor-intensive manner. Because the labor element is larger in small enterprises in relation to total value added, it is likely that wages will be lower. The small enterprise will probably operate in a market where labor is relatively more abundant and is not organized. Household labor will be used more, and in rural areas part-time labor may be used. This labor obtains possibly the larger part of its income from agriculture and might comprise owner-farmers, tenant farmers, or agricultural laborers. They will regard their industrial wage as something of a windfall and therefore will be less zealous for higher wages and perhaps in a poorer position to demand them. This situation may appear to lower the opportunity cost of this labor for agriculture, but in reality the availability of part-time employment by small enterprises probably has the effect of raising the cost of farm labor.

Labor-intensive and capital-intensive projects

Labor-intensive public works projects, rather than subsidies or tax incentives to induce labor intensity into private production, may be preferable from the standpoint of international competition, even if it is assumed that the real costs of production would not be increased by introducing labor intensity, particularly in the export sector. It would be best if labor-intensive techniques did not utilize any scarce factor of production capable of contributing to export growth.

John Lewis has listed the advantages of labor-intensive public works programs in comparison with programs encouraging small-scale industry, which he considers generally inefficient.[26] The advantages are that labor-intensive construction activities:

1. tend to be fairly cost effective
2. are likely to have less effect on the efficient sectors of the economy than other forms of make-work projects
3. will tend to benefit underpaid farm labor
4. provide a useful transition to nonagricultural employment
5. cause little adverse impact on foreign exchange.

26. John Lewis, "Designing the Public Works Mode of Antipoverty Policy," Princeton-Brookings Study of Developing Countries Income Distribution, September 1974 (draft), pp. 8–9. □

Lewis warns against some of the errors made in these programs. Mistakes include operating on too small a scale, with technology at too low a level, and without regard to the needs of general area development.

No one could quarrel with John Lewis's objectives, but, with some exceptions, these programs have proven difficult to administer. Their success has depended on the capacity and dedication of a few individuals, and the continuity of their cost effectiveness has thus been limited. A realistic appraisal of one such program, the Promotion Nationale (PN) in Morocco, has been presented by Jackson and Turner.[27]

In its approach to the employment problem, PN emphasizes the demand for labor rather than the supply price of capital. Labor is given a very low valuation in the design of the project in order to achieve maximum labor use. For ten PN schemes involving investment in agricultural development, particularly during slack periods of agricultural activity, the average financial rate of return was 14 percent and the median 9 percent.

The authors concluded that capital-intensive techniques produce more output per unit of capital invested than do labor-intensive techniques. The disadvantages of using labor-intensive techniques may, however, be offset by the fact that economic costs of labor are lower than those of capital in relation to their respective market prices.

Jackson and Turner make the valid point that the economic costs of unskilled labor used in make-work projects will be below the economic costs of skilled labor required for capital-intensive projects. More dubiously, they feel that fiscal measures to raise revenue for labor-intensive projects would have little impact on investment because they will bear on consumers rather than on savers. Of course, this may be true to the extent that the greater demand for consumer goods results in the use of excess capacity and increases profitability.

To illustrate this case, the authors use a one-factor model, that is, capital, and postulate that social marginal product starts higher but declines faster in capital-intensive than in labor-intensive activities.[28] Consequently, maximum advantage would be gained by spreading investment between these two types of activities (see figure 2). If the purpose is to achieve maximum social marginal product, it would be better to invest all the capital (OK) in the labor-intensive industry, since $EK > BK$. To achieve maximum social gross product, it would be better to invest all the

27. Dudley Jackson and H. A. Turner, "How to Provide More Employment in a Labour Surplus Economy," *International Labour Review*, vol. 107, no. 4 (April 1973), pp. 315–38.□
28. Cost in terms of labor is excluded from this calculation because it is assumed that these are make-work projects in which labor is a "free" good from an economic standpoint. Its opportunity cost is zero.□

Figure 2. Relation of Capital to Social Marginal Product, Combining
Labor-Intensive and Capital-Intensive Projects

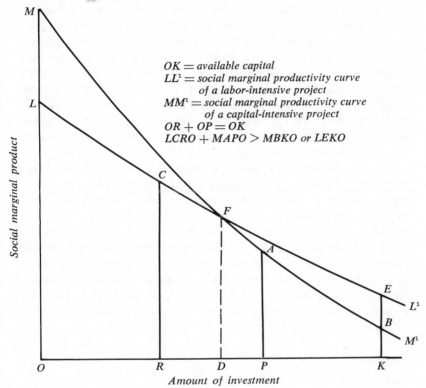

$OK = available\ capital$
$LL^1 = social\ marginal\ productivity\ curve$
$\qquad of\ a\ labor\text{-}intensive\ project$
$MM^1 = social\ marginal\ productivity\ curve$
$\qquad of\ a\ capital\text{-}intensive\ project$
$OR + OP = OK$
$LCRO + MAPO > MBKO\ or\ LEKO$

Social marginal product

Amount of investment

capital in the capital-intensive industry, since $MBKO > LEKO$ because
$MFL > FEB$. By splitting the investment between the two activities, that
is, by investing OR in the labor-intensive activity and OP in the
capital-intensive activity, a higher social gross product ($LCRO + MAPO$)
results than would be obtained by placing all the capital in either type of
activity. Presumably, in an entirely rational society investment in each
activity would be carried to the point where social marginal returns were
equal, that is, OD. This would more than exhaust the supply of capital,
however, since $2OD > OK$. Because real savings from the MM^1
(capital-intensive) activity may be assumed to exceed those from the LL^1
activity, a larger investment in the MM^1 activity may be socially desirable
in the long run.

The question of how far investment should be carried in a particular
activity is of course highly complex, particularly when there are conflicts

between employment and economic growth. Such conflicts usually arise when, in an effort to improve the distribution of income, workers are subsidized to produce goods that could be produced more cheaply, in real economic terms, by more capital-intensive methods. If a low economic price is put on the employment of labor, it may be efficient to use labor-intensive methods to save even small amounts of capital, but it will never be efficient to use methods that employ both more capital and more labor (both measured at their economic prices) per unit of output. It is quite possible that an old technique can be replaced by a newer one that saves both labor and capital. If capital can be saved by employing more labor, and if a shortage of capital is the main constraint on output, then some output and growth will have been traded for short-term employment. In some situations, such as the green revolution, an increase in current inputs requiring capital expenditure may save both land and labor per unit of output. Failure to use these capital inputs in order to employ more labor may therefore be wasteful of land.

Labor policies that raise the cost of labor above its social opportunity cost may keep firms from choosing factor combinations that will optimize output. The substantial difference among the factor combinations used by firms in the same industry may, of course, be owing to a lack of homogeneity in the factor markets (particularly the labor markets) in the same country, but it may also be because firms in the same industry differ widely in age.

Function of education

Education has an important bearing on labor supply. Berry has observed that raising the level of education has contributed to the flow of job-seekers into towns because education at the precollege or secondary school level cannot be used to advantage in agriculture.[29] This appears to argue in favor of larger allotments of funds for primary rather than secondary education. Mass education, particularly at the secondary or secondary-vocational level, also may affect the elasticity of labor supply and keep the younger members of the work force out of the labor market for a time. According to the participation ratios in table 1, however, this phenomenon is more apparent in developed countries than in developing economies.

Most commentators consider the ability to earn an adequate living as the criterion of employment rather than the conventional measure of

29. R. A. Berry, "Factor Proportions and Urban Employment in Developing Countries," *International Labour Review*, vol. 109, no. 3 (March 1974), p. 223.□

Table 1. Participation Ratios in Developing Countries and Northwest Europe

Age group	Developing countries[a] Male	Female	Northwest Europe Male	Female
0–14	6.5	4.0	1.1	0.9
15–24	78.1	36.9	76.2	60.2
25–54	96.3	40.1	96.8	41.3
55–64	86.8	29.2	83.3	28.9
65 and over	57.5	14.5	23.4	7.4
Total	53.2	22.9	61.1	28.5

Source: International Labour Organisation, from unpublished data contained in J. N. Ysikartis, "Regional Estimates and Projections of the World Labor Force" (1973), processed.
a. Data for developing countries are subject to a considerable margin of error.

working or not working. They believe (often mistakenly, I think) that the supply of labor is a function of higher real wages rather than the greater availability of work. They have a valid point, however, in that the supply of labor (the labor force) may not be independent of the wage prevailing in a given locality and that, if wages fall because of slack demand, the size of the labor force may diminish at least temporarily. As wages rise and fewer labor hours are offered, a backward sloping supply curve probably generally prevails in the longer run and possibly in the short run in primitive environments.

Labor Markets in Korea, Taiwan, Indonesia, and the Philippines

The labor markets in Korea, Taiwan, the Philippines, and Indonesia are covered in some detail in chapters 5 and 6. Comments here are limited to drawing a few comparisons among them (see table 2 for summary data). These four countries were picked in order to compare the labor markets and the utilization of labor resources in the high growth economies of Korea and Taiwan with those found in the somewhat slower growth conditions prevailing in the Philippines and Indonesia. The labor markets in high growth economies might be expected to be more "perfect," not only because of lesser redundancy in the supply of unskilled labor but also because the governments might be expected to have a more laissez-faire attitude toward employer-employee affairs. In fact these conditions do not appear to be characteristic of Korea and Taiwan, in large part because of the philosophy of the governments. In addition, both countries reflect the days of Japanese colonial rule, when job security and paternalistic relations

Table 2. *Some Features of the Labor Force in Selected Countries*

Country	Labor force as percent of working-age population[a]			Unemployment as percent of labor force			Collective bargaining	Minimum wage
	Total	In agri-culture	Male	Overall	Agri-culture	Other		
Indonesia	50.0	80–90	68.7	4.5[b]	n.a.	n.a.	Political control	Regional
Korea	56.0	49.9	63.0	1.4[b]	1.5	1.3	Weak	None
Philippines	49.9	55.0	67.3	5.2	3.8	8.1	Reasonably effective[c]	Effective[d]
Taiwan	56.6	33.0	67.0	1.3[b]	n.a.	n.a.	Weak	None

Sources: Statistical Appendix: Indonesia, Tables B8, B9; Korea, Tables A3, A10; Philippines, Table B7; and Taiwan, Tables A1, A3, A12.
n.a.: Not available.
a. For Korea and Taiwan, "working-age population" is defined as those fourteen years of age and over; for Indonesia and the Philippines, as those ten years and over.
b. Unofficial estimates are much higher.
c. Well unionized, but the right to strike is suspended.
d. Only by comparison with other countries in the area.

between employers and employed substituted in large part for free labor markets. Although the comparison between the faster and the slower growing economies reveals important differences in the supply and demand for labor, these differences are not as sharp as those between employment conditions in urban and rural areas in each country. In all the countries examined here, a strong movement of labor from the country to the cities continues, despite the fact that in all cases except Taiwan there is a surplus of labor in urban areas. Unemployment in urban areas is more evident and perhaps more politically significant than in the countryside. The general conception of the country-city problem by development economists has been much colored by the situation on the Indian subcontinent, which is markedly different from that in the smaller and particularly faster growing countries of the Far East. Even in Indonesia (with the exception of Jakarta) it is doubtful if the large influx of labor into the cities is occuring because of significant real wage differentials. Other factors, such as the often illusory hope of jobs and the attractions of city life, are more important. In Taiwan, where at the time of my visit a real labor shortage was developing as a result of the very rapid growth of the labor-intensive electronics industry, special transport facilities and other inducements such as housing and recreational facilities were used to attract labor from the rural to the urban areas. This is an exceptional situation, however, and in the three other countries there is a considerable redundancy of labor in the cities.

During a visit to the Far East in 1973 I asked planning officials in Korea, Taiwan, the Philippines, Indonesia, and Singapore about their attitudes toward the use of shadow (economic) wages. Although some academic work has been done on the subject, the response of most officials range from the skeptical to the antagonistic. Some, of course, had no conception of the significance of the problem. In some instances, such as at the University of the Philippines, economists have written on the subject but with little enthusiasm. The most forthright reaction was from a high officer of the Planning Board of Singapore, who seemed to believe that Singapore has a perfect labor market and that anyone mentioning the shadow price of labor should be severely dealt with. Estimating the economic price of labor, particularly unskilled labor, is less susceptible to precise conceptual formulation than is estimating other inputs, particularly so-called traded inputs, whether financial or physical. The reasons are not difficult to find. Of all the factors of production, human labor is possibly the least homogeneous. It also varies widely in its demands upon the economy for subsistence, irrespective of its productivity; its productive capacity in alternative employments; and its mutability and capacity to absorb training. □

{2}

Policy and Environment: Elements in the Economic Pricing of Labor

WHETHER UNDEREMPLOYMENT OR UNEMPLOYMENT EXISTS and on what scale are probably the most important considerations in the economic pricing of labor. The extent of employment may be greatly influenced by such intangible features of the labor market environment as religious and cultural characteristics. There is value in estimating the relation between the economic and market price of unskilled labor even though, for purposes of project appraisal, if an economic price for labor is used, it should usually be made project specific. This can be done by multiplying the national ratio (SWR/W) by a factor expressing the relation between hardcore long-term unemployment in the project region and the national average of unemployment.

Issues in Measurement

The three most basic questions in estimating the economic cost of a particular labor input are the following: First, will the use (or nonuse) of this labor input affect the supply of labor—and therefore its marginal productivity—for other purposes, and do these other purposes actually exist? Second, will the wages paid to this labor input appreciably increase its consumption-savings ratio? Third, if it is assumed that the answer to the second question is positive and that the employment of labor will increase consumption and reduce savings-investment over the life of the project, at what rate should this increase in consumption be discounted to arrive at its present economic value (cost)?[1] The main discussion of the estimation of

---

1. I refer here to the discount rate for future consumption (usually called the consumption rate of interest, or CRI) and not the accounting rate of interest, or ARI, the discount

(*Note continues.*)

{42}

the components of the economic wage is in chapter 3; the concern here is with some of the important but secondary issues that must be resolved before mathematical formulas can be applied.

The ratio of economic to market labor costs is the real object of the present search. The ratio is used because of its substantive importance as compared with its component variables; it is also convenient. In the more formal approach in chapter 3, it will be apparent that since both numerator and denominator are likely to be affected equally by a common factor (the numéraire) it will be possible to avoid some concern about the accuracy of that rather illusive element that is important in the Little-Mirrlees analysis.[2]

Two criticisms have been raised by readers of an early draft of this book, both of which merit a response. The first is that a two-sector model (agriculture and the rest of the economy) is unrealistically limited and that with respect to the labor market my model should have included the portion of the labor force known as the informal sector. Workers in fringe occupations are an important segment of the labor force in many developing countries, and a more exhaustive statistical investigation of them would be fruitful. It is doubtful, however, if a study of these essentially transitory workers would greatly affect the conclusions I draw from my own investigation. As pointed out in chapter 1, the relevance of this part of the urban labor market for project evaluation is questionable.

The second criticism raised was that it is more or less man-made market imperfections that produce the spread between the economic wage (which my critic considers the "supply price" of labor) and the market wage produced by minimum wage laws, labor unions, and the like. This comment seems to miss the main point, namely that the purpose here is to measure the economic impact of transferring a unit of labor from one job (or lack of job) to another, a value which cannot be ascertained by the comparison suggested. A secondary point is that "supply price" seems to have only a subjective connotation in the kind of labor market situation prevailing in most developing countries, and is therefore quite unmeasurable.

---

rate that will equate the supply of, and demand for, capital. The two are indeed related and may converge and eventually become equal when the benefits from future consumption streams and the cost of present savings (in present consumption forgone) become equal. This may not happen for a long time, which, as will be seen later, simplifies the arithmetic of the computation.☐

2. I. M. D. Little and J. A. Mirrlees, *Manual of Industrial Project Analysis in Developing Countries,* vol. 2, *Social Cost-Benefit Analysis* (Paris: OECD, 1969); and *Project Appraisal and Planning for Developing Countries* (New York: Basic Books, 1974).☐

A final general point of methodology needs comment. In other treatments of this subject, the analysis, at bottom, depends largely on certain crucial value judgments made by the supreme planning authorities. Cases in point are the relative value of saving as compared with consumption or the importance of income distribution as compared with a larger GNP. It does not seem realistic to assume that governments at the highest level would be willing (and able) to quantify their judgments on these matters, even if their advisers were able to pose the problems in terms of clear alternatives. In my examples, I therefore endeavor to derive such elements as the redistribution component and the social rate of discount from objective facts.

Another question in determining economic wage rates is how to evaluate more or less arbitrary nonmarket forces such as labor unions and minimum wage scales. The existence of such arbitrary factors may mean that labor cannot be engaged in alternative occupations at a wage lower than the minimum. A case could therefore be made for considering the minimum market wage as also the minimum economic wage, since employers will not hire additional workers if their marginal productivity is lower than the wages that the employers are legally required to pay. This reasoning, however, does not take account of the broader socioeconomic factors that enter into the computation of a real economic wage.

For the general allocation of resources, the economic pricing of labor is desirable because of imperfections in both the capital market and the labor market, although the removal of these imperfections might impose such serious hardships on the disadvantaged that the action would be entirely unacceptable on social or political grounds. Examples of such unacceptable actions would be the repeal of minimum wage laws, the suppression of collective bargaining, and the elimination of unemployment insurance that enables persons to keep their labor off the market if the remuneration offered falls below a certain minimum. If there exists in a country or region a greater body of unemployed or underemployed unskilled labor than can be explained as merely temporary frictional unemployment, the assumption is warranted that employment of such labor on a new or expanded project will involve a minimal or zero real cost to the economy, because relatively little other production will be forgone. If this is true, the economic cost of employing a worker is measured by the resulting increase in consumption rather than by any decrease in other productive activities. The measurement of the real cost of employing additional labor therefore may be reduced if the additional consumption results in the utilization of excess capacity elsewhere in the economy. In this event the benefit of deriving a larger real return from the existing stock of capital equipment may at least partially offset the cost of the additional consumption involved in raising the level of total employment.[3]

In the preceding discussion it was assumed that in the absence of interference with market forces, the worker would have produced the same output but at a lower wage. This question was discussed in chapter 1 where it was concluded that the outcome would depend on the absolute wage level. With respect to capital (defined here as investment funds), an analogous situation may arise if through government subsidy the terms of the loan are "softened," but the monetary benefit of the softening is not returned to society in the form of a lower price for the product.[4] It might then be concluded that market imperfections contrived by external agents such as labor unions or governments are the principal reasons why economic prices of labor and capital differ from market wages and interest rates, with the economic prices for labor usually less and that for capital usually more than the market price.

If this were the whole story the problem would be conceptually simple enough, though objective measurement would still be difficult. For example, how should the supply price of an individual worker in a fully unionized closed shop industry be determined? The fact is that the problem of economic as against market pricing exists in countries where neither the labor nor the capital markets are distorted by effective external intervention. In such countries the causation is more subtle but nonetheless real. The first (and sometimes the last) approximation of the economic value of unskilled labor in such an economy is what economists have long called its opportunity cost, namely the laborer's marginal productivity in his most productive alternative employment.

Responsibility for the task of economic pricing

The economic pricing of labor relative to market wage rates should be done on the basis of a general countrywide analysis (a region or province may of course be used in a large country having good regional statistics). Project appraisers should work out and apply the regional adaptation of the

---

3. This would mean in theoretical terms that the marginal cost of producing additional consumers' goods are less than the average cost. As the excess capacity is absorbed, the average cost would fall and presumably the marginal cost would rise. When the two become equal, excess capacity will no longer exist, and thereafter additional employment will give rise to real economic costs, either in the form of new investment or in other consumption forgone.□

4. Of course the person who pays the subsidy, probably the taxpayer, may not be the consumer of the product—in short, a problem of incidence arises.□

national figures. This division of responsibility between project appraisers and country economists will assure that the subject receives more attention than it has in the past, when the tendency has been for project appraisers either to impute no monetary value to unskilled agricultural (particularly family) labor or to use some arbitrary fraction of the prevailing wage rate. Although useful as a kind of sensitivity test of the benefits and costs or the internal rate of return on the project, this practice has provided little assurance that the economic return on projects has been measured as accurately as available data would have permitted.

Intensity of employment and economic wages

The existence of a relatively large number of unemployed or underemployed laborers does not in itself justify the assumption of zero or near zero economic wages. A number of factors may account for such an employment situation: for example, seasonality of employment, mobility constraints (cultural, linguistic, psychological, and socioreligious factors, to say nothing of distance), and lack of the will to work, perhaps because of nutritional deprivation. In addition, the consumption effect, when present, argues strongly against the assumption of a zero or near zero economic wage rate. All of these factors need to be examined, but the basic approach should be to compare productivity of labor in alternative occupations, together with the respective wage rates, in order to arrive at an appropriate economic wage for a particular grade and use of labor.

Relative economic cost of labor and capital

The most basic assumption that seems to apply to almost all developing countries is that whereas the financial price of capital is markedly lower than its economic cost, the financial price of labor is higher than its economic cost. Also the difference between the economic and market price of labor tends to vary inversely with the degree of skill, the gap being wider for unskilled (particularly agricultural) labor. A full study of this subject would require an investigation of both the capital and the labor markets over time in the same region or locality and in other places. It would be particularly interesting to obtain evidence of the different behavior of rural and urban labor costs. This task, however, can be dealt with here only in a general way.

Another facet of the problem of economic pricing, whether of labor or other inputs, concerns the financial subsidies that will be necessary if a project is made feasible because the economic valuation placed on a particular input or class of inputs is lower than the financial cost to the project. In the absence of a subsidy in some form, including a protective tariff, such a project may produce a financial loss even though it may yield a satisfactory economic rate of return. The situations in which this may arise vary greatly, and the subject has ramifications that extend beyond the scope of this study.

It is clear that the determination of the economic feasibility of a project requires the economic pricing of both labor and capital costs. The link between the economic cost of labor and that of capital is evident in that part of the economic cost of labor is the effect that employment has on the future level of savings and investment, the economic value of which requires a judgment about the future real cost and marginal return to capital. The techniques for measuring the economic cost of capital will not be explored here, however, but this cost will be treated as an exogenous variable in the estimation of the economic cost of labor.

Reference has already been made to the consumption-savings effect that the provision of additional employment will have with respect to the disposition of the income of the workers themselves. It is also necessary to consider how providing additional employment will affect the supply of capital for the economy as a whole. Perhaps the best illustration of this effect is the taxes imposed on the more affluent members of the community (with high propensities to save) to obtain the resources to employ workers in public works projects that are specifically designed to be more labor intensive than the level of market wages (as compared with other factor costs) would otherwise dictate. These taxes will, of course, reduce the economy's supply of capital and thus reduce future, in relation to current, consumption.

This obviously is an issue on which the economist may not—and frequently should not—have the last word. There is little merit in using pricing techniques, whether subsidies or taxes, that jeopardize a political and social order which is otherwise conducive to successful economic development. Fortunately, placing a proper economic price on labor is an economic decision that under most circumstances is likely to improve political conditions as well as economic growth and stability.

An exception might be found in a project designed and operated in accordance with the valuation of labor at its economic price and in a market economy, if so much subsidy were required to make the project financially feasible that serious inflationary pressures were produced elsewhere in the economy. This situation is likely only in an economy that is quite small in relation to the project. Of course, such projects require—but do not always get—careful scrutiny. If the economic cost of labor is put at, say, 50 percent of the market wages, and if, as a result, a large portion of the country's development program consists of projects that are made highly labor intensive, the financial burden may be substantial. The incidence of this burden will depend on other facets of public policy, such as taxes, protective tariffs, and direct subsidies. Of course public sector projects are in a better position than private projects to absorb or diffuse the cost of employing labor whose financial cost exceeds its economic value. The economic pricing of factors of production would be particularly appropriate for public works if the subsidy involved were adequately reflected in an overall financial plan that is fiscally sound.

Statistical problems in the economic pricing of labor

Unfortunately, the availability of labor market data is apt to vary directly with the activity and efficiency of the market and therefore inversely with the need for the economic pricing of labor. In addition, dual or multiple labor markets are more common than the existence of a single efficient labor market throughout the economy. In certain urban areas the labor market may be reasonably competitive (although this is more apt to be true for skilled than unskilled workers), while anything resembling a competitive labor market scarcely exists in most rural communities.

It has been suggested that in such a dual economy, the market wage established for various grades of labor in the urban areas can be used for economic wage evaluation elsewhere in the economy. This assumes, of course, a fair degree of homogeneity between urban and rural labor in categories in which relatively low degrees of skill are required. This assumption may not be too unrealistic, but it neglects the important issue of movement costs. These costs are one of the major factors in perpetuating the spread between the economic and monetary level of wage rates.

If market wages established in the more labor-intensive and labor-competitive sectors cannot be applied in areas in which no real labor market exists, what other alternatives are available? If, as is often the case, the labor shortage is largely seasonal (as during planting or harvest times), and the labor market becomes fairly competitive, the prevailing market wage and the economic wage will tend to converge during those periods—which, it is to be hoped, may last for several months.[5]

5. John C. de Wilde, "Manpower and Employment Aspects of Selected Experiences in Agricultural Development in Tropical Africa," International Labour Review, vol. 104, no. 5 (November 1971), pp. 367–85. De Wilde says that the labor constraint is the principal factor in determining the crop cycle in Africa. The attempt to escape from such constraints with large families discourages family planning programs in rural areas.□

Indirect costs and benefits

The basic objective of project evaluation is to measure the contribution of a project to the economy in relation to its real cost, as measured by the alternative benefits that would have accrued to the economy in the absence of the project. Both benefits and costs will include direct and indirect elements. Direct elements are conceptually straightforward; the direct benefit is the economic value of the output of the project, and the direct cost is the economic value of the additional production that would have occurred in the absence of the project. The indirect benefits and costs, including as they do externalities of various kinds, are more difficult both to detect and to measure. Indirect benefits will usually include, for example, education and training for the labor force that will benefit other projects, as well as backward and forward linkages that may stimulate other parts of the economy, either by rendering economic the establishment of new plants or making possible the fuller utilization of existing plant and equipment. If the project provides such elements as workers' housing that would otherwise be a drain on other real resources, this provision may also be included in indirect benefits. Indirect benefits principally account for the difference between the private and social gross benefits from the project.

Indirect costs consist of the negative effect of the project on the resource endowment of the economy over and above the resources used up in the construction and subsequent operation of the project. The most important of these indirect costs usually relate to the adverse effect of the project on air and other environmental conditions, which usually are no more readily measurable than the indirect benefits of the project. More readily identifiable are other factors such as the possible spread of disease among workers handling dangerous materials or damages to the community from the disposal of industrial wastes such as nuclear materials.

The Time Dimension of Economic Pricing

Because labor is normally required in both the construction and operation of projects, its economic cost must be estimated not only for the construction phase but also throughout the active life of the project. The problem is somewhat simpler for public works such as roads and bridges, because the continuing labor costs on such projects are usually relatively small in relation to the initial cost of construction. In any case, future problems and costs assume a smaller dimension than those of the present through the vehicle of the compound discount, which is applied to streams of both future costs and future benefits and therefore reduces (or appears to reduce) the importance of the analyst's inability to forecast the future.

Various other simplifying conventions or assumptions may be introduced. Since only one project is dealt with at a time, it may be legitimate to assume availability of a supply of labor of the kind required for that project; and with only one broad category of labor to consider, the lack of homogeneity of the labor force as a whole can be disregarded, thus enabling the calculation of the economic price of labor to serve for the entire economy. Because in this study only the economic price of unskilled agricultural labor will be calculated, the assumption of homogeneity is reasonably valid. Further, if the labor requirements for the project are likely to be small in relation to the total labor supply available, it may be possible to disregard the effects of the project on the supply price of labor and thus assume perfect elasticity of supply.

It has been suggested also that averaging earnings over periods of full and partial employment will produce a reasonable indication of the economic wage rate for the year as a whole. One obvious point favoring this proposition is that, for the rural labor force, the variation in consumption over the year will be much less than the variation in market wages, and, as indicated above, consumption may be one of the principal factors in determining the economic cost of labor.

As a matter of necessity, this and other approaches to the problem have been macro (nationwide) in character. Where comparatively small projects are involved, the variance among labor markets in different localities is usually substantial enough to require project-by-project investigation, in addition to the general approach taken here. This kind of refinement is likely, however, to run into serious statistical problems. For example, in an agricultural community with year-round water supply, the production forgone by the emergence of new employment opportunities elsewhere will be much more important in determining economic wages than in areas of rain-fed or scantily irrigated agriculture.[6] In areas with a high degree of unemployment or underemployment throughout the year, the only measure of labor's economic cost may be the subsistence provided by private or public sources to the unemployed or underemployed labor force. This subsistence often consists of the retention of a surplus of employees on the public payrolls.

6. Normally the labor-capital ratio in irrigated agriculture is likely to be lower than in rain-fed agriculture, despite the more intensive cultivation in the former. Therefore, the marginal productivity of labor will be higher and probably the spread between market and economic wages considerably less than under more primitive rain-fed conditions. One implication of this is that the more highly developed agricultural techniques become, the less important the economic pricing of labor will be. □

Relation of Broader Policies to Economic Pricing

The bearing of general fiscal and monetary policy on the optimal use of resources is considered in a formal way in chapter 4. Among the general economic conditions that make the use of economic pricing desirable for purposes of project selection or design is the lower than optimal use of the labor force. The question may arise as to whether expansionary fiscal and monetary policy may help to alleviate this problem and perhaps make the use of economic pricing unnecessary. Such policies will of course have an adverse effect on the balance of payments unless countermeasures are taken—for example, adjustments in the exchange rate or imposition of quantitative import controls or protective tariffs. Expansionary policies may also affect the distribution of domestic income by reducing real wages, because commodity prices are likely to respond faster than money wages to inflationary pressures. The effect on the welfare of low-income groups will be especially adverse. Expansionary policies will probably narrow the gap between the market and the economic price of labor,[7] but if inflationary pressures are built up, the resulting distortions throughout the economy are likely to be more objectionable than the result of an incorrect pricing of labor and other factors of production.

If expansionary fiscal and monetary policies are more likely to produce a cure worse than the disease when applied to a situation in which factor combinations and project selection are distorted by a discrepancy between the market and economic cost of labor, what would be the effect of the inverse policy of contractionary fiscal or monetary action as a means of driving down monetary wages to or nearer their economic level? Such a policy assumes that the factors that go into the economic price of labor will be less responsive to contractionary measures than will market wage rates. This assumption will probably not be valid in situations in which artificial restraints on wage flexibility are of considerable significance. In most market economies the rates of discount, as well as the economic prices of consumer goods on which the economic cost of labor largely depends, may be more likely to respond to downward pressures than is the market price of labor itself. In any case, since the market and economic costs of labor are likely to differ most when there is substantial unemployment, the use of contractionary fiscal and monetary policies to narrow this spread is unlikely to be politically acceptable.

Along with steps to improve the allocation of resources by the use of

---

7. For a formal discussion of this subject, see "Monetary Policy and Shadow Pricing" in chapter 4.□

economic pricing and costing, the effect of such a policy on income distribution needs to be considered as well as its effect on savings and investment. As a general proposition, employment-generating adjustments in the market price of labor and capital for purposes of project selection and preparation might be expected to reduce income disparity, which will in turn increase current consumption at the expense of investment. It would appear to be an oversimplification, however, to assume that such a trade-off must necessarily occur if the economy is endowed with a considerable stock of underutilized capital equipment that could be used to produce consumer goods—providing there is increased market demand to generate the proper incentive. The prevailing theory on this subject would therefore seem to overemphasize the adverse economic effect of transferring income from the capitalist to the labor elements in the economy, and it does not pay enough attention to the expansibility of the total flow of economic production as a result of such transfers. This problem is considered further in chapter 3.

The economic cost of labor in relation to its market price will of course be relevant to the economic ranking of projects with different factor combinations required in the construction and production processes. Its relevance for project preparation and implementation will depend, however, on the elasticity of substitution between labor and capital for the engineering and other technical (noneconomic) aspects of the project. There would be little point in the difficult and time-consuming examination of this problem for a project in which the maintenance of quality standards or other exogenous considerations prescribe rather strict limits to capital-labor substitutability. If technical coefficients are fixed for projects—as they are usually assumed to be for the sectors used in input-output analysis—the economic pricing of factors becomes redundant for purposes of project preparation (but not for project selection). Probably, the more complex the technology, the less the opportunity for substitution of labor for capital (or vice versa), and thus the less the relevance of economic pricing of labor. Economic pricing will also have varying degrees of relevance in different parts of the same economy. This does not mean, of course, that economic pricing of factors is not significant for interproject comparisons of economic rates of return in the same region. □

Formulation of the Economic Price of Labor

BEFORE LAUNCHING INTO A COMPARISON of the different formulas that have been proposed for estimating the ratio of economic wage to market wage, a general word of caution is in order. While I believe that the concept of accounting or shadow pricing, resurrected by Tinbergen[1] and others, has its uses, it is not a precise tool. For this reason, mathematical calculations may seem rather pretentious.

This chapter is intended to serve two purposes. The first is to examine whether the different approaches to the problem of economic pricing have enough in common to permit some sort of synthesis to be made.[2] The second is to provide a guide for determining whether the empirical data available in two of the four countries studied in chapters 5 and 6 are or can be made relevant to a solution to the problem of economic pricing.

As already stressed, the concept of differentiating between the economic cost of goods and services and their market or financial prices is not new. The term "opportunity cost" was common in academic circles at least two generations ago. That it received little outside attention was probably owing to the belief then prevalent that competitive forces in factor as well as commodity markets made the concept relatively unimportant. It began to be applied only when the economies of developing countries came under serious scrutiny and particularly when the large body of unused or underused labor in those countries became a subject of concern because much of it was on the public payroll, with perhaps a zero or even a

---

1. Jan Tinbergen, *The Design of Development* (Washington, D.C.: World Bank, 1958), pp. 23–24.□
2. See Lyn Squire and Herman G. van der Tak, *Economic Analysis of Projects* (Baltimore: Johns Hopkins University Press, 1975). This work might be considered such a synthesis, although the authors have not so described it. One difficulty in using it for the kind of calculations made in chapters 5 and 6 is that it requires governments to make value judgments, which is not usually done (at least not explicitly) in a normal planning exercise.□

negative affect on economic growth. Some economists then concluded that to measure costs in terms of market prices for such redundant factors might mean a substantial misallocation of resources and particularly an under use of labor.[3] The gap between the birth of the idea and its practical use is now being closed.

Problems in Using Available Data

The general objective is to compute from empirical evidence the value of an entity which is at best definable only in rather abstract mathematical terms, that is, the partial first derivative of the production function with respect to the factor in question, measured in terms of social (economic) value. Since the calculation must be made at the margin of investment, whereas statistical data, if available at all, will usually be expressed in terms of averages, some special stratagem for manipulation of data will be necessary. Three other major difficulties also arise in using empirical data. The first is related to the lack of homogeneity of the supply of a particular factor. The second concerns the stability of the economic price of the factor over time. The third is a familiar problem of welfare economics, namely, how to evaluate in terms of one common element the economic benefits (or costs) to persons in widely disparate economic circumstances of a particular economic activity taking place over a period of time. The lack of homogeneity may be dealt with (though not satisfactorily resolved) by defining the factor very narrowly, though in so doing the possibility of using standard statistical data may be seriously reduced. The existence of regional differences in both market and real wages must also be confronted, as well as the obvious difference between urban and rural factor markets, particularly the labor markets. The stability of real costs over time is more of a problem in applying the concept to capital than to labor, at least for the construction of the project. Construction labor will be committed only during the period of construction (perhaps four or five years), whereas the capital is committed for the life of the project. Operational labor is, of course, another matter. The third problem, that of evaluating economic benefits or costs collectively, presents the greatest difficulties and really cannot be dealt with satisfactorily given the present state

3. See I. M. D. Little and J. A. Mirrlees, *Project Appraisal and Planning for Developing Countries* (New York: Basic Books, 1974), p. 29. The authors comment, "Thus we are concerned with the application of cost-benefit analysis precisely in fields where it is considered unnecessary in developed countries," where "the price mechanism works in such a way that profits are a reasonable measure of net benefits."□

of the art. The use of the numéraire device discussed below is an attempt to solve at least part of the problem.

In addition to purely economic analysis, the economic evaluation of labor depends on many exogenous factors, including technical change and its effect on the marginal productivity of labor; technical educational programs that may affect the supply of skilled and unskilled labor; and changes in the availability of capital in relation to labor.

The most pervasive problems in analyzing the labor market in developing countries and attaching a single value to the economic wage rate may be listed as follows: (a) If, because of the seasonal nature of employment, particularly of agricultural labor, the total supply is absorbed only at periods of peak demand, the economic cost will also vary seasonally and probably regionally. (b) Because household labor lacks mobility and tends to remain unemployed in slack seasons, its opportunity cost tends to deviate more from its market price than does that of nonhousehold labor. This tendency supports the point that the deviation between economic and market wages is greater in rural than in urban areas. (c) In economic and social terms, what is the elasticity of substitution between labor and capital at the margin and how may the use of subsidies distort the optimal relation between the utilization of labor and machinery in agriculture?[4] (d) What evidence exists that the deviation between the economic and market price of labor is inversely correlated with the workers' level of skill? (e) The amount of underemployment of labor at varying degrees of skill may indicate a relationship between market and economic prices. The statistical evidence on this point is, however, likely to be very weak or nonexistent.[5]

Listing these issues is not meant to imply that data exist for their adequate analysis, but to indicate the reservations that must be attached to any calculation of economic prices of labor. This book is confined to unskilled labor because I believe skilled labor is likely to be priced at or below its economic value in developing countries. Also the lack of homogeneity of skilled labor is such as to make any generalizations about its economic cost quite meaningless. One reason for the high economic cost of skilled labor is that an existing enterprise may preempt so much of the supply of skilled labor that other prospective employers are discouraged from building plants in that area or from entering the market in other ways. The ef-

---

4. The Korean Development Institute is studying this problem.□

5. The definition of "underemployment" involves subjective as well as objective factors. Little and Mirrlees (*Project Appraisal*, p. 31) say that underemployment is when men, by working, are unable to contribute as much as they consume. This definition of underemployment received comment above, and some of its limitations were pointed out.□

fect is probably both localized and transitory but is nevertheless worth examining. If the full economic cost of the monopsonist's product is reflected in its market price, this is unobjectionable. If, however, an entrepreneur is a monopsonist in hiring labor and a monopolist or highly protected in the selling of his product, economic pricing may be necessary on both the product (output) and the labor (input) for a proper evaluation of the project. This problem is beyond the scope of the macro statistics collected for the present study.

Whatever precise formula or technique is used, as suggested above, three elements must enter into the computation of the economic cost of labor. The first two are costs to the economy of using a unit of labor for a particular new task, one on the side of production and the other on the side of consumption. The production cost is the economic value of the goods and services that the laborer would have produced or is producing in his most productive alternative employment (his opportunity cost). The consumption cost is the additional consumption that the laborer or his dependents will enjoy as a result of his employment in a particular job rather than his former job (or lack of job). The third element is a negative cost and therefore a benefit—the effect of improving general income distribution by placing a new worker on the payroll or enhancing the pay of a worker presently employed. This effect is likely to depend on the pattern of income distribution in the economy. For the reasons given in the introduction and chapter 2, the economic cost of labor does not include the disutility to the worker of working on the new job as compared with his previous employment or with being unemployed.

Even with this considerable simplification it is obvious that these problems contain some highly speculative elements. The difficulty of placing a concrete economic value on a particular laborer or group of similar laborers depends, among other things, on the quality of the labor (whether skilled or unskilled) and the supply and demand for that particular type of labor, both at present and during the foreseeable future, if long-term employment is required to implement the project.[6]

6. See I. M. D. Little and J. A. Mirrlees, *Manual of Industrial Project Analysis in Developing Countries*, vol. 2: *Social Cost-Benefit Analysis* (Paris: OECD, 1969). In this, their original treatment of the subject, the authors concluded that the cost of unskilled labor is a small component in the cost of a particular product compared with other cost elements such as materials and capital equipment, and it would not cause much error to make a rough guess as to its economic price. This conclusion seems to fail to take account of the fact that the prices of the nonlabor inputs may be distorted in economic terms because these prices contain (as costs) large labor inputs which in turn are priced at market rather than economic prices. Thus, the real cost to the economy can be identified only by converting market to economic values for the total labor input regardless of how many projects or firms may be involved at

(*Note continues.*)

To value a unit of consumption (present and future) in relation to a unit of savings (present and future)—which, as will shortly be seen, is the essence of the economic price of labor problem—rates must be found for discounting both future consumption and the fruits of present and future savings. To compute these rates requires either the use of present rates of interest (or returns on capital), with the assumption that they will remain intact in the future, or rather hazardous estimates as to the direction and extent of change. It would be convenient, of course, if both future consumption and the fruits of savings could be discounted at the same rate. That would indeed be possible in an ideal situation in which any shift of resources would upset the optimal balance between consumption and saving and thus reduce total welfare. If such an economic environment existed, however, economic pricing would probably not be needed. The evaluations referred to above require a consumption rate of interest (CRI) for ascertaining the present economic value of future consumption streams and an accounting rate of interest (ARI) for determining the present economic and social value of investing savings.[7] In the course of time CRI and ARI should converge as the economy moves toward optimal use of its resources.

One further concept that needs to be examined before considering formulas for economic pricing is that of the numéraire (or basis) for comparing values which may be identical in financial terms but different in social or economic terms (or vice versa). This difference may arise because of three factors. The first follows from the fact that tariffs, subsidies, minimum wages, and other government-imposed conditions may cause actual prices to deviate from their financial costs to the economy. The second is that a certain value in financial terms, say a thousand dollars, will have a very different economic value to the recipient depending on whether it is the first thousand dollars of income or the last in a million-dollar income. Third is the fact, already alluded to, that, since development normally im-

---

different stages in producing the product. If one accepts the original thesis of Little and Mirrlees that the labor input is small for the project under study, then the results will depend on the degree of integration of the industry, which is not a sound approach. In any event, the point seems to have been omitted in the revised version of their method (*Project Appraisal*).□

7. Unfortunately economists have not agreed on a common nomenclature for these terms. CRI is sometimes called the social rate of discount and ARI the net social marginal productivity of capital. Nor do their meanings always agree with the ones used here. In *Project Appraisal* Little and Mirrlees appear to define ARI as the rate of discount applied to project benefits and costs (measured at economic prices) that will give positive present social (economic) values and just exhaust the supply of savings. According to the authors, this value is determined by experience.□

plies saving and investing, it follows that a unit of money saved usually has a higher value to a developing society than the same unit of money used for current consumption.

Not all these differences can be eliminated by dividing financial values by a common factor or numéraire, regardless of how it is constructed. In their original analysis (*Manual of Industrial Project Analysis*), Little and Mirrlees attempted to reduce all values to "border prices" by the use of a standard conversion factor or a proper economic exchange rate. This seems to have some but not major relevance to the ratio between the economic price and the market price of labor—the principal objective of this study. In this ratio, internationally traded goods or services enter into the equation only when reflected in the marginal productivity of labor or the economic value of the laborer's consumption. There is of course no international price as such for most of the highly differentiated grades and types of labor within even a single country, let alone internationally, but the commodities a particular category of labor would produce or consume in alternative employment could be so valued if the necessary data were available. Since I am concerned with ratios rather than absolute values, I have not tried to estimate the value of such a numéraire in my examples below. As Squire and van der Tak have pointed out, the choice of numéraire does not affect project analysis because the selection of projects depends on relative prices, whereas the numéraire determines the absolute price level.[8]

In their revised formulation in *Project Appraisal*, Little and Mirrlees prefer to use a two-step numéraire. First, they reduce all values to the equivalent of freely disposable funds in the hands of the government. Then they apply a standard conversion factor to convert such funds to border price equivalents. It is difficult to determine, however, how one would derive the function to convert private expenditures or funds into such public funds.[9]

---

8. Squire and van der Tak, *Economic Analysis of Projects*, p. 28.□

9. According to Little and Mirrlees (*Project Appraisal*, p. 35) there is a case for valuing income more highly in the hands of the government than in the hands of the individual because, first, the government can see the broad picture and thus weigh the different purposes of expenditure more judiciously, and, second, the government has a greater propensity to save the proper amount. They agree that this is a controversial subject. The problem is illustrated in a practical way by the political debate that took place in the United States in the mid-1970s. The Ford administration clearly believed that, except for the most essential public services, income would be more productive if left in private hands. Critics of the administration appeared to place greater emphasis on the importance of the use of public funds in coping directly with the nation's problems, particularly unemployment. This conflict may illustrate the stability problems encountered with the Little and Mirrlees numéraire.□

The other method to be examined here was discussed in the guidelines of the United Nations Industrial Development Organization (UNIDO) and uses the economic or social value of consumption as the numéraire.[10] Since the economic value of labor in the UNIDO formula is already given in terms of consumption, I find this the more convenient methodology. Both the UNIDO formulation and the so-called Little-Mirrlees method—the two best-known and most widely discussed analyses of the economic pricing of labor—are reviewed below.

The Little-Mirrlees Approach

I have examined both the original and the revised versions of the Little-Mirrlees method and, apart from the difference in numéraire, find little significant difference between them. (See appendix A for a comparison of the two versions.) The symbols used in the original version are adopted here. It is important to note that all variables used in the Little-Mirrlees system for calculating the economic cost of labor have already been converted to numéraire values, that is, they are valued in terms of freely disposable government funds and are reduced to border values by the use of a standard conversion factor (presumably the true or economic exchange rate).

The basic assumption of the Little-Mirrlees system is that the labor that is being costed has heretofore been engaged in the agricultural sector and is transferring to the industrial sector. Before the move from agriculture to industry, the worker's consumption was larger than, or at least as large as, his marginal productivity (M). He may have consumed more than M, that is, M + a, in which case a must have been obtained from others (probably members of the family) or from previous savings. Although there is a general assumption by Little and Mirrlees that labor does not save, saving and the spending of savings within a fairly short time, say, a year, is not ruled out. The authors assume that when the worker leaves agriculture he no longer derives income from sources other than his own earnings. The a element is then consumed by others (usually family members left behind). Thus the a may be disregarded in computing the economic cost of the worker after he leaves the farm because the economic cost of labor to the economy is not affected by transferring this bit of consumption from the worker to his relatives.

Little and Mirrlees assume that the worker finds employment at once in

10. Partha Dasgupta, Amartya Sen, and Stephen Marglin, *Guidelines for Project Evaluation* (New York: United Nations Industrial Development Organization, 1972).□

industry and that there are no transfer costs such as transport, moving expenses, unemployment relief while he is looking for a new job, and similar consumption expenditures. These expenditures are, of course, often very significant in real life. Also, there is no distributional effect from the labor transfer as in the UNIDO formula discussed below.[11] Conceptually, however, these could easily be added to the Little-Mirrlees equation systems. Consumption (C) in the new job is assumed to be larger than M. As in agriculture, it is assumed that workers do not save (in the sense of contributing to the economy's stock of capital), and therefore C and W (the worker's new wage rate) are equal. Little and Mirrlees do not take account of the costs to the employer of breaking in the new worker. These costs probably will include training and could be quite substantial. If these are included in W, the values for C and W would not be equal. The basic economic cost is measured in terms of the economic cost of hiring an additional laborer as it affects the present value of the future stream of consumer goods that would have been produced in the absence of such employment. Production in the industry into which the worker has moved is increased by the marginal productivity of labor in that industry. This would appear as a benefit in the cost-benefit analysis, and therefore of no concern in estimating the economic cost of labor. Of course, if the worker moves to yet another occupation, his marginal product in his previous occupation would be a cost of employing him in the new occupation.

Other variables used in the Little-Mirrlees analysis are the rate of interest (i) at which society discounts future consumption streams and the rate of saving (r) of the nonlabor or capitalist element in society out of new income generated by investing the fund saved by not hiring the worker. This is determined by the marginal economic productivity of capital and the capitalists' propensity to save. Of course, the capitalist class also consumes, but this is not an element in the economic cost of labor. An additional parameter that must be obtained is one the authors call the wages-capital ratio (n). Not much explanation is given of this quite important element in the Little-Mirrlees equation system, but the effect on labor costs and therefore on consumption of a unit increase in capital investment is n(C − M).

Another assumption in the simplest form of the Little-Mirrlees system is that all variables, such as r, i, and n, remain constant over the life of the

---

11. Little and Mirrlees (*Project Appraisal*, p. 130) say that "if the system of accounting (economic) wages is appropriate . . . then the distribution effects of the project have been largely looked after." This would seem to imply that a distributional factor is included in their economic wage formula, but I have not been able to detect it.□

project. In their revised version the authors illustrate the effect on their equation system of relaxing this condition. They are careful to stress that the discount rate applied to future consumption depends not only on pure time preference but also on the relative satisfaction to be expected from present and future consumption. This will depend, among other things, on the growth of per capita income. The assumption is that, at year zero, consumption is less desirable than investment (future consumption), and therefore there is a real economic cost to the economy of hiring an additional laborer. At this point the rate at which future consumption is discounted (CRI) may be lower than the rate of return on incremental investment (ARI). After a time, T, however, increase in future consumption will become less desirable, CRI will have risen, and possibly ARI will have fallen till the two are equal.

The S_0, an important intermediate function in the Little-Mirrlees analysis, is the present value (the value in year zero) of the future flow of consumer goods that would have been available if, instead of hiring the additional laborer now, an amount equivalent to the increase in consumption resulting from this employment had been invested. In other words, it is the value of an investment of $C - M$ in terms of its effect on future consumption. This is calculated by discounting at rate i the stream of consumption that would have resulted from putting to productive use the growing capital stock of the economy, the initial amount of which is $C - M$. This must be multiplied by the increase in consumption resulting from each increase in the capital stock. Finally, if the project is of finite life, there will be a stock of capital at the end of the project that will be discounted back to year zero to obtain the total present value of the cost in terms of future consumption forgone resulting from the additional employment.[12]

Before coming to the algebra involved,[13] it would be well to look at the basic Little-Mirrlees assumption that, if consumption had not increased due to hiring the laborer, investment would have risen and by the same amount as his wage minus his previous marginal product. This assumption leaves out such considerations as the liquidity preference of investors, the demand effect of increased consumption in a period of unemployed labor or capital equipment, and many frictional factors that are pervasive in developing countries. In other words, the sum total of economic activity and of goods produced is assumed as given at any time, and the only ques-

12. It seems strange that the residual stock of capital should be discounted at the consumption rate of interest. The accounting rate of interest would seem more appropriate.☐
13. I should like to absolve Little and Mirrlees of any resonsibility for the algebra used here since it differs in some respects from that used in their two books.☐

tion is whether they are used for consumption or investment. This is clearly an "idealist" concept in any developing economy.

The simple case where C, M, r, and i remain constant over the life of the project will be examined. The effect of changing these parameters is to complicate the algebra but not the principles involved (see appendix A).

The present value in year zero of the stream of capital resulting from the investment of $C - M$ is:

$$C - M \left[1 + \frac{1 + r}{1 + i} \cdot \cdot \cdot \left(\frac{1 + r}{1 + i} \right)^{T-1} \right].$$

Summing this series:

$$\frac{(C - M)(1 + i)}{r - i} \left[\left(\frac{1 + r}{1 + i} \right)^{T} - 1 \right].$$

This assumes that $C - M$ and the yearly increment would be available for investment at the start of each subsequent year. Properly, however, the capital sum should be discounted by a half-year, that is, divided by $(1 + i)^{1/2}$. If, in the interest of simplicity, the term $(1 + i)$ is dropped from the numerator of the above summation, this factor will be slightly more than compensated for. The present value at the consumption rate of interest of a stream of capital is thus about

$$\frac{(C - M)}{r - i} \left[\left(\frac{1 + r}{1 + i} \right)^{T} - 1 \right].$$

To convert this to the present value of future consumption this factor must be multiplied by n, the ratio of the unskilled employed to capital investment, on the assumption that all of the wages bill is devoted to consumption. The present value of the stock of capital at the end of time T, which is $[(1 + r)/(1 + i)]^{T}$, must also be added. This results in the equation:

$$S_0 = \frac{(C - M)n}{r - i} \left[\left(\frac{1 + r}{1 + i} \right)^{T} - 1 \right] + \left(\frac{1 + r}{1 + i} \right)^{T}$$

or

(1) $$S_0 = \left(\frac{1 + r}{1 + i} \right)^{T} \left[\frac{(C - M)n}{r - i} + 1 \right] - \frac{(C - M)n}{r - i}.^{14}$$

14. If the life of the project is infinite and $r < i$, the first term will be zero and $S_0 = (C - M)n/(i - r)$. This equation gives the present social value of investing one unit now, expressed in terms of the discounted stream of consumption to which such investment will ultimately give rise. Therefore, $1/S_0$ is the ratio between the value of one unit of current consumption and one unit of current investment. Since $W = C$, C is not multiplied by S_0 in equation (3).□

If M is taken as zero (owing to unemployment in agriculture) and C is taken as 1, then:

$$(2) \qquad S_0 = \left(\frac{1+r}{1+i}\right)^T \left[\frac{n}{r-i}+1\right] - \frac{n}{r-i}.$$

Since S_0 is the cost to society of forgoing the future consumption that would be lost by hiring a worker in year zero, then the portion of this cost that is also a gain to society from his employment would be $(1/S_0)$ times whatever additional current consumption results from such employment. Since $C - M$ is the additional consumption enjoyed by the worker, the value to society of such consumption is $(1/S_0)(C - M)$. The difference between this amount and the additional consumption by the worker is of course $(C - M) - (1/S_0)(C - M)$. A further cost to society is the worker's marginal product in his previous agricultural employment. Thus, the total cost to society, or the economic cost, of employing the worker in his new employment (SWR) is $(C - M) - (1/S_0)(C - M) + M$. Rearranging the terms of this expression:

$$(3) \qquad \text{SWR} = C - \frac{1}{S_0}(C - M).$$

$$
\begin{bmatrix} \text{Economic cost} \\ \text{of hiring a} \\ \text{new worker} \end{bmatrix}
=
\begin{bmatrix} \text{Consumption in} \\ \text{new employment} \end{bmatrix}
-
\begin{bmatrix} \text{Increase in} \\ \text{consumption} \end{bmatrix}
\div
\begin{bmatrix} \text{Present} \\ \text{value of} \\ \text{investing} \\ \text{one unit} \end{bmatrix}
$$

If the actual wage in the new employment is W, and $W = C$ (no savings), then the basic equation for the ratio of economic wage to market wage is:

$$(4) \qquad \frac{\text{SWR}}{W} = 1 - \frac{1}{S_0}\left(1 - \frac{M}{W}\right).$$

As long as $S_0 > 1$ and $W > M$, then $\text{SWR}/W < 1$. Conversely, if M should exceed W (probably a rare situation unless labor is exploited in the agricultural sector), the economic wage will be above the actual market wage. Usually, the more backward the country, the larger the S_0 and also probably the higher the W in relation to M.[15]

Estimating the values of the Little-Mirrlees numéraire from impirical data poses some very difficult problems, particularly in forecasting. For this

---

15. If r and i are convergent and become equal at time T, then $S_T = 1$ and from equation (4) the wage rate in industry equals the marginal productivity of labor in agriculture. Also at this point a unit of investment has the same social value as a unit of consumption.□

reason their approach is not used in the estimates given in chapters 5 and 6. A numerical hypothetical example may, however, be useful to the reader. The savings of "nonworkers" out of their incremental income from a unit of investment is r. If the marginal economic productivity of capital is, say, 20 percent and their marginal savings rate is 25 percent, r should be 5 percent. In a relatively poor economy in which consumption is low, the consumption rate of interest (i) is likely to be fairly high, say, 10 percent. This can be expected to fall over time, but perhaps not appreciably over the twenty-year period which is assumed to be the life of a project. If n, the labor-capital ratio, is assumed to be 0.25, C and W are 1, and M is 0.4, then from equation (1) $S_0 = 2.5$. From equation (4) SWR/W = 1 − (1/2.5)(1 − 0.4) = 0.76 or 76 percent.

If the project lasted to infinity and the same variables were used, the value of SWR/W would be 80 percent. Neither of these values appears unreasonable as the ratio of the economic to the financial wage for unskilled labor.

To obtain some notion of the sensitivity of the relationship between economic and actual wages and the different variables, assume T (life of the project) is 30 years and n is 0.25; C and W are 1 and M is 0.4 as before. Thus r and i are the independent variables to be considered. If r is 6 percent and i is 15 percent, from equation (1) $S_0 = 1.9$ and from equation (4) SWR/W = 69 percent.

It will be noted that widening the spread between i and r from 5 to 9 percentage points has little effect on the economic wage–market wage ratio, even though the life of the project is lengthened by 50 percent. If the same values are taken for T, r, i, and W and M is reduced to 0.2, SWR/W will fall to 58 percent. If the spread between r and i is narrowed sufficiently SWR/W will decline further. For example, an r of 9 percent and i of 10 percent will produce an SWR/W of only 34 percent, if M is set at 0.2; if M remains at 0.4 the value would be 50 percent.

It is evident that a low marginal productivity of labor in its previous occupation will, as might be expected, produce a low economic wage almost regardless of the interest rate. It would be interesting to look at the circumstance, if any, under which SWR/W is greater than unity.[16]

It is clear from equation (4) that for SWR/W to be greater than unity, M must exceed W. That is, the wage in the new employment must be less than the marginal productivity in the old. This might indeed happen, but

16. This is very unlikely unless both the capitalist's propensity to save and the marginal productivity of capital are high. For example, if the former is 40 percent and the latter 20 percent, r would be only 8 percent.□

it would be unlikely unless labor were exploited and received less than its marginal product in its former employment.[17]

As in most simulations, the discussion above only shifts the problem from one unknown to another (in this case from SWR to i, r, and M), the valuation of which may be equally elusive. Also, the assumption that workers do not save is far from realistic, particularly when public savings are considered. To separate the elements in the problem and examine how they fit together is not without value, however, in an exercise which must yield results that are only approximate in any event.

One other problem that needs some emphasis is that various kinds of circular reasoning seem inherent in the economic pricing of labor. One example concerns the relationship between the accounting rate of interest (ARI), which under conditions of perfect equilibrium should correspond to the marginal productivity of capital, and the economic price of labor. Since all variables in the economic process are interrelated, there can be no objective determination of ARI without an assumption regarding SWR. As indicated throughout the examples above, however, the rate of capital accumulation out of an investment process (r) is both an element in determining SWR and in part a function of ARI. The problem of circularity can therefore be resolved only by value judgments concerning certain critical variables. These value judgments, which usually have important political overtones, are more clearly specified in the UNIDO method.[18]

The UNIDO Approach

In the UNIDO study Dasgupta, Sen, and Marglin use a method of measuring the economic wage rate that is basically similar to the Little-Mirrlees approach. As for estimating all other cost elements, the criterion employed is the effect of using a unit of the factor on the supply of consumption goods.[19] The algebraic formulation of the problem and the numéraire are different in the two approaches,[20] and the economic frame-

17. According to the convention adopted here, if there are no "breaking in" costs but only transfer costs, $W > C$. It is obvious that SWR would increase and might well exceed W. In this case, however, either W would have to increase or the transfer costs would have to be borne by the state, a not unlikely development. Of course, "breaking in" costs refer only to charges borne by the employer (see chapter 4). □

18. The algebra of the UNIDO method has not been rigorously adhered to, but the general line of the economic analysis has been followed. □

19. As already noted, in their revised formulation Little and Mirrlees convert the cost to its equivalent in freely expendable and convertible public funds. □

20. In the UNIDO analysis SWR is not broken down in quite the way that it is in this

(*Note continues.*)

work within which the two methods are applied is also somewhat different. The Little-Mirrlees analysis assumes that labor is shifting from agriculture to industry, whereas the UNIDO method discusses the shift of labor from private projects to those in the public sector. In this discussion, it will continue to be assumed that all wage income is used for consumption. Although the UNIDO study sets out to measure the economic wage rate in a surplus labor economy, underemployment is also considered. The authors admit the difficulty of measuring underemploynfent, which they define as a condition in which the social value of the marginal product of the worker is less than his demand price in alternative employment. This particular definition is not very helpful since the demand price for alternative employment seems unrelated to the worker's ability to perform such work. An alternative definition might be that the social marginal product of labor in the occupation in which a worker is underemployed is less than the social value of the wage he could command if fully employed elsewhere in the economy, less the transfer costs of moving to the new employment. The matter of transfer costs deserves more attention in the literature than it has been given.

A more important difference between the Little-Mirrlees and the UNIDO methods is that the latter takes into account the effect on income distribution of employing a worker in a job in which his wage and presumably his marginal productivity is higher than in his previous employment. This is a positive factor as far as the worker and the economy are concerned and therefore should be subtracted from the economic cost of labor to the economy. In the discussion of the estimate for the Philippines it may well be an element of significant size.

The authors separate the shadow (economic) wage into three elements: first, the direct opportunity cost of the worker; second, the indirect cost of employing him; and, third, the gain to the economy of the redistribution of income resulting from the employment of the worker. The direct cost is the social value of the product forgone by taking a worker from one job and putting him in another. This is the M of the Little-Mirrlees formulation, except that Little and Mirrlees measure M in terms of their numéraire, whereas the UNIDO guidelines measure it in terms of the effect on aggregate consumption. Consumption is measured in domestic prices.[21] In both approaches, if overt unemployment is widespread and continuous, M may be assumed to be zero.

---

book, but the general approach is the same. The terms have been arranged to show better SWR in relation to changes in the relative values of its constituent variables.□

21. Little and Mirrlees (*Project Appraisal*, p. 147) criticize the UNIDO numéraire of ag-
(*Note continues.*)

The second element, indirect cost, is, in UNIDO terms, the social value of the increase in consumption by labor and the reduction of savings by capitalists. This assumes, as in the Little-Mirrlees method, that all saving is out of nonwage income or that if the project is in the public sector it is financed by a levy on capital income only. In UNIDO symbolism (which I find cumbersome but which is supposed to be readily comprehensible because of its generic quality) S^{cap} is the rate of savings out of profits and thus $1 - S^{cap}$ is the rate of consumption out of profits (nonwage income). If the new market wage is W, then $(1 - S^{cap})W$ would be the consumption denied to the capitalist as a result of hiring an additional laborer. P^{inv} is the economic value of a unit of investment. Since the reduction of investment resulting from hiring an additional laborer will be WS^{cap}, its social cost (or, in the terms of this book, economic cost) will be that factor times P^{inv}. Thus the gross economic cost of hiring an additional worker would be $(1 - S^{cap})W + S^{cap}WP^{inv}$ or $(1 - S^{cap} + S^{cap}P^{inv})W$. To get the net economic indirect cost of hiring a worker, his wage is subtracted from the gross social indirect cost, as shown by the formula: $(1 - S^{cap} + S^{cap}P^{inv}W) - W$. Since W is all to be consumed and consumption is the numéraire, it requires no adjustment to be considered a social value. The above formula for net indirect (consumption) costs reduces to the simpler form $WS^{cap}(P^{inv} - 1)$.

Obviously the key parameter to be evaluated here is P^{inv}, the social value of investment. As in the Little-Mirrlees analysis, only costs are considered and therefore it is not necessary to be concerned with the production resulting from hiring the additional worker or from transferring him from one employment to another.

P^{inv} (as S_0 in the Little-Mirrlees analysis) is the value of a series which can be expressed as the present value of a stream of consumption, if it is assumed that the rate of saving and the marginal productivity of investment have a constant value, that all savings from profits are invested, and that the social rate of discount, i, is known and stable. If g is the social marginal productivity of capital and s the rate of saving from all income, then the annual return for one unit of investment may be expressed as $(1 - s)g$ units of consumption and $P^{inv}sg$ worth of investment. Thus the annual return from a unit of investment will be $(1 - s)g + P^{inv}sg$.

---

gregate consumption on the ground that consumption of different economic groups should be weighted differently, whereas uncommitted funds in government hands are homogeneous in this respect. Studies now in progress in the World Bank show, however, that public expenditure varies substantially and generally in favor of higher income groups. For this reason, funds in the hands of the government can be considered homogeneous only in a rather abstract sense. □

If the process continues to infinity and i is the social rate of discount, then:

$$(5) \qquad P^{\text{inv}} = \sum_{T=1}^{\infty} \frac{(1 - s)g + P^{\text{inv}}sg}{(1 + i)T}.$$

The sum of this geometric progression to infinity is $[(1 - s)g + P^{\text{inv}}sg]/i$. Therefore $P^{\text{inv}} = [(1 - s)g + P^{\text{inv}}sg]/i$ which can be rearranged as:

$$(6) \qquad P^{\text{inv}} = \frac{(1 - s)g}{i - sg}.$$

Substituting this for P^{inv} in the formula above for the net indirect cost of hiring an additional worker gives $WS^{\text{cap}}(g - i)/i - sg$. If n is the labor-capital ratio (as in Little-Mirrlees) the function becomes:

$$(7) \qquad nWS^{\text{cap}}(g - i)/i - sg.$$

This is the present value of consumption forgone because of hiring a worker or the indirect cost of such action.

It might be asked whether this function could be negative. That is, barring the redistribution factors discussed below, could the cost to the economy of hiring an additional worker in a new job be less than the loss of his marginal product in his former employment? This would, of course, be possible if he had been exploited in his old job and received less than his marginal product. Except in such a case, I think the likelihood of this function being negative is small. In a growing economy with surplus labor it would require either that $i > g$ and $i < sg$ or that g and sg are both greater than i.

That either of this pair of coincidences could occur seems a rather remote possibility. If $i > g$ it would mean that the project's marginal social product is less than the social discount rate and probably should not be undertaken. Of course, if i (the social rate of discount) is higher than g (the social marginal productivity of capital) it will certainly also be higher than sg since s is certain to be much less than unity. The first of the two alternative conditions may therefore be discarded. The real question is whether the social rate of discount is at all likely to be less than the social marginal productivity of capital times the rate of savings. It is possible than an affluent and very frugal economy will discount future consumption at a rate lower than the social value of additional production times the rate of savings.[22] This solution would however, be nonsensical in a poor

22. If, when Japan was saving at the rate of about 40 percent, the marginal productivity of investment was 20 percent and the social rate of discount was 7 percent, then equation (6) would be negative since $sg = 8$ percent. □

country where g and particularly s are likely to be fairly low and immediate consumption is likely to be given a high value so that i is high. There will therefore be a net indirect gain from hiring the worker, and the economic wage rate will exceed the marginal productivity of the worker in his present employment. In the long run, of course, the stock of capital would be drawn down in order to increase current as compared with future consumption until the social marginal productivity of capital (g) rose to be at least equal to the social rate of discount (i). At this stage there would be zero net indirect costs of additional employment, the economic and market rates of wages would tend to be equal, and economic pricing of labor would probably not be necessary.

The third element in the UNIDO formulation is the redistributional effect of providing a wage higher than the marginal productivity of labor, which is assumed to equal his former wage. The increase in wage is $W - M$, which is assumed to have a higher utility to the economy than income generally by a factor v, which is greater than zero. Thus $v(W - M)$ is the additional utility resulting from the worker's change of employment. This is a gain and therefore a negative factor in estimating the economic cost of labor to the economy (SWR). The worker, however, like the rest of the economy, will share in the loss of future consumption because nonworkers' savings have been diverted from investment to consumption to pay the worker's higher salary. The loss of investment per job will be $S^{cap}(W - M)$. With a social marginal productivity of g and with v, the premium on his consumption, the "cost" in terms of utility to the worker will be $nvgS^{cap}(W - M)$, where n is the labor-capital ratio. Summed to infinity at social discount rate i this results in a cost element to be included in SWR of $nvgS^{cap}(W - M)/i$. Thus the net beneficial effect to the economy of the distributional factor in SWR is $v(W - M) - nvgS^{cap}(W - M)/i$. Simplified, this becomes $v(W - M)(i - ngS^{cap})/i$. Because this is a benefit to the economy it appears as a negative factor in the SWR/W equation which, stated in the form of the SWR/W ratio, becomes:

$$(8) \quad \frac{SWR}{W} = \frac{M}{W} + \frac{nS^{cap}(g - i)}{i - sg} - v\left(1 - \frac{M}{W}\right)\frac{(i - ngS^{cap})}{i}.$$

$$\begin{bmatrix} \text{Ratio of} \\ \text{economic} \\ \text{wage to} \\ \text{market wage} \end{bmatrix} = \begin{bmatrix} \text{Direct} \\ \text{marginal} \\ \text{cost of the} \\ \text{worker} \end{bmatrix} \div \begin{bmatrix} \text{Money} \\ \text{wage} \end{bmatrix} + \begin{bmatrix} \text{Indirect} \\ \text{(consump-} \\ \text{tion) cost of} \\ \text{the worker} \end{bmatrix} - \begin{bmatrix} \text{Distribu-} \\ \text{tion} \\ \text{premium} \end{bmatrix}$$

This is the basic formulation of the ratio of economic wage to market wage.

If, instead of a project of infinite life, a thirty-year project is assumed with constant productivity over that period, equation (8) will be altered by eliminating the consumption and redistributional effects from the thirty-first year on. Thus, the equation becomes:

$$(8a) \quad \frac{SWR}{W} = \frac{M}{W} + \left[\frac{nS^{cap}(g - i)}{i - sg} - v \left(1 - \frac{M}{W} \right) \frac{i - ngS^{cap}}{i} \right]$$
$$\left(1 - \frac{1}{(1 + i)^{31}} \right)$$

Since $1/(1 + i)^{31}$ is likely to be quite small if i (the social rate of discount) is substantial, the expression $1 - 1/(1 + i)^{31}$ will be close to unity. Therefore the difference between the SWR/W ratio for a project of thirty years and a project of infinite duration is likely to be very minor and may easily be disregarded.

If the distributional premium is neglected the two formulations of the economic wage can be compared using much the same values as in the Little-Mirrlees formula. In both analyses i is the social rate of discount (consumption rate of interest) and n is the marginal labor-capital ratio. The r in Little-Mirrlees is equal to $S^{cap}g$. In testing the SWR/W ratio it is assumed that v is zero and the following values are used: 0.4 for M, 25 percent for S^{cap}, 10 percent for i, and 0.25 for n. It is also assumed that s is 10 percent and g is 0.25, which gives:

$$\frac{SWR}{W} = 0.4 + \frac{(0.25)(0.20)(0.25 - 0.1)}{0.10 - 0.025} = 50 \text{ percent.}$$

A zero value is used for v to enable some comparison with the results of the Little-Mirrlees cases illustrated above.

Before discussing the effect of including the distributional factor, it is useful to consider the question of whether the SWR/W ratio can be either negative or greater than one. If a negative economic wage rate is used, the implication is that employment has value for its own sake—more a political than an economic judgment. From equation (8) it may seem possible for SWR to be less than zero if there is a very large premium on income redistribution. This possibility is precluded if $i - nS^{cap}g$ is also negative, in which case a high v enhances the value of SWR. All this seems quite academic, however, as the examples in Taiwan and the Philippines will show. Of course, as the economy becomes more affluent v will tend to decline, and the spread between S^{cap} and s will diminish. The critical relationship, however, is that between g (the social marginal productivity of capital) and i (the social rate of discount). As these approach equality SWR will approach M, which in turn will approach W. There does not seem to be any objective proof that SWR may not be greater than W, but it appears improbable.

Comparisons

There are two rather fundamental problems in the use of both of the two formulations of the economic wage discussed above. One is the assumption of stable parameters and fixed exogenous variables over time, and the other is the problem of distinguishing between the so-called national parameters (in the UNIDO sense of parameters applicable to the whole economy) and those that are specific to particular programs, projects, or regions. This question was touched on above. A third possible complexity relates to the assumption of the Little-Mirrlees model that labor does not save out of wage income and that wages and consumption by labor are equivalent. In equation (8), however, a factor for savings is included, and C does not come into the calculation. Since the concern here is primarily with unskilled labor in developing countries, it is perhaps reasonable to assume that this kind of labor as a whole does not save in the sense of making a permanent contribution to the capital stock of the economy. Temporary savings by an individual or family will be dissaved within a fairly short period to subsist during seasonal unemployment, to pay for such things as family festivals, or to sustain old age. Saving by industrial wage earners, however, is certainly likely. The best way of adjusting for this appears to be to treat such savings as an "externality" to the economic price calculation. Therefore W is defined as the market wage of labor after savings. If unity is retained as the value of W, the actual economic wage to market wage ratio would be somewhat lower than that calculated earlier using the Little-Mirrlees approach. If the savings rate is taken as about 10 percent as in the UNIDO calculations (which do include the savings factor), SWR/W would be reduced to about 67 percent in the Little-Mirrlees example.

Because the SWR/W ratio is being calculated in relation to a specific project with a finite life span, the stability or instability of the variables in the Little-Mirrlees formulation will depend largely on the time involved. In the absence of a rather complex growth model for the economy (which would require estimates even more difficult than the components of the SWR formula) it is not possible to predict changes in the key variables. It should be possible, however, to estimate whether r's and i's are likely to change in the same or in opposite directions. Since i may decrease (that is, the cost of deferring consumption will become less) the value of S_T will approach zero. Because r is a function of the marginal social productivity of capital and of S^{cap}, it seems likely to remain fairly stable in the long run. Thus, if at the starting position discount rates are relatively high compared with savings rates, the difference between the economic and the market price of labor will tend to diminish over time. But if the social discount rate is already quite low in relation to the rate of savings, the SWR/W ratio is likely to be high (close to unity) from the outset.

The same general logic applies to the UNIDO formulation. As the economy becomes more affluent g and i should converge and v should diminish toward zero. Therefore SWR/W will increase as S^{cap} increases in relation to $(g - i)/(i - sg)$. Because S^{cap} is likely to increase more rapidly than $(g - i)/(i - sg)$ decreases, SWR/W will approach one.

In both the Little-Mirrlees and the UNIDO models, the higher the social value of investment as compared with current consumption, the lower the SWR—an indication of a social preference for projects that distribute a relatively large amount of the product to the higher income groups whose propensity to save is high.[23] If the distribution factor is disregarded, then SWR will vary directly with the rate of savings of the capitalists as long as the social marginal returns on investment, g, exceeds the social rate of discount, i, providing i is greater than the overall rate of savings, s, times g. SWR will be larger, other things being unchanged, the larger the ratio of savers to nonsavers in the economy and the higher the ratio of savers' income to nonsavers' income. The g and M variables will vary with different projects and different regions. Although it may be possible to arrive at an overall estimate of SWR/W from macroeconomic data, as in the illustrations above, the result should be adjusted to local conditions by selecting approximate values for the local marginal productivity of capital and labor.

The preceding analysis has shown the importance of selecting the appropriate social rate of discount, rate of saving, and marginal social rate of return on investment in the economy as a whole in determining the SWR. The social rate of discount is a result of subjective considerations by members of the community and will vary substantially with both intratemporal and intertemporal changes in time preference, which in turn will depend on the community's expectations regarding the future value of consumption. The social rate of discount will be very difficult to calculate from empirical data, and in the final analysis it will have to be estimated after taking account of a variety of factors, such as the economy's rate of growth and propensity to save, and a political judgment as to the degree of austerity the people would be willing to endure without unfavorable political reaction. The marginal social rate of return on investment can be estimated from economic analyses of projects, particularly from the economic rate of return on projects currently being undertaken by the development authority. The savings rate can of course be obtained from historical data,

23. Corry F. Azzi and James C. Cox, "Shadow Prices in Public Program Evaluation Models," *Quarterly Journal of Economics*, vol. 88, no. 1 (February 1974), pp. 158–65.□

supplemented by estimates of the marginal rate of savings expected during the foreseeable future. As a practical matter it may not be possible to arrive at more than a rough estimate of the subjective and objective factors listed above, but to determine the SWR it is important that the order of magnitude of the elements be identified.

There are other costs to society of employing labor in its new employment, in addition to the marginal productivity of a unit of labor in its previous employment and any increase in consumption in its new employment. These costs include such items as the use of transport facilities to get the laborer to his new employment, an unusually burdensome need to build training facilities if special training is required, and any hidden or overt subsidies required to induce the laborer to move from the old job (or lack of job) to the new. The extent of the burden of these costs on the economy will depend on whether new facilities are required to provide the services or whether excess capacity in existing facilities is sufficient to make new facilities unnecessary. This is clearly a project-specific problem.

Under normal circumstances SWR will be less than money wages because a unit of current consumption will be of less value than a unit of investment. This will be true as long as $g > i$, that is, the marginal rate of increased production made possible by increased investment exceeds the rate of discount needed to reduce a greater amount of future consumption to the value of a lesser amount of present consumption. If g increases over time, SWR will also increase because the value of investment in terms of consumption will increase.

If, say, labor and land are complementary factors of production, the use of more labor by using an SWR which is lower than W may increase the demand for land. Because the supply of land will be inelastic, the price of land will rise, whereas the price of capital (a third factor of production) may fall as a result of labor displacement. Thus, by "correctly" pricing one factor, labor, the market price of a competitive factor may be reduced, but that of a complementary factor may increase.

In the long run capital costs in most countries are expected to fall and labor costs to rise. If these expectations regarding future economic prices are reflected in current decisions, they may not result in the optimal blend of factors for meeting current national objectives. National objectives may, of course, change over time just as may the economic prices of labor and capital.

Whether the SWR/W is project specific or not, the cost of all the factors of production clearly cannot be derived from independently calculated national parameters because the economic price of labor is a function of the economic price of capital and vice-versa. The effect of this reciprocal relationship between economic factor prices is reduced for any one factor if more than two are considered—simply because the changeover from market to economic prices for a particular factor is then spread over more factors—but the principle is the same. The reciprocal relationship between the economic price of factors also depends on the nature of the production function. If the production function is not linear, the economic price relationships may be greater or less than reciprocal depending on the elasticity of substitution among the factors of production.   □

{4}

Further Considerations
Relating to Economic Wages

IF NEW JOB OPPORTUNITIES OPEN UP in an urban area and the city wage is sufficiently higher than the country wage plus transfer costs, an influx of workers from the country can be expected. It will be assumed that the worker would not move unless he expected to recover his transport costs during his first period of employment in the city.

Effect of New Urban Jobs on the Economic Wage

Before the new job opportunity arises, if N is the number employed in the city at this stage and the urban labor force is L, then the probability (p) that a worker will secure a job in the city will be N/L.[1]

After the new job opportunity arises, the probability of finding work needs to be restated. If g is the rate of growth of job opportunities in the urban area and these new jobs attract U persons from the country to the city, the city labor force will then become $L + U$ and the number of employed persons will be $N + gN$. Therefore the chance of getting a job in the city will be:

$$(1) \qquad\qquad p^1 = \frac{N + gN}{L + U}$$

It is assumed that labor will move from the country to the city if the wage in the city (W) minus transport costs (T) times the probability of securing employment there equals the marginal productivity of labor (M)

1. It has been suggested that it would be better to define the probability of securing a job as the ratio of vacancies to job seekers. I would agree if the labor market were sufficiently well organized to reveal these numbers, but I think the ratio I have used is sufficiently valid in the medium to long run. The number seeking a new job will depend in part on the ability of the unemployed to predict their chances of securing employment. Normally that capacity will be quite limited, as is evidenced by the increasing problem of urban unemployment.□

in rural areas. This assumption in turn presupposes that competitive conditions prevail in rural labor markets. Thus $(W - T)p^1 = M$ or $p^1 = M/(W - T)$ and therefore from equation (1):

(2) $$\frac{M}{W - T} = \frac{N + gN}{L + U}.$$

also from equation (1):

(3) $$gN = p^1(U + L) - N \quad \text{and}$$

(4) $$U = \frac{(N + gN) - Lp^1}{p^1}.$$

Thus those employed from the increment to the labor force (gN) naturally equals the total employed less those employed from the old labor force (Lp^1). This gives the somewhat ironic result that the total attracted to town is directly proportional to the number of jobs obtained but inversely proportional to the chances of getting a job. The economic cost of the increment to the urban labor force equals (in Little-Mirrlees symbols) their consumption (C) in the city (assuming no savings by the workers) plus their transport costs (T), less the increase in production of those securing employment, that is, $(p^1/S_0)(W - M)$, or if SWR^c is the economic cost of a new worker in the city then $SWR^c = W - (p^1/S_0)(W - M)$. Thus the total economic cost of those moving is $U \cdot SWR^c$. To take an example, let the following be assumed:

$p^1 = 40$ percent
$W = 1.3$ (includes T)
$C = 1$
$M = 0.4$
$T = 0.3$
i (the social discount rate—CRI) $= 10$ percent
r (the capitalists' marginal savings rate (S^{cap}) times the marginal social productivity of capital (K_s^1)
$S_i^{cap} = 25$ percent
$K_s^1 = 20$ percent

Therefore r is 5 percent, and the labor-capital ratio (n) is 0.25. For a thirty-year project period the computation is as follows, using equation (1) of chapter 3:

$$S_0 = \left(\frac{1.05}{1.10}\right)^{30} \left[\frac{(1 - 0.4)(0.25)}{-0.05} + 1\right] + \frac{(1 - 0.4)(0.25)}{0.05}$$

$$= 0.248[-3 + 1] + 3 = 2.5^2$$

2. Rounding 2.496 to 2.5.□

Therefore $$\frac{SWR^c}{W} = \frac{1}{1.3} - \frac{0.40}{2.5}\left(\frac{1.0 - 0.4}{1.3}\right) = 69.6 \text{ percent.}$$

If the worker had been sure of a job in town rather than having only a 40 percent chance, SWR^c/W would be 58.4 percent or about 11 percentage points lower. This is part of the price society pays for urban unemployment resulting from the attractions of urban over rural life. If, instead of migrating to the city, those who are unemployed had remained on the farm, their productivity per unit (M) would have been 0.4. If the wage (W) in the city truly reflects the marginal productivity of labor there, it is evident that if $U = 100$ workers and 40 get jobs in town, they will produce 40×1.3 or 52 units, whereas the entire 100 in the country would have produced only 40 units. Transporting the 100 to town, however, would cost 30 units, so the economy would be worse off by 18 units in the first period (30 units of transport cost, less the difference between 52 and 40). This is recouped in one and a half periods at the rate of 12 units a period.

It is interesting to note the situation in town before and after this influx. If initial population (L) of 1,000 is assumed and an unemployment rate of 40 percent, then $N = 600$. Since the influx (U) is taken as 100 and the probability of getting a job (p^1) as 40 percent, from equation (1) the rate of growth of job opportunities in town (g) is 10 percent. Of the 100 country folk who thought that they were going to get all the new jobs, 60 were deluded and joined the unemployed already in town. Of course, despite a growth in the labor force of 10 percent, the unemployment rate in town remains at 40 percent after the influx.

Price Elasticity of Supply of Labor

The price (or wage) elasticity of the supply of labor will probably be very low in the short run. It will depend on those induced to enter the labor market by higher wages or those that drop out because of lower wages. The elasticity of supply may be greater for female than for male labor. Also, the elasticity of supply of labor may be greater in more affluent economies in which, among other things, more significant savings enable workers to withdraw temporarily from the labor market. For this reason and also because of greater competitiveness in the demand for skilled labor it is assumed that the elasticity of supply of skilled labor would be greater than that of unskilled.

Social security benefits, particularly unemployment insurance, may also be assumed to increase the elasticity of the supply of labor. There are few such schemes in developing countries, however, and their effect

depends on how strictly the measures are enforced that require the unemployed to take any job that is available. In general, the greater the elasticity of supply of unskilled labor, the higher the money wage is likely to
be in relation to the economic wage rate.

In a closed or highly protected economy (as compared with the same
economy without import restrictions) the competition between capital
and labor may be reduced in favor of labor. This may cause the SWR/W
ratio to diminish. A high effective rate of protection may enable the manufacturing sector, or a substantial portion of it, to pay higher wages than
the more exposed sectors of the economy. Such wages are at the expense
of the economy as a whole, but particularly the export industries and agriculture, which normally do not enjoy a positive rate of effective protection. The money cost of labor in the protected capitalistic sectors of the
economy may therefore exceed its opportunity cost as measured by its
marginal productivity in the sectors of the economy that are exposed to
foreign competition or otherwise constrained in the pricing of their domestic value added. It is interesting to compare wage rates in protected industries with those prevailing in export industries or in other exposed
sectors of the economy. If there is a high degree of labor mobility between
industries and geographical areas, protection would be expected to have
less effect on wage rates. In this case the entrepreneur in the protected
sectors of the economy may be taking the higher value added in the form
of higher profits. To the extent that labor is exploited in this way the cost
of labor in other sectors of the economy will be reduced. Thus, in a protected sector, labor's share in the benefits of protection will be a function
of the effective rate of protection and of the nature and structure of the
labor market.

Economic waste will occur if the money wage offered by the protected
industry exceeds the social marginal product forgone in the unprotected
agricultural sector for the same quality of labor. The economic waste
would equal the excess of the social marginal product in agriculture over
the incremental consumption of labor due to higher wages in industry
minus the social marginal product in industry. Such net economic waste
would occur only if there had previously been reasonably full employment
in agriculture. There is no doubt, however, that autarkical policies have
generally boosted industrial wages in relation to those in agriculture.

Labor as Overhead Cost

Sometimes developing countries have a greater compulsion than developed
countries to keep labor on the payroll regardless of need. Thus labor costs

per unit of output tend to fluctuate not only with changes in wage levels but also with changes in output. In these circumstances the SWR/W ratio will fall off with a decline in the level of production.

Probably wage differences resulting from differences in skills are not as great in developing countries as in developed countries, though this remains to be investigated. Turner found, however, that wage differences between skilled and unskilled were greater in developing than in industrial economies, and clerical labor tends to be relatively better paid in developing countries than in developed countries in relation to manual laborers. Urban-rural wage differences have continued to increase despite growth in urban unemployment. Other imperfections in the labor market are the 2 to 1 ratios between wages paid by large and small enterprises and the political influence that keeps urban wages at a comparatively high level despite unemployment. Turner found that wage rates have recently been rising faster than labor productivity in developing countries (4 percent for wages and 1 percent for per capita GNP in Africa and 4 to 5 percent as compared to 1.5 percent for Latin America).[3] This would perhaps indicate that the SWR/W ratio has decreased.[4] As might be expected, the increase in real wages in African countries has tended both to encourage capital-intensive investment and to increase the labor surplus.

In addition to the prime effect of increasing the production of goods or services in the economy, an investment will have a secondary effect through the investment multiplier. The increase in incomes generated by the investment may stimulate demand and thus production and income elsewhere in the economy. As Gittinger points out, the benefit from this multiplier effect will depend on a number of factors, including the opportunity cost (economic price) of the factors of production employed as a result of the indirect demand that was stimulated, the elasticity of their supply, and the effect of the stimulated production on employment or unemployment elsewhere in the economy.[5] The maximum advantage from the multiplier effect of investment will be achieved if the investment is autonomous (that is, if it does not reduce other investments) and if the economic price of the factors provided new employment opportunities is low.

---

3. H. A. Turner, "Wage Policy and Economic Development," *Transactions of Manchester Statistical Society* (1962–63), pp. 1–22, especially pp. 7–8.□

4. SWR/W might rise even if W fell, if the elasticity of substitution of capital for labor were greater than one, since SWR depends, among other things, on the price of capital and its marginal productivity.□

5. See J. Price Gittinger, *Economic Analysis of Agricultural Projects* (Baltimore: Johns Hopkins University Press, 1972), pp. 280 ff.□

Monetary Policy and Shadow Pricing

As noted above, there is usually a positive spread between money wages and opportunity costs of labor in developing countries, together with a negative spread between market interest rates and the opportunity cost of capital. In the following examples a surplus labor economy will be assumed and it will be shown that fiscal and monetary policies may not be entirely neutral as far as the relative economic and money prices of capital and labor are concerned.[6] Expansionary fiscal and monetary policy lowers the market rate of interest; conversely the market rate of interest is lowered or raised to achieve fuller employment or dampen inflation. The economic price of labor and capital, however, remain more stable than their respective market prices in the short run. Therefore manipulation of the market price of labor and capital will have an effect on the relation between the economic and market prices of these factors and thus on the allocation of resources. The allocation of resources will be less affected if changes in the ratio of economic price to market price for labor and capital move together. If, however, the economic wage is below the market wage and the economic interest rate is above the market interest rate, measures to raise the market interest rate will narrow the discrepancy between the economic and market interest rates. If a secondary effect of raising the market rate of interest is to reduce employment in the urban sectors of the economy and thus drive down money wages, the spread between economic and money wages will also be reduced. For the present purpose, the importance of this measure is reduced by the fact that fiscal and monetary policies are likely to be less effective in narrowing the gap between the economic wage and money wage in rural areas where allocation of resources is a more acute problem. In the following analysis the effects of inflation as such are ignored.

The relationships between the variables involved are illustrated below using the following definitions:

W = money wage rate
SWR = economic wage rate
R = market interest rate
ARI = economic interest rate
M = money supply

The question is whether the relationship between SWR/W and ARI/R will be affected by fiscal and monetary policy and if so in which direction. It is assumed that (a) $SWR < W$ and (b) $ARI > R$.

---

6. See Milton Friedman and others, "Determinants of Wages (Real and Money) and Prices," *Journal of Political Economy*, vol. 80, no. 3 (September /October 1972), pp. 10–20.□

In case 1, constant returns to scale, the marginal productivities of labor and capital will not change by an increase in economic activity because of an increase in M. Since no other element in the SWR equation is likely to be affected, at least in the short run, it may be concluded that dSWR/dM and dARI/dM equal zero.[7] Differentiating the right-hand side of (a) and (b) by M gives dW/dM > 0 and dR/dM < 0. Thus, the increase in money supply will increase money wages relative to economic wages but decrease market interest rates relative to economic interest rates. Therefore the SWR/W ratio would decrease and ARI/R would increase. The discrepancy between the economic prices of labor and capital would increase in relation to their respective market prices, and the extent of the increase will depend on the elasticity of the supply of labor. A tightening of money supply would of course have the opposite effect, reducing money wages relative to economic wages and raising market interest rates relative to economic interest rates. Thus the discrepancy between economic and market wages in relation to economic and market interest rates should decrease.

In case 2, diminishing returns to scale, both dSWR/dM and dARI/dM are less than zero and both SWR and ARI will fall as the marginal productivity of labor and capital decline. Since dW/dM will still be greater than zero and dR/dM less than zero, with monetary expansion money wages will rise relative to economic wages and market interest rates fall relative to economic interest rates. The discrepancy between SWR/W and ARI/R may be increased because SWR/W will decrease and ARI/R will remain relatively stable (since both ARI and R will fall); the increase in the discrepancy, however, will be less than in case 1. By the same token, a tightening of monetary policy will tend to decrease the divergence, again less than in case 1.

In case 3, increasing returns to scale, both dSWR/dM and dARI/dM are greater than zero (marginal productivity rises). Since dW/dM > 0 and dR/dM < 0, monetary expansion will perhaps not change the SWR/W ratio much (since both SWR and W will rise) but it will increase the ARI/R ratio because ARI will rise and R will fall, thus increasing the discrepancy between SWR/W and ARI/R. Tightening monetary policy will again not change the SWR/W ratio, but it will raise market interest rates relative to economic interest rates and thus the divergence between the two ratios. As in case 2, the changes will be less than in case 1.

In cases of constant, diminishing, and increasing returns to scale an ex-

---

7. These are, of course, secondary derivatives of the production function. I assume the marginal productivity of labor and capital are the dominant factors in the economic prices of labor and capital.□

pansionary monetary policy will therefore increase the divergence between the SWR/W ratio and the ARI/R ratio while a contractionary monetary policy will tend to reduce it. Monetary policy will be more effective in this regard if the economy is operating under constant rather than diminishing or increasing returns. Of course, different sectors and firms do not continuously operate under any of these conditions, but it is worth noting that contractionary monetary policy, other things remaining the same, is more likely than expansionary policy to produce a symmetry between the SWR/W and ARI/R ratios. Such symmetry should tend to reduce any misallocation of resources between capital-intensive and labor-intensive industries.

Empirical data are needed to support this link between monetary policies and the relationship between economic and market prices. Evidence is needed, first, to demonstrate the flexibility of money wages and long-term interest rates in response to the easing or tightening of the supply of money by the manipulation of interest rates or other more direct means; and, second, to reveal the price movements that enter into the cost of living (consumer goods) at various levels of income in relation to labor and capital market prices, so that it can be determined which category of prices is the more elastic in response to changes in fiscal and monetary policy.

Effect of Agricultural Growth on the Economic Price of Industrial Labor

Lele and Mellor have pointed out that if the price of food falls because of technological advances in agriculture, industrial growth may speed up. This is partly because income elasticity of demand for food by the rural beneficiaries of technological change (the large farmers) is low, and also because industrial growth is largely a function of the real cost of labor in off-farm occupations, which will be reduced by the more abundant and hence cheaper cost of food.[8] If this process evolves far enough it will have a secondary reaction on the supply price of farm labor because of the rise of real wages in the urban areas. Nevertheless, since the relative absorption of labor in industry is likely to be less than the release of labor in agriculture, real wages in agriculture are not likely to rise very much. Of course, as the authors point out, the importance of the initial transfer of labor from agriculture to industry will depend on the labor intensity of industrial

8. See Uma J. Lele and John W. Mellor, *The Political Economy of Employment Oriented Development*, Occasional Paper no. 42, Department of Agricultural Economics, Cornell University, 1972.□

development, which in turn may be increased by a decline in the real cost (in terms of food) of industrial labor. Lele and Mellor have developed a model showing the possible interrelationships between agricultural and industrial development through changes in the cost of labor and other factors. Part of the model is sketched, with some comments, in appendix B.

Scott has attempted to estimate the relative values of market and shadow (economic) wages in Kenya for workers on small and large farms, workers in the informal urban sector, and unskilled labor in the formal urban sector.[9] He breaks down the shadow (economic) wage rate in a particular (new) employment as a function of three elements: first, the social cost of labor in its previous employment; second, the social cost of the increase in wage required to attract labor into new employment; and, third, the benefits to the family from the higher wage in the new employment.

Scott's method uses a large number of functions with elasticities so that in the final analysis the results are only educated guesses. The author relies on ILO studies of the wage structure of Kenya for his basic wage data and on a model of the rural-urban migration for some estimates.[10] For conversion factors he uses the revised Little-Mirrlees method, his numéraire being foreign exchange in the hands of the government. Basic to his analysis is the critical wage level (margin of subsistence) in rural and urban environments. At this wage, by definition, the shadow wage and the money wage would be equal. Thus only the deviations from the critical wage level need adjustment to convert from market to economic wages.

Since Scott is comparing shadow wages in real terms in rural and urban employments, he must know the comparative prices of the same basket of consumer goods in the two areas. By real wages he means the wage in terms of its utility to the wage earner. In this connection he makes the rather heroic assumption that the elasticity of marginal utility for income at different levels is unity.

He concludes that the following SWR/W ratios prevail in Kenya:

Worker on a small farm	0.75
Worker on a large farm	0.60
Worker in the informal urban sector	0.65
Worker in the formal urban sector	0.60

9. Maurice FitzGerald Scott, "Estimates of Shadow Wages in Kenya," Nuffield College, Oxford University, February 1973, processed. Part of this study is summarized in appendix C.□

10. J. R. Harris and M. P. Todaro, "Wages, Industrial Employment and Labor Productivity: The Kenyan Experience," *East African Economic Review*, vol. 1, no. 1 (June 1969), pp. 1–15.□

Stability of Economic Wage Rates

The question of the stability of SWR/W ratios has already been alluded to in the discussion of monetary policy above. The issue is whether economic wages are likely to change in the same amount and direction and at the same time as market wages or by different amounts, directions, or time intervals. Of concern here are general or average wave levels rather than specific wages. It has been pointed out that labor is not a homogeneous factor that remains constant in terms of productivity over time.[11] Individuals and groups will change in proficiency on the job. The productivity of labor will be a function of both subjective factors, which can be acquired by training and experience, and the whole gamut of technological and economic factors, both internal and external to the firm or other establishment in which labor is employed. Furthermore, although the marginal productivity of labor may equal the market wage, it does not necessarily determine it, particularly when nonmarket forces are present, such as trade union activity and the alternatives to employment provided by social security benefits. To the extent that economic wages are determined more by intrinsic economic factors than are market wages, it might be expected that economic wages would be more stable or at least would respond to somewhat different economic forces and therefore that the SWR/W ratio would change more because of changes in the denominator than the numerator.

In this study there is no intention to present a thorough analysis of the factors that determine the monetary wages of different grades of labor in comparison with the factors that affect the economic prices of similar grades of labor. Analyses of the economic pricing problem, including this one, tend to concentrate on unskilled labor because of the underlying assumption that skilled labor is sufficiently rare and valuable a factor and has sufficient bargaining power in the market so that the SWR/W ratio for it will approach unity and be relatively stable over time. This seems a reasonable assumption in developing countries, though it lacks a body of empirical support. It may be worth noting that the ratio of skilled to unskilled wages has tended to decline over time both in developed economies such as the United States and in countries such as Thailand.[12] In Thailand in 1969 the average income in urban areas was about two and a half times that in rural areas. Recently, however, the rise in rice prices

---

11. Malcolm R. Fisher, *The Economic Analysis of Labour* (New York: St. Martin's Press, 1971), pp. 7–9.□

12. In Malaysia a sample survey showed that wages for skilled labor were only 40 percent higher than for unskilled.□

has tended to increase wages in the rural areas relative to the urban areas. This is perhaps at least indirect evidence of the narrowing spread between the incomes of unskilled rural workers and more highly skilled urban workers.

In both the Little-Mirrlees and UNIDO formulations the social rate of discount and the propensity to save of the nonwage earning population are significant factors in determining SWR. These factors do not seem likely to change substantially in the short run, whereas money wages of unskilled labor are likely to be quite vulnerable to short-term changes in economic conditions, such as commodity prices and the level of economic activity. I believe, therefore, as stated above, that economic wages may show greater stability than market wages over time. This is an important consideration when estimates of economic wages enter into project appraisals. The stability of economic wages over time is usually assumed primarily because prediction can be made only by an elaborate and fallible growth model that in turn usually requires assumptions regarding the stability of variables that are difficult to predict. ☐

{5}

Korea and Taiwan

BECAUSE OF CERTAIN SIMILARITIES in their economic orientation and performance, Korea and Taiwan may be conveniently analized together. Data on the labor situation in the two countries, particularly Taiwan, are more ample and relevant than for most developing countries. Furthermore the market forces affecting the price of labor seem rather more active than in the Philippines and Indonesia—though if this is true there will be less need for the economic pricing of labor in Korea and Taiwan. First, it is desirable to get a feel for the labor situation in these two countries and how it has developed in recent years. The available data are summarized in a number of tables in the statistical appendix.

Korea and Taiwan have relatively full employment economies, though not as full as official statistics would indicate. Hence, it might be supposed that wages would correspond fairly closely to marginal productivity and therefore to the economic price of labor. There do exist some controls on both the upward and downward movement of wages. On the downward side are minimum or basic wage scales, which may or may not be well enforced and which are said to be used mainly by companies in the public sector. On the upward side, controls are exercised indirectly through labor federations that appear to be instruments of quasi-official control over the incipient labor movements rather than representatives of the interests of the labor community as are their Western counterparts. Apart from such official or quasi-official controls, it was noted that all TV manufacturers in Taiwan had about the same starting wage for female labor (the type most in demand in the electronics industry) and also about the same standard increment in salary after the first year. Company unions predominate in both Korea and Taiwan.

Comparison of the Labor Forces

Some comparison of the composition and utilization of the labor forces in Korea and Taiwan is useful. The growth of the overall population of these countries has been declining quite rapidly. Between 1962 and 1972 the rate of population increase in Taiwan declined from 3.2 percent a year to 2 percent, and in Korea from 2.9 to 1.8 percent. Over this same period the population of Taiwan increased from about 11.5 million to nearly 15.3 million; by 1990 it is estimated that it will reach about 24 million, an increase of about 57 percent over 1972. This would mean an annual increase of about 2.3 percent a year or somewhat higher than that of 1972. Korea's population rose from 26.2 million to 32.4 million over the 1962–72 decade, an increase of about 23.6 percent. The growth rate appears to have stabilized at about 1.8 percent a year, however, which would mean a population of about 53 million in 1990, although the Korean planners expect the rate to decline further to around 1.3 percent by 1980. The growth of population in Taiwan is believed to be negatively correlated with the education of women and with expenditures on the family planning program, and positively correlated with the proportion of the population engaged in agriculture. The portion of the population living in urban areas has been fairly stable, but there was an absolute decline in the number of workers in agriculture near the end of the 1960s.

There is a decline in the dependency ratio in Taiwan and Korea.[1] In Taiwan the dependency ratio is projected to fall from 75 percent in 1970 to 60 percent by 1980. In Korea it was 79 percent in 1960 and was probably slightly lower in 1970, but by 1980 it may fall as low as 56 percent. Thus this ratio is following much the same downward course in both countries. In contrast, participation ratios[2] have remained relatively stable, although in Taiwan where the ratio has been considerably higher than in Korea (see table A2) it has shown a slight tendency to decline. These two rapidly growing countries have a higher percentage of their population in the recognized labor force than do developing countries generally. According to ILO data most developing countries have a participation rate of about 40 percent; in 1972 Korea's was about 56 percent and Taiwan's 60 percent. The substantial decline in eligible male participation in the labor force in Taiwan between 1963 and 1972 is illustrated in table A2, together with a small increase in female participation. The greater emphasis on education is certainly one explanation for this. The same trends are apparent in Korea, but less forcefully. Table A6 indicates that in Taiwan in the short period from 1968 to 1972 illiterates declined from 17.3 to 14.9 per-

1. The dependency ratio indicates those below fifteen and over sixty-four years of age in relation to those between fifteen and sixty-four; it is expressed here as a percentage.□

2. Those in the labor force expressed as a percentage of those of working age and over (fourteen years for Korea and fifteen years for Taiwan).□

cent of the labor force, while those with high school or vocational school qualifications increased from 22 to over 25 percent.

The age composition of the population is also changing. In Korea those of working age are expected to increase from about 59 percent of the population in 1966 to 71.5 percent in 1981. In fact the growth of population and that of the labor force have been moving in opposite directions for some time in Korea as shown in table 3. The Taiwan labor force has been growing at a much slower rate than the Korean—1.3 percent from 1967–70—and it is expected to grow even more slowly in the future.

Table A2 shows the sex composition of the labor force of Korea and Taiwan over the decade ending in 1972. The sharp decline in the male participation rate, particularly in Taiwan, has already been noted. For the two countries together, the female portion of the labor force did not change perceptibly in the decade, increasing only from 31.0 to 33.3 percent, while the female participation ratio increased by about the same comparatively small percentage.[3] In view of the influx of labor-intensive electronic industries into Taiwan it is rather surprising that the female portion of the labor force did not increase more, particularly in view of the decline in the male participation ratio in that country. There was probably a considerable shift of woman workers from agricultural to industrial employment in Taiwan. Table A10 shows the predominance in Korea of male workers in the professional and technical categories but the near equality of females to males among skilled workers in manufacturing.

Tables A4 and A5 show the increase in workers under twenty-five in the Taiwan labor force and the decline in those over sixty-five, though the latter did not exceed one percent from 1965 to 1972. Workers over sixty-five approximated 2 percent of the Korean labor force in 1971 and 1972, perhaps because of the greater importance of agriculture. It is a mark of economic development in Taiwan that the proportion of paid employees increased by 7.6 percent and unpaid family workers declined by 5.6 percent of the employed labor force from 1968 to 1972 (see table A8). Family labor also declined in Korea from 1964 to 1971 by 5.8 percent of the employed labor force (see table A9). Family workers represented 26.7 percent of the employed labor force in Korea in 1971 as compared with only 18.8 percent in Taiwan. Tables A11, A12, and A14 show roughly the same evolution of the sectoral composition of the labor force with economic growth and development in the two countries. Thus, in Korea the portion of the labor force in agriculture declined from 63 to 45 percent (18 percentage points) between 1963 and 1971, while the proportion of the

3. Unadjusted participation ratios are higher because they cover workers under age fourteen.□

Table 3. *Average Annual Growth of Population and Labor Force,*
Korea, 1955–70
(Percent)

Period	Population	Labor force
1955–60	3.20	2.20
1960–66	2.63	2.52
1966–70	1.90	2.54

Source: Assembled for the author by the Korean Development Institute.

labor force in primary industry (mainly agriculture) in Taiwan declined from 51 percent in 1960 to 36 percent in 1971 (15 percentage points). Apparently the growth of labor absorption in secondary industry (manufacturing) was somewhat faster in Korea than in Taiwan. In the manufacturing and mining sectors it rose from 9 to 16 percent of the total labor force in Korea between 1963 and 1971. In Taiwan the share of secondary industry in the labor force increased from 21 to 30 percent from 1960 to 1971. Thus the relative growth in the percentages in manufacturing was 78 for Korea and 48 for Taiwan. Taiwan started the decade at a much higher level of industrialization, which is reflected in the sectoral distribution of the labor force. The tertiary (service) sector increased its claims on the labor force in both countries, but in this sector too Korea somewhat exceeded Taiwan in the growth of labor absorption. Later in this chapter the change in the labor force within a sector will be compared with the change in the sectoral contributions to GNP.

Employment

Because of definitional and statistical problems any discussion of employment, underemployment, and unemployment in developing countries must be approached with a good deal of trepidation.[4] This may be less true for Taiwan and Korea than for, say, the Indian subcontinent or Indonesia. It is easier to accept a figure of 2 to 3 percent of the labor force for unem-

4. Most observers feel that unemployment data understate the case inasmuch as the unemployed are defined as those who are seeking jobs and who have not worked at all for one month prior to the sampling date. This definition is used in most countries in the Far East and probably gives a downward bias to the official rate of unemployment because people are reluctant to admit that they are seeking work and not finding it. Some countries, such as Malaysia, draw a useful distinction between the active (those seeking work) and the passive (those not seeking work) unemployed. The failure to seek work presumably is largely the result of a belief that no work exists.□

ployment in Taiwan than in almost any other developing country. But the official estimates in table A15, which show a drop from 3.10 percent in 1963 to 0.85 percent in 1972, do seem dubious. The official index of employment rose by 37.5 percent between 1965 and 1973 and the index of unemployment fell by over 46.5 percent. These two sets of data obviously do not agree. Also in Taiwan, in contrast with other developing countries, the underemployed segment of the labor force is small and declined by two-thirds from 1965 to 1972. Over this period the potential labor force (those doing housework or going to school) remained stable at about one-third of the working age population.

Skepticism regarding the official estimates of unemployment for Taiwan is increased because estimates of the Manpower Development Committee (table A13) are much higher than those given by the Labor Force Survey (table A15), whereas in Korea the unemployment rates produced by the Korean Development Institute for 1965 to 1968 are not much higher than those of the Office of Labor Affairs (compare tables A16 and A17). I would assume that unemployment has been considerably lower in Taiwan than in Korea but that the difference is probably not as great as the official estimates indicate. Table A17 indicates that in Korea unemployment in farm households is low (as official statistics show it to be in most developing countries), while in nonfarm households it is quite high (though it declined by over 50 percent from 1963 to 1971). This, of course, reflects not only the urban drift but also Korea's increasing capacity to cope with it by rapid industrialization.

In Korea workers aged ten to fourteen years are included in the labor force, but since they constitute only 1.3 percent of the labor force they do not explain the high rate of urban unemployment. As indicated in table A18 unemployment rates in Korea in the 1960s were roughly comparable with those in the Philippines, which had a much slower rate of economic growth. In fact, with an economic growth rate of about 10 percent a year and a population growth of not much over 2 percent, an even greater absorption of the labor force would be expected than the rate of unemployment indicates.[5]

---

5. One well-informed source estimated that about 10 percent of the potential labor force in urban areas in Korea is unemployed. He said that a good deal of the unemployment is attributable to the fact that boys leaving school delay seeking employment until they have completed their army service. Although the extended family system provides a substitute for social security, it may also reduce the incentive to seek work outside the family. The government is attempting to reduce the considerable flow of unskilled labor into the cities from the rural areas by slowing its housing program in the cities and by encouraging decentralized industrialization.☐

The seasonality of unemployment in Taiwan is not apt to be a serious problem. Table A19 shows that from 1969 to 1972 unemployment peaked in October and employment peaked in April. The average incidence of unemployment was 8 percent below the annual average in April and 8 percent above in October. The spread between the peak and the trough averaged only 0.28 percent of the labor force, however, and it was quite unstable from year to year.[6]

In Korea employment was about evenly divided between farm and non-farm households in 1970 and 1971. If June, the high point, is taken as 100, farm employment was 70.5 percent in March, 91.2 percent in September, and 56.5 percent in December. Thus the seasonal fluctuation of agricultural employment is over 50 percent greater in Korea than it is in Taiwan.

Labor mobility and growth of the labor force

The mobility of labor among industrial sectors and between urban and rural communities has a bearing on the relation between the economic and the market price of labor. As noted in chapter 4, such mobility will generally tend to raise the economic cost of labor relative to its market wage rate. With fairly high mobility (that is, a large percentage of the labor force changing employment over a given period) the SWR/W ratios would be expected to be higher than with less mobility. Other things being equal, greater mobility indicates a more active labor market.

As might be expected in rapidly developing countries, the movement of labor from primary industry (mainly agriculture) to secondary and tertiary industry is considerably greater than the movement from secondary and tertiary industries to the primary industries. Information on the mobility of labor between sectors is summarized in tables A22 to A24 for Taiwan (1967–72) and in table A25 for Korea (1970 and 1971).

Despite the Taiwan economy's rapid rate of development, the mobility of labor seems to have been fairly limited. Over the five-year period from 1967 to 1972 only a little more than 5 percent of those in primary industry

---

6. The data collected in the Labor Force Survey (table A19) are partly contradicted by data collected by other agencies (table A20) which show a seasonal demand for labor in agriculture, the high months being July, October, and November. In the 1967–71 period, the average level of employment for these three months was 22.4 percent above the annual average and 36.9 percent above the average of the three lowest months, namely, February, May, and September. The only explanation (aside from bad statistics) is that the labor force in agriculture increases by more than the increase in jobs during the fall months and the opposite is true during the spring months.☐

moved to secondary and 3.7 percent to tertiary industry. The movement from tertiary and secondary industry to primary industry was only a little over one percent. Only 6.28 percent of those in tertiary industry in 1967 moved to secondary and 6.87 percent of those in secondary moved to tertiary.

Tables A23 and A24 also give some notion of the relative attractiveness of the different sectors to new entrants to the labor force. Secondary industry obviously had the greatest appeal to newcomers and primary industry the least; of those in primary industry in 1972 only about 10 percent were new entrants since 1967 (around 2 percent a year). Comparable figures for secondary and tertiary industry were 39 percent and 26 percent for the five-year period. Only 12.3 percent of those in primary industry in 1972 were either new entrants to the labor market or had shifted from the other two categories. For secondary and tertiary industry the comparable figures were 51 percent and 33 percent. From these data it appears that about 8.5 percent of the 1967 labor force had shifted sectors between 1967 and 1972. If the new entrants are included but those dropping out of the labor market in the interim are excluded, the mobility percentage was only 6.8 percent or about 1.4 percent a year. But for secondary industry, if those that dropped out of the labor force are excluded, the 1967 labor force in that sector was augmented 22.5 percent by transfers from other sectors. The comparable figure for primary industry was 2.1 percent and for tertiary industry 8.6 percent.

Teng-Hui Lee has attempted a longer range analysis of mobility and its causes as it pertains to agriculture in Taiwan.[7] Taking a small sample of 129 workers going from agriculture to industry, he found that 26 percent were "pushed out" and 74 percent were "pulled out." Lee points out that the movement of labor from agriculture to industry is a function both of changes in the wage spread and of new job opportunities in manufacturing. Table 4 shows that in recent years daily wages in agriculture have risen relative to those in industry.

Lee calculated the relation between the movement of labor out of agriculture and farm family income deflated by agricultural prices, employment opportunities, the average industrial wage deflated by consumer's price index, and the degree of urbanization. He found that the flow of labor from agriculture is strongly influenced by change in farm income and by employment opportunities off the farm. But for the 1967–72 period, I found almost no correlation between change in real wages in manufacturing and the percentage increase in migration out of agriculture. Lagging

7. Teng-Hui Lee, "Wage Differentials, Labor Mobility and Employment in Taiwan's Agriculture," paper presented at Sino-American Conference on Manpower, Taipei, June 26–July 1, 1972.□

Table 4. *Average Daily Wage in Industry and Agriculture,*
Taiwan, 1965–70
(Taiwan dollars)

Year	Industry	Agriculture	Ratio of agricultural to industrial wage
1965	47.93	38.76	80.86
1966	56.88	41.26	81.86
1967	56.88	43.93	71.50
1968	64.29	50.99	79.31
1969	65.99	60.60	91.83
1970	74.57	67.28	90.22

Sources: "Industry of Free China" and "The Report on Price Received and Paid by Farmers," Provincial Bureau of Accounting and Statistics.

statistics on migration out of agriculture one year behind changes in real wages in manufacturing produces a coefficient of correlation of only 0.2.

There is more correlation between migration from agriculture and changes in money wages in manufacturing. Again with one year's lag in migration behind changes in money wages, the correlation coefficient is about 0.7. Therefore it would seem that labor in Taiwan is more responsive to changes in money wages than to changes in real wages. Of course, such factors as employment opportunities in a new field and the chance for advancement enter into a farm worker's decision to try his luck in the city.

According to the Council for International Economic Cooperation and Development (CIECD) in Taiwan, the migration from agriculture to other sectors averaged 2.35 percent of the agricultural labor force from 1953 through 1968. It rose rapidly to 4.7 percent in 1969 and to 6.8 percent in 1970. For the period as a whole (1953–70), the average migration was 2.73 percent a year.[8] The coefficient of variation for the first sixteen years was about 34 percent.

Similar data are not available for Korea. Table A25 shows the percentage of the labor force that joined or left the mining, manufacturing, and construction sectors in 1971 and 1972. These data would seem to indicate a fairly rapid turnover. In 1970 nearly 65 percent of those in manufacturing took on a new job during the year (if all had shifted the index would be 100 percent) and 72 percent left an old one; in 1971 the comparable figures were 48.6 and 65 percent.

---

8. Growth rate of employment in agriculture decreased from 0.6 percent in 1953–61 to 0.26 percent in 1961–70. Manufacturing employment increased by 6.95 percent and 9.31 percent respectively in the two periods or by 8.20 percent a year for the two periods combined. For the period as a whole total nonagricultural employment increased by 5.89 percent a year and total employment by 3.17 percent.□

Wages and Productivity

The relation between wages and productivity may be analyzed by re-
viewing the labor markets and wage structures in the two countries.

Labor markets

In Korea, out of an employed labor force of about 4 million (about half
in secondary and service industries) only 500,000 belong to labor organizations, and these workers are effectively barred from strikes and most other
collective bargaining devices. The principal government activity in the
labor market is to serve as a clearinghouse between the unemployed
workers and prospective employers, and there is also a great deal of government involvement with wages and working conditions. Though
standby legislation has been drafted, there is no effective minimum wage.
The government has established guidelines for wages in export industries
the equivalent of 25 to 30 U.S. dollars a month, but the effectiveness of
these guidelines is limited. Though the relatively low level of unemployment might indicate that wages compare fairly well with the marginal productivity of labor, restrictions on the mobility of labor and its lack of effective bargaining power probably keep the market wage rate somewhat
below its potential level. (It should be recalled that these observations
refer to 1973–74.)

The government pressure to keep wages low is partially offset in Korea
by workmen's compensation and many other fringe benefits. One month
of severance pay is usually given by private employers. The army and government service have pension systems, but other social security is the
responsibility of the private employer. There is a plan to introduce a nationwide social security system. Labor disputes are settled by compulsory
mediation, which amounts to compulsory arbitration.

The Office of Labor Affairs of Korea is conducting a vocational training
program with emphasis on training people for off-season employment; five
vocational training centers are contemplated, two of which have already
been established. One large factory that I visited had established its own
vocational training school. The government also runs an overseas training
program, for which 50 million U.S. dollars have been provided, and has
sent many technicians to such countries as West Germany.

Labor organizations seem to have about the same role in Taiwan as in
Korea.[9] Social security and minimum wage requirements may be somewhat superior in Taiwan. In 1968 the minimum wage was 31 percent of

---

9. In 1970, 18 percent of nonagricultural civilian employees belonged to unions.□

the average wage in manufacturing, which compares with 34 percent in 1964 and perhaps a little under 50 percent in 1956. It indicates that wages are fixed mainly by market forces rather than by the minimum wage. Vocational education seems to be better organized and is financed by a payroll tax. Stress is placed on vocational training because the working-age population is expected to be fairly stable during the next decade and improvement in the quality of the labor force has high priority.

Wages

Table A26 shows money and real wages for Taiwan by sector from 1968 through 1972.[10] Real wages increased about 6.3 percent more in agriculture than in manufacturing, but this increase was not sufficient to prevent a net reduction of the amount of labor in agriculture. It is difficult to compare absolute wage rates in agriculture and industry because, among other things, there are differences in the sex composition of labor in the two sectors and more seasonal variations in agricultural wages (see table A27). On the basis of a twenty-four-day work month it appears that wages for males in manufacturing in mid-1972 were about 11 percent higher than wages in agriculture. Comparable wage figures for mining, public utilities, and personal services were higher than agricultural wages by 20.8, 36.2, and 27.9 percent respectively (see table A28).[11]

There is no significant correlation between the increase in real wages from year to year and the variation in wages paid by different firms. The increase in real wages produced no significant reaction on the variation in wages in different industries during both the inflationary period of the 1950s and the comparatively stable period of the 1960s.

Wage statistics are not as complete for Korea as they are for Taiwan. In Korea the average earnings for an employee in manufacturing increased 14.2 percent between April 1970 and April 1971 (table A31). This compares with an increase of 10.9 percent during the following year. In Taiwan average money wages in manufacturing increased 9.4 percent in 1970–71 and 8.6 percent in 1971–72. But if the increase in money wages in Korea is adjusted for the depreciation of the official exchange rate, the

---

10. Table A29 indicates that real wages in agriculture increased over 90 percent in the decade of the 1960s. Between 1954 and 1970 real wages in manufacturing increased 69.4 percent and in mining 143.6 percent.□

11. In July 1972 the wage rate for males was 69 percent over that for females in manufacturing and 41 percent more in personal services. Skilled labor in cotton spinning and chemical industries is now said to be earning the equivalent of 450 U.S. dollars to nearly 700 U.S. dollars a month. This supports the view that the Taiwan economy has a tendency toward high labor costs.□

percentages for the two countries (showing the adjusted relative changes in wage rates) are: Korea 12 percent, Taiwan 9.4 percent for 1970–71, and both Korea and Taiwan 8.6 percent for 1971–72. Thus exchange rate adjustments by 1971–72 had fully compensated for the somewhat larger increases in money wages in Korea. The consumer price index rose in Korea by 6.8 percent in 1970–71 and 11 percent in 1971–72, making it appear that for industry as a whole (excluding agriculture) real wages rose 3.5 percent in 1970–71 but declined slightly in 1971–72, whereas in Taiwan real wages increased in all sectors during both of these years.

In the longer run (1963–72) Korea's growth in real wages was 7.5 percent a year in urban manufacturing and 6.5 percent in rural areas. The difference is estimated at about 17 percent. Therefore the goal of achieving parity by 1981 is quite an ambitious one.

Opportunities for rural workers to supplement their incomes by off-farm work are fewer in Korea than in Taiwan because industrial production is concentrated in Seoul, Inchon, and Pusan. In Korea 17 percent of the income of rural dwellers is earned off the farm, compared with 55 percent in Taiwan. The Korean government has introduced a self-help program (the Sae Maeul) to improve the rural standard of living and in 1973 earmarked 6.6 percent of total public outlay for this program. During recent years price supports for rice and barley have tended to improve the position of rural households as compared with urban. For example, the ratio of household income in rural areas to household income in cities fell from 116.3 to 60.1 from 1963 to 1967 but rose from 60.1 to 83.0 from 1967 to 1972. (This comparison of course does not reflect changes in the relative sizes of households in rural and city areas.)

The productivity of labor has increased substantially in both Taiwan and Korea, with perhaps a marginally faster increase in Taiwan. The CIECD of Taiwan has estimated that labor productivity increased by 4.25 percent a year in 1953–61, and 5.98 percent in 1961–70. Data for the growth of real wages over these periods are not available for Taiwan. Real wages in agriculture increased about 6.5 percent a year during the decade of the 1960s, and, at least during the latter part of the decade, this increase was somewhat faster in agriculture than that in manufacturing (table A26). It seems safe to conclude that the increase in real wages and in productivity were about the same over this decade. The rate of growth in labor productivity is compared with the growth rates of other factors in table 5.[12]

Chi-Ming Hou, Charles Dana, and Yu-Chu Hsu have analyzed some of

12. Difficulties arise when comparing productivity between countries, both in measuring labor inputs and in calculating value added after adjustment for effective rates of pro-

(Note continues.)

Table 5. *Rate of Growth of Various Parameters, Taiwan, 1953–70*
(Percent)

Item	1953–61	1961–70	1953–70
Labor productivity	4.25	5.98	5.17
Employment	2.62	3.66	3.17
Gross domestic product	6.98	9.86	8.50
Labor force	2.76	3.54	3.17
Population	4.17	2.63	3.35
Unemployment	5.97	1.25	3.47

Source: Prepared for the author by the Council of International Economic Cooperation and Development (CIECD), Taiwan.

the factors entering into the growth of labor productivity in the nonagricultural sector of Taiwan.[13] They concluded first, that capital per worker declined by about a third from 1952 to 1969, but output per worker increased at 9 percent a year from 1952 to 1970. This apparent paradox may be the result of changes in the composition of capital. Many overhead facilities, such as buildings, were built in the early 1950s, and these have a lower marginal return than other forms of capital.

The second conclusion was that real wages have been rising in Taiwan despite a cyclical surplus of labor—which is contrary to the Lewis surplus labor theory. For nonagricultural sectors in 1954–58 the average increase in labor productivity was 4.89 percent and in the real wage, 5.8 percent.

The final conclusions concern factor intensity and growth. Compared with such countries as India and the Philippines, Taiwan has followed a labor-intensive pattern of development. Unemployment has been low, actually as well as statistically, and this has narrowed any gap between economic and market wage rates. Employment growth was considerably faster than population growth in the 1960s. Because the intensity of labor or of capital varies a great deal from sector to sector, however, there does not appear to be a simple relationship between labor intensity and output growth. Public utilities, transport, and communications have the highest capital-labor ratios and the highest growth rates. The spread between growth rates in different sectors is not as great as the spread between capital-labor intensities in different firms. The same is true for subgroups in manufacturing. As might be expected, the relation between labor pro-

---

tection. This subject requires further study. It will be assumed here that effective rates of protection are about the same in Taiwan and Korea.□

13. Chi-Ming Hou, Charles Dana, and Yu-Chu Hsu, "Non-agricultural Employment, Factor Intensity, and Growth: The Case of Taiwan," paper delivered at Sino-American Conference on Manpower, Taipei, June 26–July 1, 1972.□

ductivity and the capital-labor ratio is closer than that between the growth rate and the capital-labor ratio.

Marginal productivity of labor in Taiwan

For the shorter run (1968–71) the productivity of labor in Taiwan increased by 3.5 percent a year in agriculture and by 7.3 percent in industry, a greater spread than in earlier years. During this period the annual average increases in real wages were about 8.5 percent for agriculture and about 7 percent for manufacturing. Money wages, however, increased by about the same percentage in both sectors and in absolute terms were of course higher in industry. This appears to be further confirmation of the point made earlier that changes in money wages rather than real wages are the principal motivating force for the mobility of labor.

To summarize the relation between productivity and real wages in Taiwan, from 1953 to 1970 the average annual increase in real productivity of labor in agriculture was 3.67 percent and 4.21 percent in all nonagriculture sectors. During the first part of this period, however, productivity of labor grew more rapidly in agriculture (3.62 percent) than in the nonagriculture sectors (3.26 percent). This was largely because of a negative increase in labor productivity in construction and a relatively small increase in commerce. In manufacturing and mining the growth of productivity was considerably higher than in agriculture in both the 1950s and the 1960s. If the change in productivity in the different sectors is compared with the change in real wages, it should be possible to infer whether the relation of economic wage to real wage in agriculture is higher or lower than that in manufacturing. The results are given in table 6.

In relation to real wages, productivity in manufacturing increased about 57 percent more than in agriculture from 1960 to 1969.[14] If equilibrium is assumed between the two sectors with respect to the ratio of real wage to productivity in 1960,[15] the productivity of labor in agriculture fell to 64 percent of parity with manufacturing by 1969. This is a rough indication of the relation of marginal productivity of labor in agriculture to real wages in industry. In other words, it may be used as a rough measure of the overpayment of labor in agriculture compared with manufacturing in which labor is assumed to earn its economic wage.

14. $\dfrac{1.57}{1.21} \div \dfrac{1.55}{1.87} - 1 = 0.57.\square$

15. Employment statistics indicate (table A12) that 1960 was near the start of a large shift of labor from agriculture to industry and services after a considerable period of stability. I assume that this shift was brought about by disequilibrium between income and output in the sectors. $\square$

Table 6. Ratio of Labor Productivity to Real Wages, Taiwan

Year	Agriculture	Manufacturing
1960	1.87	1.21
1965	2.02	1.31
1969	1.55	1.57

Source: Prepared from table A33.

Despite the relative increase in the ratio of labor productivity to real wages in manufacturing in comparison with agriculture, the export-oriented industries in which Taiwan has specialized in recent years are more labor intensive than industries that compete with imports. The labor-capital ratio appears to be about 13 percent higher for export-oriented industries. It is doubtful whether this will continue as labor becomes more scarce and additional capital-intensive technology is imported.

Comparison of labor productivity in Korea and in Taiwan

Data concerning the relation of productivity to real wages are considerably sparser for Korea than for Taiwan. In comparisons of agriculture and industry it must be noted that the seasonality of agricultural employment is greater in Korea than in Taiwan. Korea's peak employment in June is about 75 percent above the low in December; a comparable percentage for Taiwan would be about 40 percent. Nonfarm employment shows very little seasonality in either country. Therefore, labor productivity by sectors may not be too meaningful.

A study by OECD[16] estimated that if the whole Korean economy is taken as 100, productivity per employed person was only 61 in agriculture and 148 for the rest of the economy. The comparable figure for manufacturing and mining is 164. Between 1968 and 1972 (1971 for agriculture) the productivity of labor in agriculture increased 25.2 percent, and in manufacturing 56.2 percent or 24.8 percent more.

Unfortunately no long-term data for real wages (or income) in agriculture are available for Korea. It is known, however, that agriculture's contribution to real GNP increased by 41 percent from 1968 to 1972. It is possible of course that Korean agriculture became more capital intensive

16. David Turnham and Ingelis Jaiger, *The Employment Problem in Less Developed Countries* (Paris: OECD, June 1970), pp. 1–10.□

during this period. Table A14 indicates that the number of employed persons in agriculture increased only 4 percent between 1968 and 1972—which strongly suggests that the productivity of agricultural labor rose considerably, as estimated by OECD. A sectoral study of Korean agriculture by the World Bank in 1973 indicates that the real income of the farm worker increased 18 percent from 1968 to 1971. The report also estimated that output per farm worker might increase about 5 percent a year over the next decade, along with a decline in the work force of 1 percent a year. From these data it would seem reasonable to assume that the real income of the Korean farm worker from 1968 to 1972 increased about 23 percent or a little less than the increase in productivity of labor in agriculture cited above. Labor's share of output was increasing at just over 60 percent of the rate of growth of agricultural GNP.

As for manufacturing in Korea, between 1968 and 1972 real wages increased 33 percent, as indicated in table A30. Since labor's real productivity in manufacturing increased by over 56 percent, the ratio of the increase in labor's productivity to the increase in real wages was about 1.7, compared with 1.8 for agriculture.

In Taiwan the comparable ratio for 1960 to 1969 was 1.3 for manufacturing and about 0.96 (from 1960 to 1971) for agriculture. It seems reasonable to conclude that the ratio of real income to productivity of labor in agriculture has shown relatively little change in Korea over recent years, and in manufacturing the real wage of Korean labor in relation to its productivity increased by less than half as much as it did in Taiwan. This does not necessarily mean that labor in manufacturing was exploited in Korea relative to Taiwan. To make that sort of judgment, it would be necessary to know the change in factor combinations in the two countries. The inference is merely that the economic price of labor in Korean manufacturing industry is much closer to its real income than in Taiwan and may even be above it. In Korean agriculture, however, indications are that the economic price of labor may be below its real market price.

The previous paragraphs on changes in the productivity of labor in agriculture and manufacturing in Taiwan concluded that, if the proposition is accepted that the relation between marginal product and real wages was in equilibrium (approximate equality) for agriculture and manufacturing in 1960, the productivity of agricultural labor in Taiwan in relation to its real wage had fallen to about 64 percent by 1969. Although data over the same period were not available for Korea, from 1968 to 1972 real wages and productivity in Korean agriculture seemed to move about in tandem. In further support of the thesis that the productivity of labor in Taiwan was relatively lower in relation to real wages than in Korea, it was found that in manufacturing the ratio of labor's rise in productivity to the rise in real wages between 1968 and 1972 was 1.7 as compared with 1.3 for Taiwan over the same period.

Sectoral comparison of productivity

In further examination of this question I have endeavored to compare changes in the relative productivity of labor in the main sectors of the two countries with rates of change in the relative rates of growth of the labor force in the different sectors. This should give some indication of comparative changes in the marginal productivity of labor.

An indication of the relative productivity of labor in the different sectors for Taiwan may be obtained by dividing the proportion of GDP contributed by each sector in 1953, 1961, and 1970 by the proportion of the total labor force engaged in that sector in the respective years. Unfortunately similar data are not available for these years for Korea. Table A43 shows the contributions of the various sectors to the GNP of that country for 1965 and 1973.

As might be expected, the ratio of the contribution per unit of labor to GNP or GDP is lower in agriculture than in manufacturing and mining (mining is quite small in both countries) and much lower than in the service fields in both countries. Also, with respect to the relation between agriculture and manufacturing, the ratio of productivity of agricultural labor to that of industrial labor increased in Taiwan from about 0.48 to 0.62 between 1963 and 1970 and increased in Korea from 0.88 in 1965 to 1.67 in 1973. The ratio of GNP or GDP to labor input for agriculture was exactly the same for Taiwan in 1970 as for Korea in 1973, but in the secondary industries the evolution was quite different in the two countries. In Taiwan the productivity ratio changed little from 1961 to 1970, decreasing only about 5 percent, whereas in Korea it increased by 36 percent. This further supports the assumption that the marginal productivity of labor in Taiwan was falling relative to its real wages. Interestingly, the increase in the productivity ratio for Korea in the 1960s was about the same as that for Taiwan from 1953 to 1961, which was 38 percent. For the tertiary sector the change was about the same in amount and direction over the respective periods in the two countries. The portion of national product produced by the tertiary sector tended to remain quite stable at about 50 percent, but in contrast to the situation in agriculture, the portion of the labor force in the tertiary sector rose, as it did in the secondary sector, but by a smaller percentage in the former than in the latter.

Tables A44 and A45 compare the growth of the labor force in each sector with the growth of that sector's portion of GNP or GDP. Again the periods differ substantially, with 1953 to 1961 for Taiwan and 1965 to

1972 for Korea. In both countries the small absolute increase in the agriculture labor force (there was even a decline from 1965 to 1968 in Korea) was accompanied by a continuing increase in agricultural production. These trends combined make agriculture look like a more efficient user of labor than manufacturing. More interesting than intersectoral comparisons are comparisons between the same sector in the two countries. The efficiency of labor utilization by Korean manufacturing is apparent from table A45. In Taiwan from 1953 to 1970 the labor force in manufacturing grew 5.1 percent a year and the sector's contribution to GNP grew by 13.37 percent, a ratio of 2.62. The similar ratio for Korea from 1965 through 1972 was 3.3. This is more impressive in view of the fact that the Korean ratio rose from only 1.53 in 1965–68 to 11.17 in 1968–72, whereas the Taiwan ratio fell from 4.2 for 1953–61 to 2.0 for 1961–70. The ratio for the service sector in both countries and periods is relatively low. Although the period is rather short it might be concluded that the elasticity of labor absorption with respect to output is falling in Korea and rising in Taiwan.[17]

Ranis has concluded that the Korean devaluation in 1963 and the increase in interest rates in 1964 had important effects. They stimulated export-oriented industry, which in his view tended to be more labor intensive than import-substitution manufacturing. The hike in interest rates also was calculated to increase the use of labor in place of capital whenever possible. The data in table A45 certainly reflect a significant increase in labor absorption relative to output during the 1965–68 period, but the increase does not seem to have been sustained from 1968 to 1972 when output grew rapidly but labor absorption was modest. A study of each industry would be needed to ascertain the cause of this difference between the two periods. In Taiwan the difference between the 1953–61 period and the 1961–70 period probably illustrates the change in industrial structure that took place as electronics and other consumer goods industries with great labor-absorbing potential became more important in relation to the more capital-intensive industries producing or processing raw materials. Thus the ratio of GDP growth to labor absorption was reduced from 4.2 to 2.0 This would indicate a considerable flexibility in technical coefficients (capital and labor per unit of output) over time.

The following conclusions seem apparent from these data: First, the crude labor productivity (without allowance for other inputs) in manufac-

17. See Gustav Ranis, "Industrial Sector Labor Absorption," Economic Growth Center, Discussion Paper 116 (New Haven: Yale University, July 1971), pp. 30–32. The author concludes that elasticity of labor absorption with respect to output tends to fall over time in developing countries. A growth of 8 to 10 percent is required to produce a labor absorption of 2 to 3 percent.□

turing rose sharply between 1953 and 1961 in Taiwan and between 1965 and 1972 in Korea. Second, this process continued to a lesser extent in Taiwan from 1961 to 1970; although productivity ratios declined for all sectors, the decline in manufacturing was less than in agriculture and services. Third, in both countries services tended to produce about half of the national product, but they did this with a steadily increasing portion of the labor force. Fourth, productivity per unit of labor in Korea increased more in agriculture relative to manufacturing than the respective increases in Taiwan even though the data cover a considerably longer period for Taiwan. By inference this seems to support the point made above that Taiwan farm labor may have been paid more in 1970 in relation to its productivity than in 1960. Thus, the real wage of agricultural labor exceeded its marginal product more than did the real wages of labor in manufacturing. Manufacturing wages were reasonably competitive in both periods.

Economic Wage of Agricultural Labor in Taiwan

Clearly only an approximate conclusion can be reached regarding the economic price of labor from the statistical analysis above. To arrive at the inference that Taiwanese farm labor might be somewhat overpaid in real terms in relation to its productivity, two assumptions were made. The first was that labor in secondary industry was not underpaid in relation to its marginal productivity; the second was that in 1960 a reasonable equivalence existed between productivity and real wages in Taiwan's agriculture. There does not seem to be similar evidence that farm labor in Korea is paid more than its economic wage. In fact the reverse may be the case.

In addition to the M/W ratio other elements are used in the Little-Mirrlees and UNIDO formulas to derive the SWR/W ratio. The more important parameters needed are the rate of savings from nonlabor income, the social rate of discount, and the social marginal productivity of capital. Deriving these parameters from normal macroeconomic data obviously requires some rather heroic assumptions. The income distribution factor is another element useful in the application of the UNIDO method.

Table A35 shows that between 1964 and 1970 the distribution of income in Taiwan became somewhat more even and that in 1970 it was considerably more even than in most developing countries. This process has probably continued along the same lines, and I have estimated the Gini ratio at about 0.3.[18]

---

18. The Gini function measures the inequality in the distribution of income; zero indicates an even distribution and one an extremely uneven distribution. The Gini function for

(*Note continues.*)

As for the social marginal productivity of capital (the g of the UNIDO formula), table A36 gives both the annual output (value added) and the amount of fresh investment per worker for 1964 to 1971 at constant prices. Since the marginal productivity of capital is $\Delta P/\Delta K$, the incremental output per worker (lagged by a year) divided by the fresh capital invested per worker gives a fairly good idea of the marginal productivity of capital. For the 1968–71 period the estimated marginal product was found to decline fairly steadily from 25 percent to about 20 percent. I will use 20 percent, the 1971 figure, because there was practically no change in real wages or in the labor force between 1970 and 1971. It is also necessary to know the labor cost per unit of investment (n in the Little-Mirrlees and UNIDO formulas). From the data above this seems to be about 0.5. This figure seems rather low, however, and investment per unit of labor cost is probably greater in manufacturing than in agriculture. Since the concern here is with agriculture, a value for n of 0.7 will be used.

The remaining factors to be estimated are the savings rate for the investor class (S^{cap} in the UNIDO or r/g in the Little-Mirrlees formula) and for the country generally (s), and the social rate of discount (i). Table A34 indicates that the overall rate of saving was 9 to 10 percent. For those in the income class of 80,000 Taiwan dollars and above, the savings rate approached 20 percent. It is assumed that most investors fall in this class and an S^{cap} of 20 percent is assumed. The value of i (social rate of discount) is largely a matter of public policy. At the present level of affluence of Taiwan an i of 12 percent seems reasonable. To summarize, the following will be used: $M/W = 64$ percent, $n = 0.7$, $g = 0.2$, $S^{cap} = 0.2$, $i = 0.12$, and $s = 0.10$. These values are applied to the following formula:

$$\frac{SWR}{W} = \frac{M}{W} + \frac{nS^{cap}\ (g - i)}{i - sg} - v \left(1 - \frac{M}{W}\right)\left(\frac{i - ngS^{cap}}{i}\right).$$

Without taking account of the distribution factor (that is, taking v as zero) an SWR/W ratio of 75 percent is obtained.

In Taiwan, which has a fairly even income distribution compared with many developing countries, the distributional weight should not have a significant effect on the SWR/W ratio. Any decision on that score is bound to be very arbitrary. If the v in the UNIDO equation is taken as 0.15

Taiwan has been estimated at 0.27 for 1972 and 0.33 for 1964. See Shail Jain, *Size Distribution of Income: A Compilation of Data* (Washington, D.C.: World Bank, 1975), p. 108.□

(half the Gini function), the effect of the redistribution factor would be about 5 percent. Thus the SWR/W ratio would be 71 percent.

For lack of the necessary data, particularly those needed to compute the marginal productivity of agricultural labor, I have not attempted to calculate the SWR/W ratio for Korea. Studies of the Korean Development Institute, though not specifically directed at this subject, suggest that in certain public utilities this ratio may be only a little less than 100 percent. My general impression, as indicated above, is that the SWR/W ratio for Korean agricultural labor is higher than that of Taiwan.   □

{6}

Indonesia and Philippines

THERE IS MUCH LESS SIMILARITY between the labor forces of the Philippines and Indonesia than between those of Korea and Taiwan. Some useful comparisons are, however, possible.

Comparison of the Labor Forces

Labor data are more abundant for the Philippines than for most other developing countries in the Far East. Unfortunately, publication of the data lags about two years behind the period to which it applies. The labor force was 12.9 million as of August 1971 or about half the population in the eligible age group. As in Indonesia, this group is defined as the number of people over ten years of age. Males accounted for 67.3 percent and females for 32.7 percent of the labor force. The average number of hours worked monthly was somewhat higher for men than for women. In comparison, females constitute about 28 percent of the labor force in Taiwan and 36 percent in Korea. The Philippine labor force is divided about equally between agricultural and nonagricultural pursuits, with only about 11.7 percent employed in manufacturing. As might be expected, the proportion employed in agriculture is declining and that in manufacturing slowly rising. The 61.5 percent of the labor force employed in agriculture in 1962 shrank to 48.9 percent in 1971. Meanwhile, manufacturing labor increased from 10.9 to 11.6 percent of the labor force. The growing importance of the service sectors, including government employment, is apparent.

Fairly detailed but somewhat obsolete data are available on unemployment in the Philippines and appear more realistic than the data for most other developing countries. A survey conducted in 1971 by the Bureau of the Census and Statistics placed unemployment at 5.4 percent of the labor force, which was less than in earlier years (see table B7). Owing to the slow-down of construction during the rainy season there is some seasonality, but it is comparatively minor. Philippine statisticians attempt to adjust unemployment data to account for partial unemployment or underemployment. With this adjustment the percentage of the labor force not at work was 7.4 percent in August and 9 percent in May of 1971. In other words, the degree of underemployment as a fully unemployed equivalent is about 2 percent of the labor force. A somewhat larger proportion of women than men suffer from unemployment since men accounted for 60.9 percent of the unemployed and women 39 percent as compared with their respective participations in the labor force of 67.3 and 32.7 percent. That a large percentage of the unemployed are "floaters" is indicated by the fact that over two-thirds of the unemployed are unmarried. In August 1973, 26.8 percent of urban males who had never married were unemployed, but only 7.1 percent of the rural "never-married." On a national basis the incidence of unemployment among this group was about twice the overall percentage.

An interesting aspect of the labor situation in the Philippines is that the unemployment rate in 1971 was 8.1 percent in the urban areas and 3.8 percent in the rural areas. In Manila and its suburbs it was over 11 percent. The unemployed are defined as those who have not worked at all during the week prior to the survey date. Among the sectors, agriculture had the lowest rate of unemployment (1.7 percent) and construction the highest (9.9 percent) in August 1971. This high rate for construction is largely explained by the fact that August is in the rainy season. Although the percentage of full-time unemployment in agriculture is very low, the incidence of part-time work (underemployment) in agriculture is nearly twice as large as in nonagricultural industries, namely 31 percent as compared with 16.5 percent. In manufacturing, underemployment is estimated to be 25.9 percent of the labor force in that sector. The higher incidence of underemployment in agriculture does not make up for the much higher rate of complete unemployment in the nonagricultural occupations.

Since 1970 there has been a minimum wage of 8 pesos a day for industrial labor in larger units and 4.75 pesos for agricultural labor. That these wage rates have some teeth is evident from the fact that the overall average weekly wage for all workers in August 1971 was 47 pesos a week or about 8 pesos a day.[1] The components of this average varied from 83 pesos

1. Tito A. Mijares of the School of Economics, University of the Philippines, has calculated that the effect of raising the minimum wage in 1965 from 3.50 to 4.75 pesos a day for agriculture and from 6.00 to 8.00 pesos a day in manufacturing (35.7 percent and 33.3 percent respectively) was to increase the weighted average wage costs by about 46.5 percent. This reflects indirect effects (for example, higher working capital costs) as well as the direct effect of wage hikes.□

a week for technical and professional workers to 38 pesos for manual workers. In the Philippines, as in Indonesia, certain firms and industries appear to pay wages higher than required by the labor market. Firms which have a large foreign participation and industries with strong trade unions fall in this category. The government sector pays wages which average well above those paid in the private sector.

There are about six thousand registered trade unions in the Philippines but only about half are engaged in collective bargaining, and many operate as labor contractors, supplying labor for work projects. About two million of the labor force or about 15 percent are unionized, but outside agriculture the percentages are quite high. All mining is unionized and 75 percent of the manufacturing. This is in sharp contrast to other countries in the Far East. Before martial law was proclaimed in 1972, there were about a hundred strikes a year, but strikes are now banned and compulsory arbitration is used.[2] The sugar workers, who are among the most depressed labor groups in the Philippines, are now open to unionization, which was forbidden before martial law because of pressure by the sugar producers and their political supporters. In many plants there is a good deal of competition among different unions. In general, labor unions appear to be a fairly strong economic force in the Philippines but they are not organized politically. Provisions for social security are more advanced in the Philippines than in most other countries of the Far East. Employers are required to pay 3.5 percent and workers 1.5 percent of the wage into provident funds, which provide a lump sum to the workers after a certain age or after a certain number of years of employment. There is no unemployment insurance.

Because of underemployment in agriculture the average agricultural laborer works about ten hours a week less than the nonagricultural worker. Another interesting point is that the unemployment rate appears to increase with the amount of schooling received.[3] There is also a large amount of underemployment among the highly educated.

Information on the labor market in Indonesia is limited in both its coverage and reliability. Data from a population census taken in 1971 and spot surveys can be accepted with reservations. Although the economi-

---

2. Compulsory arbitration, first introduced in 1935, was replaced in 1953 by Republic Act 875 (Magna Carta of Labor). By the time this act was suspended in September 1972, there were six thousand labor unions. The Presidential Decree of October 1972 (no. 21) outlawed strikes and lockouts and in effect restored compulsory arbitration, vesting control in the National Labor Relations Commission of the Department of Labor.□

3. This is also true of Indonesia up to the college level, after which unemployment seems negatively correlated with the level of education.□

cally active population of Indonesia covers a wider age span than that of Korea and Taiwan, partial census data indicate that it constitutes a lower percentage of the population than in the other two countries. Just under 50 percent of the population of Indonesia is economically active, compared with 57 percent in Taiwan. The census recorded 68.7 percent of the males and 32.1 percent of the females over the age of ten as included in the Indonesian labor force. These percentages are about the same as in the Philippines. The participation of urbanites in the urban labor force was about 10 percent less than a similar ratio for rural areas. About 42.8 percent of the urban and 52.1 percent of the rural population were classified as economically active. These low percentages may indicate unemployment rather than a low labor force participation ratio. Payrolls in Indonesia, perhaps more than in other developing countries, tend to be padded because of the red tape involved in reducing personnel.

The unemployment rate indicated by a sample of the census is lower than in Taiwan, which is growing much faster than Indonesia. About 2.4 percent of economically active men and 1.8 percent of the economically active women were registered as unemployed in 1971. As in other countries of the Far East the unemployed are defined as those seeking work but not finding it during the month (or week, in the case of the Philippines) prior to the recording date. According to competent observers, pride, the small amount of work needed to qualify as employed, and recording that is probably faulty or incomplete tend to make the official data well-nigh meaningless. Data on urban unemployment normally mean more than data on rural unemployment. Unemployment among the men in the urban labor force was recorded as about 5 percent and among the females as about 4.5 percent. Actually, the Labor Department takes a serious view of the unemployment situation and reckons that 20 percent of the labor force is less than fully employed. (A proposal by the department to provide funds for labor-intensive small-scale industry is still only an idea rather than a program.) It has been conjectured that the decline in the participation ratio over a recent three-year period was because better educational opportunities were drawing youths out of the labor force. This phenomenon was also noted in Taiwan. The minister of labor, Dr. Subroto, would not confirm this explanation but referred to the heavy rate of dropout from secondary schools as indicating that educational activities were not absorbing a larger portion of the labor force.

Except in the case of Jakarta, which is receiving an influx of about 140,000 new residents a year, the movement of population from rural to urban areas has not been as pronounced in Indonesia as elsewhere. Rural-urban migration has been limited by such factors as multiple cropping (half the area devoted to rice now has more than one crop a year) and the official transmigration program to move people out of Java. About 950,000 are said to be employed in rural work relief programs. Because of the nature of the crops grown (tea and rubber) there is relatively little possibility for the mechanization of agriculture in Indonesia, particularly on the estates.

The industrial wage structure of Indonesia is extremely complex. The general principle seems to be that wages are determined by the ability to pay of different firms. Foreign firms, particularly the oil and mining companies, pay several times as much as the small indigenous plants. No doubt they also get the best people. The policy is that foreign firms should pay at least 30 dollars a month equivalent, but Stanvac and Caltex pay their labor about 40,000 rupiah a month (1973) or something approaching a hundred U.S. dollars, whereas a newly established tobacco factory in the same locality pays about one-fifth that amount. Sweatshop wages as low as 35 rupiah a day are not uncommon. According to the Statistical Bureau of the Jakarta Municipality, the average yearly salary of employees in Jakarta has increased from about 48,000 rupiah in 1969 to 74,000 rupiah in 1970. The minimum wage for Jakarta, which applies only to municipal workers, is 140 rupiah or roughly 34 cents a day. Other regions also have minimum wages. That of the central government is 4,300 rupiah (about US$10.36) a month plus ten kilos of rice for each person in the family—usually the most important component in the wage bill. The government has established a National Wages Board to study the desirability of a national minimum wage. There are 112 labor offices in Indonesia, but they are understaffed and have to perform safety inspections and mediate labor disputes as well as act as labor exchanges. These offices deal with the unemployed mainly by assisting workers who want to leave Java for work in the outer islands. Inasmuch as the family structure of Indonesia is becoming less vertical, a public social security system appears to be necessary. At present, apart from the government and the army, employer participation in social security programs (such as workmen's compensation and old age pension) is still voluntary.

Labor disputes are handled by what amounts to compulsory mediation or arbitration. Labor union activity in the Western sense is rare in Indonesia. At present the only labor federation in the country has a membership of about twenty industrial unions. Formerly there were twenty-six federations, each with a number of unions that were sponsored by political factions. The total number of unions is said to be about four hundred. The objective of the government is to have one union in each plant (organized by industry), because plants without unions are more apt to have strikes than those with.

Labor Force and Employment

The International Labour Office (ILO), assisted by other agencies, made a thorough study of Philippine labor and related matters, which has been valuable in preparing this section.[4] Table B1 indicates that the population of the Philippines was about 37.4 million in 1970 and is expected to increase to over 51 million by 1980, with males slightly outnumbering females throughout the period. In May 1972 the population was estimated at 39.15 million. At its present growth rate of about 3.1 percent a year the population would reach the 100 million mark sometime shortly after the year 2000.

In mid-1971 the population of Indonesia was estimated at 119.2 million and the growth rate at about 2 percent a year. This compares with an estimated population of 97 million in 1961 (table B2).

Participation ratios

Accepting the official statistics, which categorize all those ten years of age and over as eligible for employment, the participation ratio in the Philippines in August 1972 was 67.8 percent for males and 31.9 percent for females or an overall ratio of about 50.2 percent. This compares with Indonesia's 49.9 percent.[5] The secular decline in the participation ratio (tables B3 and B4) in both urban and rural areas has been much more pronounced for the female component, in which the participation ratio fell from 41.0 percent to 31.9 percent from 1956 to August 1972. The male participation ratio fell only from 73.4 percent to 67.8 percent over the same period. In order to have a basis for comparison with Taiwan and Korea I have excluded those under fifteen from the labor force of the Philippines and Indonesia, since they are not counted in the former two countries. A comparison of tables A2 and B6 reveals that whereas the participation ratio in Korea in 1972 was about the same as that of the Philippines, the former has been quite stable since 1963 whereas the latter has declined by about 4 points. The ratio for Taiwan declined about half as much as that for the Philippines, but the Taiwan ratio in 1972 was still about the same as that for the Philippines in 1965. I do

---

4. *Sharing in Development: A Programme of Employment, Equity and Growth for the Philippines* (Geneva: ILO, 1974).□

5. The ILO Year Book of Labor Statistics for 1968 shows a participation ratio of 53 percent for Indonesia and 47 percent for the Philippines. There was a sharp drop in the Philippines between 1967 and 1968. Since then there has been some recovery. Indonesia data must be rough estimates at best.□

not have a useful time series for the change in the adjusted participation ratio in Indonesia. In 1971 the participation ratio was about 57.1 percent or only slightly higher than in the Philippines. This is rather surprising since the urban concentration of the labor force in Indonesia is only about 15 percent as compared with nearly 30 percent for the Philippines. In neither country is there much difference between the rural and urban participation ratios and what difference there is favors rural areas. In the Philippines the percentage of employment provided by the urban manufacturing sector declined slightly in the decade of the 1960s. Services and commerce took up the slack, with the result that, even with the poor showing in manufacturing, the urban labor force increased faster than the total.

Unemployment

As already noted, unemployment data for the Philippines (table B7) seem to be fairly realistic whereas the information on Indonesia (table B8) does not seem to bear much relation to facts. While the former is based on quite a thorough series of special sample surveys, the latter is a sample of general census material. There is some seasonality in unemployment in the Philippines, which is of course much more significant in rural than in urban areas. Although underemployment is likely to be high in the country, rural unemployment percentages are only about a third as high as the urban, and the seasonal swings in overall unemployment are therefore reduced (table B13). It appears also that the participation ratio is lower when unemployment is seasonally high, reflecting the natural tendency to withdraw from the labor force when the chance for employment is reduced.[6] In August 1971, the last month for which data were available, the rural unemployment rate was 3.8 percent and the urban 8.1 percent. This compares with 3 percent and 9 percent for May of that year. The overall rate of unemployment was 5.4 percent in August and 4.8 percent in May 1971.

6. The ILO reports that in May 1965, 76 percent of the males (ten years of age and over) were in the labor force and 39 percent of the females. In October when unemployment is higher the participation ratios were 71 percent and 35 percent. The male participation rate was 79 percent in rural and 70 percent in urban areas in May as compared with 73 percent and 66 percent in October. The female participation rate did not show much seasonal variation, nor did the "invisibly underemployed" (those working 40 hours a week or more but wanting more work), who in 1965 constituted 13.1 percent of the labor force. The visibly underemployed (working 40 hours a week or less and wanting more work) made up 11.6 percent of the work force. Thus in May 1965, although unemployment was only 8.2 percent, the visibly unemployed plus the partially unemployed constituted 32.9 percent of the labor force.□

The pattern of unemployment in Indonesia appears to be much like that in the Philippines, though the percentages are clearly much too low. The unemployed make up only 2.1 percent of the labor force (age fifteen and over) on a crude basis, and only 1.2 percent if only experienced people are counted (those that are not looking for their first job). As in the Philippines, recorded urban unemployment is two to three times rural unemployment on a percentage basis (tables B9 and B10), and male unemployment is higher than female in both urban and rural areas. Over half the urban unemployed in Indonesia are said to be looking for their first job. This group may include those who have left school and are holding out for better jobs, a situation common to most developing countries.

Employment and unemployment by sector

The growth of the Philippine labor force from 1966 to 1972 is shown in table 7. Employment grew slightly faster than the supply of labor during this period, and unemployment declined slightly in percentage,[7] although the number unemployed increased nearly 8 percent. As already noted, the decline in the relative importance of agriculture was marginal during this period. In agriculture 1,436,000 were seeking additional work in 1966, and 1,004,000 in 1972, or 12.2 and 7.1 percent of the labor force. When those seeking additional work in nonagricultural pursuits are added, the underemployed were 12.2 percent of the labor force in 1966 and 12.4 percent in 1972.[8] The total in search of some or more work declined from 29.3 percent of the labor force in 1966 to 19.3 percent in 1972.

The incidence of unemployment by sector is given in table 8. Because May is a month of normally high agricultural employment, in May 1972 54.2 percent of the total employed were in agriculture,[9] but only 30.7 percent of the unemployed with prior work experience were attached to that sector. Of the underemployed, 57 percent were also in agriculture and constituted over 14 percent of the agricultural labor force. Table B11 indicates the preponderence of male labor in agriculture. About 50 percent of the

7. From 7.1 to 6.9 percent of the labor force.□

8. According to the ILO study, since 1960 the labor force has grown by 2.9 percent a year and employment in agriculture at less than one percent. Over the decade of the 1960s the urban manufacturing sector accounted for only 12 percent of total employment, and its share declined over the decade from 12.1 to 11.5 percent. Agriculture declined from 61.2 to 50.4 percent. Commerce increased from 8.8 to 12.4 percent and services from 11.4 to 17.3 percent. These changes would normally mark the maturity of the economy, but in the Philippines they probably reflect the flow of rural labor into the cities where it seeks employment but finds it only in underemployed urban sectors.□

9. This compares with 59.8 percent in agriculture in May 1961.□

Table 7. Distribution of the Labor Force, Philippines, 1966 and 1972

| | 1966 | | 1972 | |
Sector	Thousands	Percent	Thousands	Percent
Total labor force	11,822	100	14,120	100
Employed				
Agricultural	6,135	51.9	7,022	49.7
Nonagricultural	4,512	38.2	5,606	39.7
Total at work	10,647	90.1	12,628	89.4
With job but not working	337	2.8	589	4.2
Total with jobs	10,984	92.9	13,217	93.6
Unemployed				
Worked before	308	2.6	397	2.8
Not worked before	530	4.5	506	3.6
Total unemployed	838	7.1	903	6.4

Source: Bureau of the Census and Statistics, Philippines.

underemployed in agriculture were self-employed and 21 percent were unpaid family workers.

In manufacturing it is estimated that in 1972 over 25 percent of those employed were seeking more work (as compared with 14 percent in agriculture), a decrease from 46 percent in 1969. If both the underemployed and the unemployed are included in the total, full unemployment in manufacturing was 24.9 percent of the labor force in manufacturing in 1966,

Table 8. Employment by Major Sector, Philippines, May 1972

Sector	Employed (thousands)	Percentage of total employed	Experienced unemployed (thousands)	Percentage of total experienced unemployed
Agriculture	7,166	54.2	122	30.7
Mining	58	0.4	4	1.1
Manufacturing	1,467	11.1	53	13.4
Construction	456	3.4	46	11.6
Transport[a]	519	3.9	22	5.5
Commerce	1,674	12.7	55	13.8
Services[b]	1,878	14.2	95	23.9
Total[c]	13,217	100.0	397	100.0

Source: Interim Manpower Plan for FY 1974–1977, National Manpower and Youth Council, Philippine Department of Labor, Quezon City, 1974.
  a. Includes electricity, gas, water, and sanitary facilities.
  b. Includes industry not reported.
  c. Figures may not add to totals because of rounding.

27.8 percent in 1967, 24.3 percent in 1968, 28.7 percent in 1969, and 27.0 percent in 1971. Apart from the educated unemployed, it is the lower levels of the work force that are generally most affected by underemployment as well as unemployment.

As noted above, the incidence of outright unemployment in the Philippines is very much lower in rural than in urban areas. In May 1971, 56 percent of the unemployed were urban although less than 30 percent of the labor force lived in urban areas. Manila and its suburbs had 17.5 percent of the total unemployment in the country in 1966 and 16.6 percent in 1972, although in 1971 only 8 percent of the Philippine families lived there. Thus the incidence of unemployment was about twice as severe in metropolitan Manila as in the country as a whole. In contrast, the Manila area together with central and southern Luzon had 47 percent of Philippine unemployment and about 46 percent of the population of the republic in 1972. The Visayas, which had about 26 percent of the population, had only 22 percent of the unemployed. In 1972 unemployment rates by job category were as follows: wage and salary workers 7.4 percent, self-employed 12.7 percent, and unpaid family workers 5.2 percent.

The *Interim Manpower Plan for FY 1974–1977*, published by the National Manpower and Youth Council (NMYC) of the Department of Labor in 1974, projected expansion of employment at 4.4 percent a year through 1977. Its projections are given by sector in table B12. Inasmuch as the labor force is expanding at about 3.4 percent a year, unemployment would be reduced by only about 15 percent of its 1972 level each year, quite a modest target. The NMYC plan suggests that the labor intensity of investment be increased by both fiscal incentives and qualitative controls. Philippine industrial policy in the past has been criticized for encouraging capital-intensive investment through tax incentives, interest rate concessions, and foreign exchange management policies designed to reduce capital equipment costs.[10] Tax exemptions of the kind used in the 1950s for new enterprise would be neutral in their effect on labor intensity and capital intensity.[11] Accelerated depreciation as well as minimum wage laws and social security taxation could have the effect of encouraging capital-intensive investment, and these measures have been prominent in more recent legislation.[12] The problem is to enact labor laws that will pro-

10. See John H. Power and Gerardo Sicat, *The Philippines: Industrialization and Trade Policies* (London: Oxford University Press, 1971), pp. 79–80.□

11. The period of the tax holiday did not increase with the amount of investment, as it did in Malaysia.□

12. Board of Industry data show that the largest portion (65 percent) of the incentives provided by the government went to the most capital-intensive sectors such as oil, petroleum products, mining, paper, nonmetallic products, transport equipment, chemicals, and

(*Note continues.*)

tect the economically weak position of the labor force without raising market wages above their economic level.

I have not examined in detail the future labor requirements for Indonesia by sector. A recent education sector study by the World Bank produced some interesting estimates of the relation of economic growth to demand for labor. The ratio of incremental employment to output for 1961–71 was estimated at 0.5, but at only half that level for the last half of the decade. If the lower ratio continues it would require a growth rate in employment of 8 percent to accommodate the probable increase in the labor force of at least 2 percent a year. This projection may be unduly pessimistic, however, because in 1965 there was a considerable redundancy of labor on Indonesian payrolls that still exists. Output could increase without a normal increase in the demand for labor. Probably an employment-output ratio of 0.3 to 0.4 is not unreasonable.

Sectoral and occupational distribution of labor in Indonesia

The difference between the industrial structures of Indonesia and the Philippines is indicated by comparing tables B11 and B14. Agriculture commands 9.7 percent more of the labor force in Indonesia than it does in the Philippines and manufacturing 3.5 percent less. To put it more sharply, if the proportion of the labor force engaged in manufacturing is taken as an index of industrialization, the Philippines is about 63 percent more industrialized than Indonesia. The average growth in agricultural employment in Indonesia has been only 0.5 percent a year for the last decade, compared with an estimated 4.1 percent a year in mining, manufacturing, construction, and public utilities. In proportion to the size of the male and female components of the labor forces in the two countries, females stand out in the manufacturing sectors in both countries. Females are proportionately nearly twice as important as males in the Philippines and nearly 80 percent more important in Indonesia, though in absolute numbers males in manufacturing somewhat outnumber females in both countries.

In view of the higher income levels and the generally more highly developed economy of the Philippines it is rather surprising that the por-

---

machinery, whereas only 35 percent went to food manufacturing, textiles, footwear, and forest products. For tax purposes, the law allows export industries to deduct from their net incomes the cost of direct labor and local raw materials (up to 25 percent of total export revenues). The ILO holds that granting incentives for raw materials may bias investment against more labor-intensive industries, such as electronics, which use imported materials.□

tion of the labor force classified as professional, technical, and managerial workers is almost the same in both countries: 5.7 percent for Indonesia and 5.9 percent for the Philippines according to recent census surveys.

Mobility of labor in the Philippines

Information on the mobility of labor between sectors of the economy is not available for the Philippines as it was for Taiwan. Some indication of the problem is given by the time it takes for a man to find employment in another sector after leaving agriculture. According to the *Interim Manpower Plan,* the average time required was 11.6 weeks in 1966, 8.4 weeks in 1969, and 13.1 weeks in 1972. To ease the problem, ten regional Manpower Development Centers have been established to provide training for skilled and semiskilled jobs.

Chapter 4 contained a discussion of the proposition that equilibrium in the labor market does not necessarily require equalization of real wages for comparable skills in different sectors of the economy. A number of factors besides wage differences enter into the mobility of the labor force. These include tangible and intangible transfer costs and whether they are borne by the worker, the employer, or the government. In addition to simple transport expenses for the worker and his family, there are costs of resettlement and training for a new job. There are also intangibles such as the psychological disutility of distance from friends and family and difficulty with an unfamiliar language or dialect. These intangible costs are striking in the Philippines because of the geographical dispersion of the population.

If, as often happens, these costs are not compensated by the superior social and environmental attractions of urban life, the supply price of agricultural labor for urban employment may be considerably higher than its marginal productivity in agriculture. This will be true even if its marginal product in the rural area is very low or even zero. If labor is assumed to be receiving its marginal product in the old and the new locations, an equilibrium situation (zero migration) would be one in which the difference in marginal productivities equals the transfer costs cited above, which are borne by the worker.

DeVoritz has collected data for 1948 to 1960 which indicate quite high ratios between those migrating into certain provinces of the Philippines and the average populations of those provinces. Manila and its suburbs showed the highest ratio, with immigration over the period being equal to about 52 percent of the population in 1960. The average for northeastern Mindanao, Davao, Cotabato, and Zamboanga was about 31 percent. DeVoritz also examined the relation between the gross increase in population between 1948 and 1961 and the growth in per capita income in these different provinces. That he found little correlation would seem to support the view that factors other than income differences may be chiefly responsible for population transfers. DeVoritz also attempted to evaluate population movements in relation to a number of exogenous variables, such as language and distance. Some of his conclusions are helpful in evaluating the factors influencing migration. One conclusion was that income gains account for only a small portion of the movement, but those with superior education and therefore with a higher income potential are more prone to move than others.[13]

Income Distribution in the Philippines

The *World Bank Atlas* (1973) gives the per capita GNP in the Philippines for 1971 as 240 U.S. dollars, or exactly three times that of Indonesia. The figure of 80 U.S. dollars per capita for Indonesia has been in use for several years. The per capita GNP for Korea and Taiwan are given as 290 U.S. dollars and 430 U.S. dollars respectively for 1971. By 1974 increases in the prices of petroleum and other raw materials had probably increased Indonesia's per capita income to 100 U.S. dollars or more.

Income distribution by source for the Philippines is available on a comparable basis for 1965 and 1971 and on a roughly comparable basis for 1961. As might be expected in a slow-growing economy, the proportion of total family income coming from wages and salaries increased from 41.9 to 44.2 percent from 1961 to 1971 (table B16). Nearly all of this increase went to wage and salary earners in nonagricultural sectors (2.2 percent), leaving an increase of only 0.1 percent in agricultural sectors. The portion of total family income coming from agricultural wages and salaries is quite small, only 6.3 percent in 1971. It is significant that the portion of total family income resulting from entrepreneurial activity in agriculture declined over the decade from 24.4 to 21.5 percent, and that accruing (presumably to landowners) as a share of crops, livestock, and poultry raised by others declined from 2.8 to 2.5 percent. The total of these three identifiable sources of agricultural income declined between 1961 and 1971 from 33.3 percent of total family income to 30.3 percent. There may have been some increase in the share of total family income accruing to agricultural landlords from cash rentals, but this is not clearly identifiable

---

13. Don J. DeVoritz, "Migration in a Labor Surplus Economy," *Philippine Economic Journal,* vol. 11, no. 21 (First Semester 1972), pp. 58 ff.□

from the statistics and cannot have exceeded 0.3 percent. There was also a decline of 1.6 percent in the share of total family income accruing to the nonagricultural entrepreneurs. This seems to have been largely among entrepreneurs in the trading category.

These changes in the distribution of family income over this decade, though certainly not spectacular, are nevertheless of some significance. In agriculture the changes seem to indicate a small relative improvement for labor as compared with entrepreneurs (including of course those who own and operate their own farms), but they indicate a much more substantial gain by nonagricultural labor as compared with both agricultural labor and the entrepreneurial group in nonagricultural pursuits, including manufacturing. It may be significant also that this relative gain by labor was made during a relatively slack period in the Philippine manufacturing industry.

This relative gain in the position of nonagricultural labor does not appear to have been achieved through the more or less normal working of market forces. The urban (or at least nonagricultural) labor supply was increasing relative both to demand for such labor and to the supply of labor in the rural areas where economic progress was relatively faster than in the cities. Thus it would appear that nonmarket forces such as minimum wage laws, labor unions, and social security may have been responsible for the relative improvement in the position of urban labor. Of course, all of the preceding discussion pertains to the share of various segments in the economy as a whole and not to their per capita position.

The distribution of family income by occupational group and income class is shown (at constant prices) in table B17. A striking development of the decade is that the portion of family income derived from wages rose from 36 to 43 percent of the total, while the portion derived from entrepreneurial activities showed a corresponding decline from 58 to 51 percent. The mean family income increased 9.7 percent in real terms from 3,405 pesos to 3,736 pesos. This might be construed as indicating some improvement in income distribution during the decade, but an analysis of the figures shows only marginal improvement, if any. In fact, the lowest 20 percent of families in the income scale received 5.7 percent of total family income in 1961 and only 4.9 percent in 1971. The top 20 percent also received a little smaller portion, namely, 54 percent in 1971 as compared with 56.5 percent in 1961. Thus families that make up the 60 percent in the third through the seventh decile increased their take from 39.3 to 42.4 percent. No striking change occurred in income distribution over this decade. From figure 3 it seems that income distribution was only a little more equitable in urban areas than in rural areas. A calculation of the extent of the deviations of family incomes from equality (the Gini

Figure 3. Distribution of Family Income in the Philippines, Urban and Rural, 1971

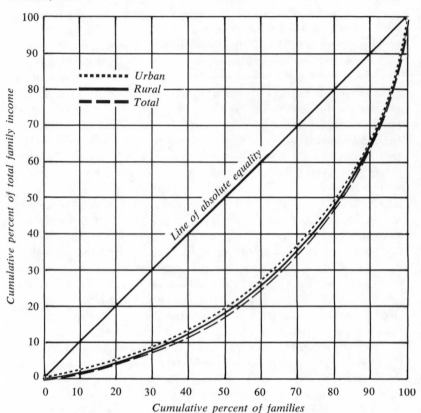

Source: Philippines Bureau of the Census and Statistics, Survey of Households on Family Income and Family Living Expenditures, conducted in May 1971.

function) results in a figure of about 0.52 for the Philippines[14] compared with 0.3 estimated for Taiwan.

The Bureau of the Census and Statistics has made some interesting studies of income distribution over this decade. Table B19 confirms my estimate of the Gini function and shows the similarity between rural and urban areas. The bureau also calculated the ratio between the median fam-

14. The Gini function for the Philippines has been estimated at 0.5139 for 1965. See Shail Jain, *Size Distribution of Income: A Compilation of Data* (Washington, D.C.: World Bank, 1975), p. 90.□

ily income and the arithmetic mean and found that for rural families this ratio increased from 1.34 in 1961 to 1.44 in 1971, whereas in urban areas it decreased from 1.65 to 1.48. This would indicate that although at the start of the decade income distribution was more even in rural than in urban areas, at the end of the period there was little difference, mainly because of an improvement in income distribution in the urban areas. The urban-rural gap in average family income also narrowed somewhat, the income of urban families being nearly 2.5 times that of rural families in 1961, as compared with 2.1 times in 1971. In Manila and its suburbs, of course, average family income was considerably higher than in other urban centers in the Philippines—nearly a third higher in 1971 (see table 9). Excluding metropolitan Manila, the other urban centers on the islands had a decrease in their income superiority over the rural areas from 99 percent in 1961 to 82 percent in 1971. Average family income in Manila increased 25 percent less rapidly than those in other urban areas and 30 percent less

Table 9. Annual Wages for Unskilled Labor in Manila, 1950–71

Year	Money wage (pesos)	Price index	Real wage (pesos)
1950	1,072.5	1.068	1,004.0
1951	1,157.5	1.092	1,060.0
1952	1,237.5	1.062	1,165.0
1953	1,272.5	1.037	1,227.0
1954	1,257.5	0.994	1,265.0
1955	1,295.0	1.000	1,295.0
1956	1,315.0	1.026	1,282.0
1957	1,300.0	1.058	1,229.0
1958	1,307.5	1.082	1,208.0
1959	1,317.5	1.100	1,198.0
1960	1,320.0	1.158	1,140.0
1961	1,352.5	1.188	1,138.0
1962	1,392.5	1.238	1,125.0
1963	1,467.5	1.330	1,103.0
1964	1,482.5	1.393	1,064.0
1965	1,585.0	1.430	1,108.0
1966	1,702.5	1.488	1,144.0
1967	1,782.5	1.570	1,135.0
1968	1,982.5	1.639	1,135.0
1969	2,075.0	1.738[a]	1,194.0[a]
1970	2,303.8[a]	1.981[a]	1,163.0[a]
1971	2,459.2[a]	2.253[a]	1,092.0[a]

Source: Central Bank of the Philippines, Monthly Statistical Bulletin, various issues.
a. Based on April–June 1972 Statistical Reporter.

rapidly than incomes in rural areas. The greater incidence of unemployment in Manila has already been noted.

Although the income gap between urban and rural areas has been narrowing somewhat, it is still significant and probably will remain so. This income disparity may be reflected in the different patterns of consumption. These patterns did not change appreciably from 1961 to 1971 (table B20). In 1965 families in rural areas spent about 20 percent more of their incomes on food than families in Manila, and 15 percent less on housing. Certainly the long-time overvaluation of the peso, together with import controls, contributed to the rural-urban income gap because the principal beneficiary of these measures was urban industry. Though protective tariffs have replaced quantitative import restrictions, trade liberalization and devaluation should tend to move the terms of trade more in favor of the rural areas. This has not, however, stemmed the flow of people to the cities. Lack of personal security in rural areas is a noneconomic factor in swelling urban population and has been a long-standing problem in the Philippines.

The factor distribution of income is one of the main concerns here. As might be expected in a maturing economy, those dependent on wages and salaries increased in relation to the total, as shown in table B17 and as noted above. But for those in the lowest family income bracket (below 3,000 pesos) the proportion relying on wages and salaries declined in the decade of the 1960s. This was true for both small farmers and those in small-scale or cottage industry in that income bracket. Relief recipients and retirees took up the slack. A surprising feature in the Philippines is that families relying on wages and salaries received larger average incomes than those engaged in entrepreneurial and self-employed activities. Farmers predominate in the latter group and show the widest dispersion by income level.

In view of the general assumption in economic wage analysis that workers do not save, some data in the ILO report are interesting. In rural areas 12.3 percent of families with incomes below 3,000 pesos saved as compared with 10.6 percent of urban families in that income bracket.

In the main, the observed trend in the income distribution of rural and urban families in the Philippines appears to run somewhat counter to the experience of other developing countries. The usual trend is for income distribution to become less equal among urban families and more equal among rural families. The reason for such behavior is the movement of people toward the urban centers, where there is proliferation of ghettoes or squatter areas whose inhabitants generally belong to the low-income groups. The income disparity between such groups and the high-income group in the urban center becomes wider. In contrast families in rural areas without permanent sources of income tend to migrate to the urban centers, thus reducing the income disparities among the families remaining.

Income Distribution in Indonesia

Data on income distribution in Indonesia are not adequate for a satisfactory comparison with that of the Philippines or Taiwan. A rough indication of income distribution in Indonesia is shown in the distribution of population by monthly expenditure classes in table B21. The 25 percent of the population with the lowest income had expenditures averaging about 580 rupiah (US$2.10) a month, and the highest 25 percent had average monthly expenditures of almost 2,900 rupiah (US$10.50).[15] In other words, the highest 25 percent consumed about five times as much as the lowest 25 percent. In the Philippines in 1971 the 25 percent with the highest income probably had an average income about ten times that of the lowest 25 percent. Even if an allowance is made for savings by the upper 25 percent in Indonesia of, say, 20 percent of their incomes and no savings by the lowest 25 percent, there would be a ratio of about 6.3:1. Thus, Indonesia has a considerably more equitable distribution of expenditure than the Philippines. As might be expected, consumption expenditure is distributed more evenly in the rural than the urban areas and is more nearly even in Java than in other parts of the archipelago.

Data do not permit even a rough estimate of the SWR/W ratio for Indonesia, and any generalization about such a heterogeneous country would be meaningless. Table B22 shows the substantial variance in daily wages paid on the different types of estates.[16] An indication of the poverty of Indonesia in relation to the Philippines is given by the fact that in 1971 the average family in the Philippines spent 53.7 percent of its total expenditure on food, compared with 76.1 percent for Indonesia in 1970 (January to April).

As on the estates, wages in industry in Indonesia vary widely depending on the location, the ownership, and the size of the establishment. In Jakarta in 1970 the firms rated as large paid an annual average wage of 86,545 rupiah (US$255), while those rated of medium size paid only two-thirds of that amount.[17] In Jakarta the average wage for both skilled

15. The 1969 major export exchange rate was used for these conversions.□
16. The standard deviation was about 36 percent of the mean for January to December 1970.□
17. The rating depends on the industry. In textiles, for example, the average large firm had over 4,400 employees and a medium-sized firm about 2,700. In electrical machinery the average large firm employed about 2,200 and the medium 1,350.□

and unskilled labor paid by foreign-owned firms was about double that paid by Indonesian firms in 1971. The same relationship did not prevail outside of Jakarta because of different industrial mixes of foreign and locally owned firms. The unweighted average monthly wage for skilled labor paid by Indonesian firms in fourteen cities in 1971 was about 8,000 rupiah a month and 4,720 rupiah for unskilled. In Jakarta at the same time the comparable wages were 12,000 rupiah for skilled and 7,900 rupiah for unskilled labor, while foreign firms were paying an average of 27,500 rupiah for skilled and 14,000 rupiah for unskilled. Again, it should be borne in mind that the newer foreign-owned firms probably require labor of higher quality and training than the domestic firms.

Productivity and Wages of Agricultural Labor in the Philippines

Various estimates have been made of the average productivity of labor in Philippine agriculture, and it has been compared with productivity in the other sectors of the economy and in foreign countries. An OECD study estimated the productivity of labor in agriculture as a percentage of productivity in the nonagricultural sectors. The percentages were 36 percent for the Philippines, 42 percent for Indonesia, and 41 percent for Korea.[18] I have attempted to make a rough estimate of the ratio of wages per employee in agriculture to wages in other sectors. Table B16 shows that in 1971 wage income paid in agriculture was 6.3 percent of total family income in the Philippines, whereas that paid in nonagricultural occupations was 38.0 percent. It seems likely that this figure drastically understates the remuneration of labor in agriculture because it does not take account of income such as wages earned in kind as shares of crops and the rental value of owner-occupied housing. If it is assumed that the landowner received 40 percent of the crops, then the farm tenants' share of total family income from that source would have been about 3.7 percent (2.5 times 1.5) in 1971. It seems reasonable also to add about 30 percent of the rental value of owner-occupied housing as income of farm labor. This would be an additional 2.1 percent of total family income. If these two amounts are added to the 6.3 percent referred to above, a total of about 12 percent of total family income is seen as accruing to farm labor. In May 1971 those employed in agriculture constituted 50 percent of the total employed work force. Thus the ratio of wage income per person employed in agriculture to wages of those employed elsewhere in the economy appears to be about 32

18. *Employment Problems in Less Developed Countries* (Paris: OECD, January 20, 1970).□

percent. This compares with the 36 percent which the OECD has estimated as the productivity of labor in the agricultural sector as a percentage of the productivity of labor in the nonagricultural sectors of the Philippine economy.

Of course, both the productivity of labor in agriculture in relation to that in the manufacturing industry and, to a lesser extent, agricultural wages in relation to wages in manufacturing are reduced by the effective rate of protection, which benefits the industrial sector almost exclusively. The average effective rate of protection has been variously estimated at 40 to 50 percent. If the productivity of nonagricultural labor is adjusted for the beneficial effect of protection to the industrial sector (which contributes about 25 percent of the GNP), the ratio of productivity of labor in the agriculture sector to the productivity of those employed elsewhere in the economy would increase to about 40 percent.[19] Thus it can be concluded that the ratio of the average productivity of agricultural labor to wage income is about 40 (instead of the 36 percent estimated by OECD) to 32 or 1.25, when the ratio of average productivity of labor to the wage rate in the rest of the economy is taken as unity.

Thus far the relation between average productivity and wages has been considered, but the estimation of the SWR/W ratio requires calculation of the ratio of the marginal productivity of agricultural labor to nonagricultural wages. That is, how would the ratio of output to wages have been affected if no change had occurred in any input other than the addition of a unit of labor? This value is very easy to conceptualize but difficult to estimate from empirical data, particularly in view of the importance of technical change (the green revolution) in recent years. The following analysis does not pretend to be precise.

The obvious assumption is made that if all inputs including labor increase at the same rate, then output would increase in proportion to labor input and average and marginal productivity of labor would be equal. Externalities such as technical change are thus ignored. Such simultaneous increase in all inputs would be a rare occurrence indeed, however, and certainly has not been true in the Philippines. Without extensive field work, conclusions must be drawn from aggregated data and will of course not apply to any specific part of the country or to particular crops.

As a result of research done at the University of the Philippines data are

---

19. The productivity per employed person in the nonagricultural sectors is 157 and in agriculture is 57 before adjustment (whole economy = 100). Since industry is 25 percent of GNP and the effective rate of protection is 50 percent, the 157 would have to be reduced by 50 percent of 25 percent or 12.5 percent to adjust for protection. Therefore the 157 becomes about 145. The ratio of 57 to 145 is 39.3.□

available on the principal inputs and outputs of Philippine agriculture over the 1949–68 period. (Needless to say, those who have compiled these data are not responsible for the use made of them here.) A shorter period, say, 1958–65 (after postwar reconstruction but before the impact of the green revolution) would have been desirable, but the longer period is used to smooth out the effects of weather and other exogenous events, such as the change in trade arrangements with the United States, which are important in the Philippines.[20]

During this twenty-year period total agricultural production increased by about 120 percent (4.1 percent a year) and labor input by about 50 percent (2.1 percent a year). If all the other inputs had increased only in proportion to the increase in output, an inference might be drawn that the marginal productivity of labor was rising substantially. During this period, however, the cropped area increased by 3 percent a year, fixed capital in agriculture by 6.9 percent, and off-farm current inputs (chiefly fertilizer) by 11.2 percent annually.

Economic Wage of Agricultural Labor in the Philippines

In estimating the SWR/W ratio for the Philippines, as in Taiwan, the following equation will be used:

$$\frac{SWR}{W} = \frac{M}{W} + \frac{nS^{cap}(g - i)}{i - sg} - v\left(1 - \frac{M}{W}\right)\left(\frac{i - ngS^{cap}}{i}\right),$$

where M = marginal productivity of agricultural labor
W = wage of nonagricultural labor
n = labor cost/capital ratio
S^{cap} = rate of savings out of capitalists' income
g = social marginal productivity of capital
s = the overall rate of savings
i = social rate of discount
v = redistribution of income factor.

The most difficult element to estimate in this equation is M/W, since standard statistical information does not reveal the value of M. The ratio will be estimated from data selected for other purposes, particularly that assembled by Crisostomo and Barker. Attention will be focused on M since table 9 shows practically no change in annual real wages for unskilled

20. C. Crisostomo and R. Barker, "Growth Rates of Philippine Agriculture, 1948–1969, *Philippine Economic Journal*, vol. 11, no. 1 (First Semester 1972), pp. 88–148.□

urban labor from 1961 to 1971. This would indicate that the increase in the share of GNP accruing to urban labor of 2.2 percent from 1961 to 1971 was the result of an increase in number of workers rather than an increase in wages. Since the period of table 9 corresponds roughly to that of the Crisostomo-Barker study it is assumed that W was constant over the twenty-year period, and for convenience it will be given a value of unity.

One of the factors used to calculate the value of M will be the OECD estimate of the average productivity of labor in agriculture in the Philippines (36 percent of average productivity in nonagriculture pursuits) as changed here to 40 percent to allow for the effective protection enjoyed by industry. According to the OECD study the average productivity of labor in agriculture increased by 47 percent from 1949 to 1965. If all other factors had changed proportionally it might be concluded that the marginal productivity of labor increased by at least 47 percent. This was not the case, however. The increase in land per unit of labor was 20 percent, but fixed capital investment and current inputs per unit of labor increased over 150 percent and 500 percent respectively (the latter starting of course from a very low base). If constant returns per unit of capital investment and an incremental capital-output ratio of 3:1 are assumed, output per unit of labor could increase about 50 percent because of the increase in fixed capital investment. This is very close to the 47 percent increase in the average output per worker that occurred. In view of the sharp increase in the current inputs, Philippine authorities estimate that if corresponding increases in other factors had been available, these inputs might have increased output per worker by as much as 60 percent, or 13 percent more than the increase in average productivity that actually occurred.

Thus, there are two factors to work with in ascertaining the relation between the marginal and the average productivity of labor. On the one hand, the fact that the increase in land was 27 percent less than the increase in the average productivity of labor would normally have meant that the marginal productivity of labor was greater than the rise in its average productivity. On the other hand, the increase in current inputs might have increased output per worker by 60 percent. If these two factors are taken together, it might be concluded that the marginal productivity was roughly about 33 percent higher than the increase in average productivity over this period. On the basis of personal observation of Philippine agriculture in the early 1950s, it is assumed that the average and marginal productivity of labor were about the same at that time. This would imply a value of M of 133 percent of the 40 percent ratio calculated above between the average productivity of labor in agriculture and that in other pursuits. Thus the value of M/W is about 0.53.

In addition to the M/W ratio the following estimates are needed in order to apply the UNIDO formula: the ratio of labor to capital (n), the capitalists' savings rate (S^{cap}), the social marginal productivity of capital (g), the overall rate of savings (s), and the social rate of discount (i). Also estimated is the distribution factor (v), which is relatively high in the Philippines because of the degree of inequality in the distribution of income. This inequality is estimated at 0.52 (see footnote 14). As in Taiwan, half this will be used for v.

The *Annual Survey of Manufactures*, published by the Philippine government, estimates the ratio of payrolls to fixed capital over a period of years as ranging from 20 to 30 percent. The average was falling in the late 1960s and early 1970s with the decline in real wages. If working capital were included, it would of course be higher, and it would also be higher in the service sectors of the economy. The value of 0.7 used for n in Taiwan may be on the high side for the Philippines; in view of the lower wages and the more capital-intensive character of Philippine industry perhaps a value of 0.5 may be reasonable.

The gross national savings rate in the Philippines has been in the range of 15 to 20 percent of GNP. In 1972 the World Bank used a figure of 17.2 percent. But for present purposes the net savings rate should be used. Ten percent, the same rate used in Taiwan, should be satisfactory, but it should be more than doubled for capitalists, whose propensity to save (and invest in expensive real estate) is probably quite high. A value for S^{cap} of 25 percent will be used here.

The social marginal productivity of capital will vary both with the monetary return on invested capital and with the social value of the product. A prominent accounting firm estimated the average net return on equity capital at 16 to 17 percent from 1967 to 1970.[21] This is the best information available. In Taiwan, where investment probably yields a higher return, a figure of 20 percent was used. Probably in the Philippines the return on investment in manufacturing should be discounted somewhat because of the high rate of effective protection and the high propensity for investment of low social value. A value for g of 15 percent will be used here.

Finally, at what rate should future consumption be discounted in the Philippines? In Taiwan a figure of 12 percent was used, but because of the slower growth rate in the Philippines a higher value should probably be placed on future consumption and thus a lower discount rate used—say, 10 percent.

---

21. Sycip, Corres, Velayo and Co., "A Study of About 300 Companies, 1962–68, and Trends and Ratios in Industrial Firms, 1967–70," processed.□

When these values are applied to the UNIDO equation the following is obtained:

$$\frac{SWR}{W} = 0.53 + \frac{(0.5)(0.25)(0.15 - 0.10)}{(0.10 - .015)}$$
$$- \frac{(0.26)(0.47)(0.10 - 0.019)}{0.10}$$

$$= 0.53 + 0.07 - 0.10 = 50 \text{ percent}[22]$$

The SWR/W ratio is thus about 21 percentage points lower than Taiwan. This seems reasonable in view of the higher level of unemployment in the Philippines and the lesser degree of mobility in the labor market there. If the distributional factor is disregarded, the SWR/W ratio would be about 60 percent or 15 percentage points lower than Taiwan.

If again the distribution factor is not taken into account, as long as the social marginal productivity of capital (g) exceeds the marginal social rate of time preference (i) the economic cost of labor is likely to exceed its marginal productivity. An exception to this rule might occur if the rate of savings by nonwage earners were sufficiently high that this rate times the social marginal productivity of capital exceeded the marginal social rate of time preference ($i < S^{cap} g$). The distribution factor can be very important, however, and can reduce the economic wage rate below the marginal productivity of labor in agriculture even if the market wage is well above marginal productivity.

It is worth pointing out again that, without regard for the distribution factor, the ratio of the economic cost to the market wage will exceed the ratio of the marginal productivity of labor to the market wage as long as the social marginal productivity of capital exceeds the social rate of discount (consumption rate of interest) unless, coincidentally, the rate of savings times the social marginal productivity of capital exceeds the consumption rate of interest. The latter is highly unlikely but the former is not impossible in a very poor country that discounts future consumption at a high rate. For example, if the marginal productivity of capital is 15 percent, but the consumption rate of interest is not 10 but 20 percent, and the other parameters are the same as those assumed for the Philippines, and if the distributional factor is still disregarded, then the SWR/W ratio is 0.44. If the savings rates are made sufficiently high, say S^{cap} is 50 percent and s is 15 percent, then even with the distributional element included the SWR/W ratio will be higher than the M/W ratio. □

22. With a project life of thirty years the SWR/W ratio would be about 41 percent.□

In Conclusion

THE QUESTION MAY WELL BE ASKED whether, in view of the complex formulas needed to derive an approximation of the economic price of labor, the task is worth the candle. The margin of error is bound to be substantial even if considerably more time is spent on preliminary statistical analysis than was possible for the exercise described above. My answer to the question would be a qualified yes. The qualification depends on the general features of the labor market, particularly the mobility of labor between agriculture and industry, since a high degree of mobility tends to raise the SWR/W ratio. The qualification also depends on the importance of labor costs in the project and in the production process. If labor costs are very small, calculating the economic price of labor would probably not be worthwhile. In that case, however, the project might well be rejected on other grounds, particularly if it involved large outlays of foreign exchange.

In view of the general conditions in the labor markets of Taiwan and the Philippines, the results obtained in this book appear to be fairly good approximations of the ratio of economic wages in agriculture to market wages in the nonagricultural sectors of the economies—about 71 percent for Taiwan and 50 percent for the Philippines. In both countries meaningful results were obtained for the economic price of labor by the use of macro data which, suitably refined for local conditions, would be a useful tool in project analysis. But a study of labor and capital markets that is oriented to the local project would not be likely to produce satisfactory results. Whatever the area covered, a more reliable result will be obtained by tackling the problem systematically rather than by using guesswork based on the labor market conditions that appear to prevail in a particular locality.   □

Appendixes

{A}

The Revised
Little-Mirrlees Method

THIS APPENDIX WILL ANALYZE briefly what appear to be the more important changes introduced by Little and Mirrlees in the revision of their methodology. It will be recalled that in chapter 3 the formulas of the original *Manual of Industrial Project Analysis* were used in explaining their approach.

As noted earlier, the numéraire was changed from simply values at border prices to values in terms of freely disposable funds in the hands of the government converted to border prices by using a standard conversion factor. The merit of this modification was questioned because of operational problems. In any case the change perhaps causes more of a problem when establishing accounting prices for commodities than when deriving the SWR/W ratio, since whatever numéraire is used it will presumably affect the numerator and denominator of that ratio in about equal degrees. This is shown in the example below.

The formula suggested by Little and Mirrlees[1] for the social value of government income in relation to private consumption is as follows:

$$\bar{S}_0{}^2 = \bar{v}g + \frac{(1 - g)(C - M)n + \bar{v}gr}{i - r},$$

where $\bar{v}$ is the relative weight of public consumption expenditures at accounting prices as compared with market prices, g is the proportion of government income devoted to consumption, and of course $1 - g$ is the proportion devoted to investment. C, M, n, i, and r have the meanings assigned to them in chapter 3. The value of $\bar{S}_0$ obviously is quite dependent

---

1. *Project Appraisal*, p. 255.□
2. $\bar{S}_0$ is used here to distinguish this value from that of a unit of investment in terms of its effect on future consumption, S_0, which was used to describe the Little-Mirrlees method in chapter 3.□

upon the value assigned to $\bar{v}$. If $\bar{v}$ is 2; if three-quarters of government expenditure goes for consumption and one-quarter for investment; and C is 1, M is 0.4, n is 0.25, i is 15 percent, and r is 6 percent, then the value of $\bar{S}_0$ is 4.3. If $\bar{v}$ is unity, $\bar{S}_0$ is 3.05.

In the discussion of the original Little-Mirrlees method in chapter 3, the same values for C, M, n, r, and i were used to obtain a value of 2.5 for S_0 when measuring the value of private investment in relation to consumption. Of course the higher the S_0 the higher the SWR/W ratio. If W, C, and M were converted to their economic price equivalents instead, on the basis of $2:1$,[3] the SWR/W ratio would have been 73 percent or very close to the 76 percent obtained in chapter 3 without using numéraire conversion values. Thus it would appear that since the numéraire will affect the numerator and denominator of the SWR/W ratio in about the same way, it is not very important in determining this ratio.

A more significant change is the introduction into the SWR equations of the concept of C^1, which is supposed to measure not just consumption by the worker and his family (the W where there are no savings by the worker), but other costs connected with his change of employment, such as transport costs and special training.[4] These costs are considered at the beginning of chapter 4 and an indication is given of how the SWR/W ratio may increase as a result of them. The basic Little-Mirrlees equation then becomes:

$$\frac{SWR}{W} = \frac{C^1}{W} + \frac{1}{S_0} \frac{(C - M)}{W},$$

where C, M, and W have their usual definitions.

Another innovation in the revision is the introduction of the idea of the base consumption level.[5] The hypothesis is that at a certain level of consumption by the worker an increment of consumption would equal in social value an equal increment of uncommitted public income. Scott used this concept in calculating the shadow price of agricultural labor in parts of Kenya (see appendix C). The task of making the necessary conversions is difficult and probably the results would be quite erratic. Inasmuch as economists have not been able to measure utility by any objective standard—human reaction is the only device and that measures only in

3. A unit of funds for government investment equals two units of private consumption in terms of social value.☐
    4. Little and Mirrlees, *Project Appraisal*, pp. 270–82.☐
    5. Little and Mirrlees, *Project Appraisal*, p. 238.☐

terms of "more or less"—it is difficult to see how the base consumption level could be established except by value judgments of an arbitrary nature. Of course the same type of problem is encountered in the UNIDO approach when distributional weights are assigned to changes in income, but at least the consumption and the income distribution functions can be used as a general guide. □

{B}

The Lele-Mellor Model

THIS MODEL ATTEMPTS TO ESTABLISH the conditions and assumptions for equilibrium between the price of labor in agriculture and in the rest of the economy.[1]

Definitions:

A Agricultural production
l_a Labor force in agriculture
l_i Labor force outside agriculture
s_a Share of labor in agricultural output
M_s Share of agricultural production sold to nonagricultural sector
C Landlord's consumption of agricultural products
I Investment outside agriculture
b Portion of laborer's income spent on food
r Proportion of agricultural labor in total labor force
N Total labor force
P Price of agricultural products in terms of nonagricultural products
K Nonagricultural capital stock
W/P Wages of nonagricultural labor in terms of agricultural product
X Production of nonagricultural sector
Y Per capita income of agricultural labor in terms of agricultural product
M_d Market demand for food outside agriculture
W_d Demand for labor outside agriculture
W_s Demand for labor in agriculture

---

1. Uma J. Lele and John W. Mellor, *The Political Economy of Employment Oriented Development*, Occasional Paper no. 42 (Ithaca, N.Y.: Department of Agricultural Economics, Cornell University, 1972).□

Assumptions:
1. Agricultural labor's share of income allocated for food is negatively related to P and s_a. That is, labor will use a smaller proportion of its income on food as the price of food rises in relation to nonfood, and as labor's share of total agricultural income rises.
2. Food consumption by nonlaborers is constant (their price elasticity for food is zero).
3. Agricultural output is a function of labor input and technology (capital in agriculture is considered as embodied labor).
4. Diminishing returns prevail in agriculture.
5. Transfer of labor from agriculture to industry is a function of technological change in agriculture.
6. Labor consumes all its income (no savings).
7. Supply of agricultural commodities is price inelastic.
8. Equilibrium in food market is when $M_s = M_d$.
9. Equilibrium in labor market is when $W_s = W_d$.

Equations derived from assumptions:

(1) $$\frac{dA}{dl_a} > 0 \text{ and } \frac{d^2A}{dl_a} < 0 \text{ (diminishing returns)}$$

(2) $s_a = \dfrac{dA}{dl_a} \cdot \dfrac{l_a}{A}$ (share of labor in agricultural production depends on marginal productivity of labor in agriculture)

(3) $$M_s = (A - C) - s_a b$$

(4) $$b = f(PY), \frac{\delta b}{\delta P} < 0, \text{ and } \frac{\delta b}{\delta Y} < 0$$

(5) $$Y = \frac{S_a}{rN} = \frac{S_a}{l_a}$$

(6) $$M_d = \frac{W}{P} \cdot l_i$$

Equations derived from Cobb-Douglas production functions ($a = 1/X$):

(7) $$X = K^a l_i^{1-a}$$

(8) $W_d = \dfrac{dX}{dl_i} = K^a \left(\dfrac{1-a}{l_i^a}\right) = \dfrac{K^a(1-a)\,l_i^{1-a}}{l_i} = (1-a)\left(\dfrac{X}{l_i}\right)$

(9) $\dfrac{Ws}{P} = \dfrac{s_a}{rN}$ = wage rate in both agriculture and industry as labor moves from agriculture to industry.

Equilibrium in food market $M_s = M_d$; therefore from equations (2) and (6):

$$(10) \qquad A - C - s_a b = \frac{W}{P} l_i.$$

In equilibrium the share of agricultural and nonagricultural labor in agricultural product will be proportional to their relative numbers. Therefore:

$$\frac{W}{P} l_i = b s_a \frac{(1 - r)}{r} \text{ and from equation (10)}$$

$$(A - C) - b s_a = b s_a \frac{(1 - r)}{r} \text{ or}$$

$$\frac{A - C}{b s_a} - \frac{1 - r}{r} = 1 \text{ and}$$

$$\frac{A - C}{b s_a} = \frac{1}{r} \text{ and}$$

$$(11) \qquad r(A - C) = b s_a.$$

This says that labor in both agriculture and nonagriculture consumes agricultural products in proportion to their relative numbers.

Equilibrium in the labor market is when $W_s = W_d$ and therefore from equations (8) and (9):

$$\frac{(1 - a) K^a}{l_i^a} = \frac{P s_a}{rN}$$

and from equation (5) $Y = s_a/rN$. Therefore:

$$PY = \frac{(1 - a) K^a}{l_i^a} = \frac{dX}{dl_i} = \text{marginal productivity of nonagricultural labor and}$$

$$(12) \qquad P = \frac{(1 - a) K^a}{l_i^a} \cdot \frac{rN}{s_a} = (1 - a) \frac{X}{l_i} \cdot \frac{rN}{s_a}.$$

Therefore:

$$(13) \qquad \frac{dP}{dr} = \frac{(1 - a) X}{l_i} \cdot \frac{N}{s_a} > 0.$$

As the labor force in agriculture increases, the ratio of the price of nonagricultural products to agricultural products also increases.   □

{C}

"Estimates of Shadow Wages in Kenya" by M. FG. Scott

SCOTT[1] USES THE METHODOLOGY of the revised Little-Mirrlees method.
Definitions:

W_{ij}^* Shadow wage of worker moving from occupation i to occupation j

W_i^* Shadow wage of worker in occupation i

W_j, W_i Market wage rates in the two occupations

h_j, h_i Ratios of wages after direct taxes to wages before taxes in the two employments

k_r Fraction of the increase in income accruing to family r (r could be the number in the household)

fcr   Accounting (standard conversion) ratio for consumption of family r

$s_r a_r$ The social cost per unit of increase in income for portion that is saved

$1 - s_r$ Social cost per unit of increase in income for portion that is consumed

b_r The social benefit to family r because of the increase in money income from W_i to W_j

E_j External benefits of employing one more person in occupation j (Scott assumes this to be zero)

Y_r Family income of family r

Y_{cr} Critical income level of family r

Scott's general formula for the shadow wage of workers moving from occupation i to occupation j is as follows:

1. Maurice FitzGerald Scott, "Estimates of Shadow Wages in Kenya," Nuffield College, Oxford University, February 1973, processed.□

$$W_{ij}^* = W_i^* + (h_j W_j - h_i W_i) \cdot kr \cdot \text{fcr}(s_r a_r + 1 - s_r) - b_r + E_j.$$

The expression b_r is subtracted because it is not a cost to the economy.

Scott's formula is included here to illustrate the effect of adding the complexities of taxes and savings. If, as in the Little-Mirrlees and UNIDO formulations, taxes are ignored (or assumed to be nonexistent) and all wages are assumed to be spent, then h_j and h_i are equal to unity and $s_r = 0$. If it is also assumed that all the increase in income accrues to the worker's family (no transfer costs, for example) then $k_r = 1$. Therefore:

$$W_{ij}^* = W_i^* + (W_j - W_i) \text{ fcr} - b_r.$$

Scott suggests that if the worker were previously unemployed $W^*{}_i$ may be considered zero. In a modern welfare state, however, there would be some social gain from transferring the worker from welfare (whether provided by his family or not) to employment where he could be self-sustaining. In this case, of course, $W^*{}_i$ would be negative.

There are numerous ways in which labor is transferred from one occupation to another. For example, the transfer may take place within an industry or between industries; it may be in the usual pattern from rural to urban areas. The cost of living may differ between the locality of the old job and the new. Scott discusses the economic consequences of these various alternatives in the Kenya context. Here, however, only the derivation of fcr and b_r will be discussed.

The quantity fcr is the conversion factor for changing a unit of income into the numéraire used by Scott, which is foreign exchange in the hands of the government. To derive this he assumes that there is a "critical income level," designated as Y_{cr}, at which the government is indifferent as to whether income is in its hands. Scott then assumes that the elasticity of the marginal utility of income is constant $(U/dU)(dY/Y)$ in the eyes of the government. With these assumptions the increase in income beyond Y_{cr} is equivalent to its foreign exchange cost by definition. If W_i is the critical level of income for a rural household, then:

$$(W_j - W_i) \text{ fcr} = (W_j - Y_{cr}) \text{ fcr}.$$

To derive b_r a utility function is required. Scott takes as his utility function $U = B - AY_r^{1-e}$ so that:

(1) $$dU/dY = -A(1 - e) Y_r^{-e},$$

where $-e$ is elasticity of marginal utility of income, which is assumed to be constant since it is the weight given by the government to increases in its income. For a rural household at the critical level dU/dY_r by definition $= 1$. Therefore $- A (1 - e) Y_{cr}^{-e} = 1$ or $-A = \dfrac{Y_{cr}{}^{e}}{1 - e}$ and substituting in equation (1):

$$(2) \qquad \frac{dU}{dY} = \left(\frac{Y_{cr}}{Y_r}\right)^{e}$$

If $e = 1$, $dU/dY = Y_{cr}/Y_r$. Y_{cr}/Y_r is the total utility to family r of an increase in income from W_i to W_j or b_r. $\qquad\square$

{Statistical Appendix A}

Korea and Taiwan

Table A1. Age and Sex Distribution of Population, Taiwan, 1950–80
(Thousands)

Age group	1950 Male	1950 Female	1960 Male	1960 Female	1970 Male	1970 Female	1980 Male	1980 Female
0–4	652	625	1,008	955	992	934	1,141	1,073
5–9	493	465	909	861	1,033	975	981	925
10–14	481	457	626	590	988	937	986	931
15–19	463	391	485	455	900	856	1,028	972
20–49	1,915	1,354	2,505	1,896	2,946	2,483	3,784	3,562
50–64	251	250	414	374	702	543	1,101	767
65 and over	75	113	112	156	194	235	365	372
Total by sex	4,330	3,655	6,059	5,287	7,755	6,963	9,386	8,602
Grand total	7,985		11,346		14,718		17,988	

Source: Data provided the author by Council for International Economic Cooperation and Development (CIECD), Taiwan.

Table A2. Sex Composition of the Labor Force, Korea and Taiwan, 1963–72
(Population in millions)

	Korea[a]						Taiwan[b]					
		Percent of popu-lation[c]	Male		Female			Percent of popu-lation[c]	Male		Female	
Year	Labor force		Number	Percent[c]	Number	Percent[c]	Labor force		Number	Percent[c]	Number	Percent[c]
1963	8.7	55.2	5.6	76.4	3.0	36.3	4.2[d]	62.4	3.3	89.2	1.0	32.4
1964	8.9	54.4	5.8	75.7	3.1	35.4	4.3	62.1	3.3	86.8	1.1	34.4
1965	9.2	55.4	6.0	76.6	3.2	36.5	4.5	61.8	3.4	87.1	1.1	33.3
1966	9.3	55.4	6.1	76.5	3.2	36.2	4.6	61.4	3.5	85.4	1.2	34.8
1967	9.5	55.4	6.2	76.0	3.3	36.8	4.8	61.0	3.5	83.3	1.2	33.4
1968	9.8	56.0	6.2	76.1	3.5	38.2	4.9	60.4	3.6	81.8	1.3	34.8
1969	9.8	55.9	6.3	76.6	3.5	37.5	5.1	60.4	3.7	82.2	1.4	35.9
1970	10.0	55.9	6.4	75.1	3.6	38.5	5.2	60.3	3.8	80.9	1.4	34.1
1971	10.2	55.3	6.4	74.2	3.7	38.5	5.4	60.3	3.9	81.3	1.5	35.7
1972	10.5	56.0	6.7	74.1	3.8	38.9	5.4	60.1	4.0	80.0	1.5	34.4

Sources: Office of Labor Affairs, Yearbook of Labor Statistics, Korea, 1972; Taiwan Provincial Labor Force Survey and Research Institute, Quarterly Report on the Labor Force Survey, October 1973.
a. Refers to persons fourteen years of age and over.
b. Refers to persons fifteen years of age and over.
c. Participation ratio.
d. October 1963.

Table A3. Age Structure and Dependency Ratio, Taiwan, 1951–71

Year (at mid-year)	Total population (thousands)	Age 0–14		Age 15–64		Age 65 and over		Dependency ratio (percent)[a]
		Thousands	Percent	Thousands	Percent	Thousands	Percent	
1951	8,150	3,259	40.0	4,700	57.7	191	2.3	73.4
1952	8,472	3,412	40.2	4,862	57.4	198	2.3	74.3
1953	8,788	3,559	40.5	5,023	57.2	206	2.3	75.0
1954	9,108	3,718	40.8	5,178	56.8	212	2.3	75.9
1955	9,448	3,889	41.2	5,340	56.5	219	2.3	76.9
1956	9,799	4,072	41.6	5,501	56.1	226	2.3	78.1
1957	10,131	4,248	41.9	5,650	55.8	233	2.3	79.3
1958	10,463	4,423	42.3	5,798	55.4	242	2.3	80.5
1959	10,815	4,617	42.7	5,945	55.0	252	2.3	81.9
1960	11,169	4,834	43.3	6,073	54.4	262	2.4	83.9
1961	11,522	5,058	43.9	6,191	53.7	273	2.4	86.1
1962	11,873	5,257	44.3	6,334	53.3	282	2.4	87.4
1963	12,228	5,426	44.4	6,507	53.2	295	2.4	87.9
1964	12,583	5,565	44.2	6,707	53.3	310	2.5	87.6
1965	12,932	5,674	43.9	6,933	53.6	326	2.5	86.5
1966	13,273	5,745	43.3	7,185	54.1	343	2.6	84.7
1967	13,594	5,781	42.5	7,453	54.8	360	2.6	82.4
1968	13,910	5,812	41.8	7,722	55.5	377	2.7	80.1
1969	14,233	5,841	41.0	7,998	56.2	394	2.8	78.0
1970	14,556	5,856	40.2	8,284	56.9	417	2.9	75.7
1971	14,880	5,856	39.4	8,583	57.7	441	3.0	73.4

Source: Assembled for the author by Manpower Development Committee, CIECD, Taiwan.
a. The dependency ratio is the total of those from zero through fourteen years of age and those sixty-five and over divided by those from fifteen through sixty-four.

Table A4. Labor Force by Age Group, Taiwan, 1965–73
(Percentage distribution)

Year	|			Age group				
	15–19	*20–24*	*25–34*	*35–44*	*45–54*	*55–64*	*65 and over*	*Total*[a]
1965	16.86	10.96	28.06	22.69	14.97	5.57	0.93	100.00
1966	16.95	10.31	27.54	24.26	15.09	5.21	0.74	100.00
1967	17.78	10.11	27.05	23.94	14.83	5.56	0.84	100.00
1968	18.58	9.84	26.67	23.34	15.04	5.75	0.78	100.00
1969	19.57	9.32	25.72	24.03	14.44	6.08	0.84	100.00
1970	19.59	10.59	25.15	25.76	14.57	5.75	0.61	100.00
1971	19.34	11.49	24.88	23.63	14.71	5.43	0.52	100.00
1972	18.92	12.59	23.11	23.87	15.34	5.70	0.49	100.00
1973[b]	18.13	12.46	22.63	24.82	15.32	5.98	0.49	100.00

Source: Quarterly Report on the Labor Force Survey, Taiwan, various issues.
a. Figures may not add to totals because of rounding.
b. January.

Table A5. Labor Force by Age Group, Korea, 1971 and 1972
(Thousands)

Age group	1971	1972
14	130	183
15–19	1,289	1,463
20–24	1,085	1,099
25–29	1,099	1,162
30–34	1,402	1,427
35–39	1,361	1,373
40–44	1,099	1,121
45–49	960	950
50–54	693	745
55–59	535	518
60–64	314	298
Over 65	198	187
Total	10,165	10,500

Source: Assembled for the author by Economic Planning Board, Korea.

Table A6. Labor Force by Educational Level, Taiwan, 1968–73
(Percentage distribution)

Year	Illiterate	Self-educated and primary school	Junior high and vocational school	Senior high, vocational, and normal school	University and graduate school	Total
1968	17.34	56.26	11.96	10.14	4.30	100.00
1969	18.33	56.95	11.69	9.38	3.65	100.00
1970	15.36	53.52	11.35	9.89	9.88	100.00
1971	16.19	56.97	12.43	10.46	3.95	100.00
1972	14.90	56.56	12.82	11.38	4.34	100.00
1973	14.91	55.06	13.27	11.86	4.90	100.00

Source: Quarterly Report on the Labor Force Survey, Taiwan, various issues.

Table A7. Employed Persons by Educational Level, Taiwan, 1968–73
(Thousands)

Year	Illiterate	Self-educated and primary school	Junior high and vocational school	Senior high vocational, and normal school	University and graduate school	Total
1968	732	2,346	490	414	177	4,159
1969	824	2,534	510	406	160	4,434
1970	756	2,604	545	468	175	4,541
1971	777	2,715	580	482	185	4,739
1972	736	2,775	617	537	208	4,873
1973	753	2,772	657	573	242	4,997

Source: Quarterly Report on the Labor Force Survey, Taiwan, various issues.

Table A8. Distribution of Employed by Class of Worker, Taiwan, 1968–72
(Percent)

Year	Employers	Self-employed	Unpaid family workers	Paid employees			Total[a]
				Private	Public	Total	
1968	3.3	26.7	22.7	32.8	14.4	47.2	100.0
1969	3.0	26.3	21.7	36.8	12.8	49.6	100.0
1970	3.2	26.0	20.3	38.2	12.6	50.8	100.0
1971	3.3	25.7	18.8	40.2	12.5	52.7	100.0
1972	3.6	25.2	17.1	42.5	12.3	54.8	100.0

Source: Quarterly Report on the Labor Force Survey, Taiwan, various issues.
a. Figures may not add to totals because of rounding.

Table A9. *Percentage Distribution of Employed by Class of Worker,*
Korea, 1964–71

Year	Self-employed	Family workers	Regularly employed	Temporarily employed	Daily workers	Total[a]
Whole country						
1964	37.0	32.5	11.8	7.6	11.1	100.0
1965	36.7	31.2	13.4	8.3	10.4	100.0
1966	36.2	30.5	15.0	7.4	10.9	100.0
1967	36.2	28.7	17.2	7.0	10.9	100.0
1968	35.0	27.7	19.4	6.5	11.4	100.0
1969	34.8	27.2	21.5	5.6	10.9	100.0
1970	34.2	27.0	22.9	5.3	10.6	100.0
1971	34.1	26.7	23.0	5.7	10.5	100.0
Farm households						
1964	40.6	46.1	3.2	3.6	6.5	100.0
1965	40.1	45.2	4.1	4.2	6.4	100.0
1966	40.9	45.0	3.8	3.8	6.5	100.0
1967	42.0	43.6	4.5	3.4	6.5	100.0
1968	41.4	42.6	4.8	3.1	8.1	100.0
1969	41.7	42.2	5.8	2.8	7.5	100.0
1970	40.7	43.3	5.4	1.8	8.8	100.0
1971	40.3	44.0	5.0	2.2	8.5	100.0
Nonfarm households						
1964	30.4	8.2	27.2	14.7	19.5	100.0
1965	31.3	8.5	28.4	15.0	16.5	100.0
1966	28.9	8.0	32.4	13.0	17.2	100.0
1967	28.0	7.8	34.9	12.2	17.1	100.0
1968	26.7	8.3	38.4	11.0	15.6	100.0
1969	26.3	9.2	40.7	8.8	15.0	100.0
1970	27.0	9.0	42.3	9.3	12.4	100.0
1971	27.9	9.5	40.9	9.3	12.4	100.0

Source: *Yearbook of Labor Statistics*, Korea, 1972.
a. Figures may not add to totals because of rounding.

Table A10. *Composition of Nonagricultural Labor Force by Industry, Sex, and Occupation, Korea, 1971* (Thousands)

Industry	Total			Engineers			Technicians			Skilled workers			Semiskilled workers			Apprentices		
	Total	Male	Female	Total	Male	Female	Total	Male	Female	Total	Male	Female	Total	Male	Female	Total	Male	Female
Mining	32.4	31.8	0.6	1.0	1.0	0.0	2.4	2.4	0.0	14.7	14.5	0.2	12.0	11.8	0.2	2.3	2.1	0.2
Manufacturing	546.3	278.0	268.3	12.3	12.2	0.1	34.2	32.0	2.2	229.6	109.7	119.9	157.5	78.9	78.6	112.7	45.2	67.5
Electricity, gas, and water	7.6	7.6	0.0	1.3	1.3	0.0	2.5	2.5	0.0	3.0	3.0	0.0	0.7	0.7	0.0	0.1	0.1	0.0
Construction	11.6	11.5	0.1	3.0	3.0	0.0	3.2	3.2	0.0	3.5	3.5	0.0	1.4	1.4	0.0	0.5	0.4	0.1
Transport, storage, and communications	7.9	7.6	0.0	0.9	0.9	0.0	1.3	1.3	0.0	3.4	3.3	0.1	1.4	1.3	0.1	0.9	0.8	0.1
Total[a]	605.8	336.5	269.3	17.6	17.5	0.1	43.6	41.4	2.2	254.2	134.0	120.2	173.0	94.1	78.9	116.5	48.6	67.9

Source: Obtained by the author from Office of Labor Affairs, Korea.

a. Figures may not add to totals because of rounding.

{148}

Table A11. Employment by Agricultural and Nonagricultural Sectors,
Taiwan, 1969–73

Period	Number of persons (thousands)			Percentage		
	Total	Agricultural	Nonagricultural	Total[a]	Agricultural	Nonagricultural
1969 average	4,434	1,728	2,706	100.00	38.97	61.03
January	4,258	1,619	2,639	100.00	38.02	61.98
April	4,370	1,710	2,660	100.00	39.13	60.87
July	4,606	1,878	2,728	100.00	40.79	59.21
October	4,500	1,705	2,795	100.00	37.89	62.11
1970 average	4,546	1,672	2,874	100.00	36.78	63.22
January	4,480	1,635	2,845	100.00	36.50	63.50
April	4,473	1,662	2,811	100.00	37.16	62.84
July	4,723	1,804	2,919	100.00	38.20	61.80
October	4,508	1,587	2,921	100.00	35.20	64.80
1971 average	4,739	1,667	3,072	100.00	35.18	64.82
January	4,658	1,607	3,051	100.00	34.50	65.50
April	4,720	1,652	3,068	100.00	35.00	65.00
July	4,786	1,761	3,025	100.00	36.79	63.21
October	4,793	1,647	3,146	100.00	34.36	65.64
1972 average	4,873	1,609	3,264	100.00	33.02	66.98
January	4,804	1,612	3,192	100.00	33.56	66.44
April	4,836	1,565	3,271	100.00	32.36	67.64
July	4,966	1,660	3,306	100.00	33.43	66.57
October	4,885	1,600	3,285	100.00	32.75	67.25
1973 January	4,977	1,548	3,449	100.00	30.98	69.02

Source: *Quarterly Report on the Labor Force Survey*, Taiwan, various issues.
a. Figures may not add to totals because of rounding.

Table A12. *Employment Distribution by Industrial Sector, Taiwan, 1950–71*

	Primary industry		Secondary industry		Tertiary industry		
Year	Thousands	Percent[a]	Thousands	Percent[a]	Thousands	Percent[a]	Total
1950	1,560	58	513	19	638	24	2,711
1955	1,575	54	580	20	736	25	2,891
1960	1,648	51	680	21	881	27	3,209
1965	1,670	46	812	22	1,151	32	3,633
1966a[b]	1,586	43	850	23	1,211	33	3,647
1966b[b]	1,613	44	1,003	27	1,051	29	3,622
1967a	1,705	43	1,001	25	1,267	32	3,973
1967b	1,695	43	1,123	28	1,151	29	3,966
1968a	1,652	40	1,032	25	1,475	35	4,159
1968b	1,606	39	1,250	31	1,221	30	4,059
1969a	1,728	39	1,171	26	1,539	35	4,434
1969b	1,705	40	1,317	30	1,301	30	4,270
1970a	1,672	37	1,284	28	1,590	35	4,546
1970b	1,692	38	1,342	30	1,395	32	4,429
1971a	1,667	35	1,434	30	1,640	35	4,739
1971b	1,668	36	1,443	31	1,533	33	4,645

Source: Data for 1950–65 are from Shirley W. Y. Kuo, *The Economic Structure of Taiwan, 1952–1969,* Graduate Institute of Economics, National Taiwan University, 1970. Data for 1966a–71a are from *Quarterly Report on the Labor Force Survey,* Taiwan, October 1973. Data for 1966b–71b are from Manpower Development Committee, CIECD, Taiwan.
a. Percentages may not total 100 because of rounding.
b. Two estimates are shown between 1966 and 1971 for comparability with the earlier years.

Table A13. *Labor Force, Employment, and Unemployment, Taiwan, 1966–71*
(Thousands)

Year	Midyear popu- lation	Civilian population fifteen years and over	Labor force	Employ- ment	Unemploy- ment	Rate of unemploy- ment (percent)
1966	13,265	6,911	3,863	3,662	201	5.20
1967	13,594	7,205	4,174	3,966	208	4.98
1968	13,912	7,494	4,237	4,059	178	4.20
1969	14,236	7,784	4,467	4,270	197	4.41
1970	14,558	8,094	4,613	4,429	184	4.00
1971	14,880	9,023	5,438	4,645	188	3.46

Source: Manpower Development Committee, CIECD, Taiwan.

Table A14. Industrial Breakdown of Employed Persons, Korea, 1963–72
(Population in thousands)

Year	Total				Agriculture[a]					Manufacturing and mining					Other				
	Male	Female		Total	Male	Female		Total	Percent	Male	Female		Total	Percent	Male	Female		Total	Percent[b]
		Number	Percent			Number	Percent				Number	Percent				Number	Percent		
1963	5,146	2,801	35	7,947	3,097	1,925	38	5,022	63	496	193	28	689	9	1,553	683	31	2,236	28
1964	5,327	2,883	35	8,210	3,140	1,944	38	5,084	62	509	217	30	726	9	1,678	722	30	2,400	29
1965	5,499	3,023	35	8,522	3,068	1,932	39	5,000	59	630	249	28	879	10	1,801	842	32	2,643	31
1966	5,634	3,025	35	8,659	3,066	1,947	39	5,013	58	662	278	30	940	11	1,906	800	30	2,706	31
1967	5,763	3,151	35	8,914	2,979	1,945	40	4,924	55	786	352	31	1,138	13	1,998	854	30	2,852	32
1968	5,867	3,394	37	9,261	2,877	1,986	41	4,863	53	876	419	32	1,295	14	2,114	989	32	3,103	33
1969	5,998	3,349	36	9,347	2,902	1,896	40	4,798	51	891	444	33	1,335	14	2,205	1,009	31	3,214	35
1970	6,052	3,522	37	9,574	2,819	2,015	42	4,834	49	941	444	31	1,369	14	2,292	1,079	32	3,371	37
1971	6,095	3,613	37	9,708	2,716	1,993	42	4,709	45	909	466	32	1,464	16	2,470	1,154	32	3,624	39
1972	n.a.	n.a.	n.a.	10,026	n.a.	n.a.	n.a.	5,078	51	n.a.	n.a.	n.a.	1,423	14	n.a.	n.a.	n.a.	3,525	35

Source: Yearbook of Labor Statistics, Korea, 1972.
n.a. Not available.
a. Includes forestry, hunting, and fishing.
b. Percent of employed labor force.

Table A15. Labor Force and Others Fifteen Years of Age and Over, Taiwan, 1963–72
(Percent)

Year	Persons 15 years of age and over	In labor force				Unemployed	Not in labor force		
		Fully employed	Under-utilized	Total employed	Total[a] labor force		Potential labor force[b]	Others	Total[a]
1963	100	n.a.	n.a.	55.90	59.00	3.10	33.95	7.04	41.06
1964	100	n.a.	n.a.	56.07	58.63	2.56	33.96	7.41	41.37
1965	100	52.81	1.73	54.60	56.51	1.91	35.53	7.91	43.49
1966	100	51.66	1.31	52.96	54.66	1.70	37.23	8.12	45.34
1967	100	54.28	1.16	55.44	56.75	1.31	35.82	7.44	43.25
1968	100	55.43	0.69	56.12	57.10	0.98	35.18	7.74	42.90
1969	100	55.32	1.27	56.57	57.63	1.08	33.75	8.62	42.36
1970	100	55.09	0.86	55.95	56.92	0.97	33.77	9.32	43.08
1971	100	55.01	0.64	55.65	56.60	0.95	34.28	9.14	43.40
1972	100	55.31	0.62	55.93	56.78	0.85	34.15	9.09	43.23

Source: Quarterly Report on the Labor Force Survey, Taiwan, various issues.
n.a. Not available.
a. Figures may not add to total because of rounding.
b. The potential labor force consists mainly of those engaged in housework or in school.

Table A16. *Labor Force and Employment, Korea, 1965–68*
(Population in thousands)

Date	Population ten years of age and over	In labor force[a]	Employed[b]		Unemployed[c] (percent of labor force)
			Number	Percent of labor force	
October 1965	20,261	10,764	10,101	93.8	6.2
October 1966	21,336	11,757	10,936	93.0	7.0
October 1967	21,524	11,776	10,867	92.3	7.7
October 1968	22,932	11,371	10,471	92.1	7.9

Source: Korean Development Institute, unpublished data.

a. Persons ten years of age and over who are employed or unemployed according to footnotes b. and c.

b. Employed persons include unpaid household workers and those not currently working but due to start work within thirty days. Part-time employed workers are those working less than forty hours. Underemployed workers are those wanting additional work.

c. Unemployed workers include all those reported as seeking work on a full-time basis, as well as those wanting work but not seeking it because of temporary illness, belief that no work exists, or some other factor.

Table A17. *Male and Female Unemployment in Farm and Nonfarm Households as a Percentage of the Labor Force, Korea, 1963–71*

Year	Whole country			Farm households			Nonfarm households		
	Labor force	Male	Female	Labor force	Male	Female	Labor force	Male	Female
1963	8.1	8.7	7.2	2.9	3.3	2.1	16.4	16.5	16.3
1964	7.7	8.8	5.6	3.4	4.2	2.2	14.4	15.5	11.9
1965	7.4	8.4	5.5	3.1	3.8	1.8	13.5	14.4	11.5
1966	7.1	8.1	5.4	3.1	3.9	1.7	12.8	13.3	11.5
1967	6.2	6.6	5.4	2.3	2.7	1.8	11.1	11.1	11.6
1968	5.1	5.6	4.2	1.9	2.1	1.6	8.9	9.3	8.1
1969	4.8	5.1	4.3	2.2	2.6	1.5	7.8	7.5	8.4
1970	4.5	5.3	2.9	1.6	1.8	1.3	7.5	8.5	5.1
1971	4.5	5.2	3.2	1.5	1.7	1.2	7.3	8.1	5.7

Source: Yearbook of Labor Statistics, Korea, 1972.

Table A18. *Unemployment as a Percentage of the Labor Force in Selected Countries, 1960–70*

Country	1960	1961	1962	1963	1964	1965	1966	1967	1968	1969	1970	Average[a]
Canada	7.0	7.1	5.9	5.5	4.7	3.9	3.6	4.1	4.8	4.7	5.9	5.2
Japan	1.1	1.0	0.9	0.9	0.8	0.8	0.9	1.3[b]	1.2	1.1	1.2	1.0
Korea	n.a.	n.a.	8.4	8.1	7.7	7.4	7.1	6.2	5.1	4.8	4.5	6.6
Philippines	6.3[c]	7.5	8.0	6.3	6.4[c]	7.2	7.3	8.0	7.8	6.7[c]	n.a.	7.1
Taiwan	n.a.	n.a.	n.a.	n.a.	n.a.	3.3	3.1	2.3	1.7	1.9	1.7	2.3
United States	5.5	6.7	5.5	5.7	5.2	4.5	3.8	3.8	3.6	3.5	4.9	4.8

Source: ILO, *Year Book of Labor Statistics,* 1972.

n.a. Not available.

a. Arithmetic average for years for which data are available.
b. Change in design of sample.
c. Refers to different months than elsewhere in the series.

Table A19. Unemployment Rates, Taiwan, 1969–73
(Percent)

Period	Unemployment rates		
	Overall	Without experience	With experience
1969 average	1.88	0.97	0.91
January	2.12	1.06	1.06
April	1.55	0.65	0.90
July	1.85	0.98	0.87
October	1.99	1.18	0.81
1970 average	1.70	0.86	0.84
January	1.47	0.79	0.68
April	1.63	0.79	0.84
July	1.58	0.81	0.77
October	2.13	1.02	1.11
1971 average	1.66	0.86	0.80
January	1.63	0.74	0.89
April	1.61	0.73	0.88
July	1.75	1.01	0.74
October	1.62	0.94	0.68
1972 average	1.54	0.78	0.56
January	1.38	0.66	0.72
April	1.38	0.60	0.78
July	1.66	0.93	0.73
October	1.54	0.93	0.61
1973 January	1.32	0.67	0.65

Source: Quarterly Report on the Labor Force Survey, Taiwan, various issues.

Table A20. Monthly Variation in Demand for Labor as a Percentage of the Yearly Average, Taiwan, 1967–71

Month	Agriculture	Mining	Manufacturing
January	96.51	102.90	97.03
February	88.93	102.32	96.28
March	99.37	101.07	96.16
April	91.62	101.53	98.26
May	90.47	100.52	100.10
June	90.50	100.63	100.93
July	122.41	99.91	103.49
August	104.49	100.02	104.22
September	77.11	98.10	101.24
October	118.55	97.17	99.58
November	126.45	98.22	99.28
December	93.56	97.62	103.43

Sources: Department of Agriculture and Forestry, Provincial Government of Taiwan, *Report of Farm Record-Keeping Families in Taiwan;* Department of Statistics, Ministry of Economic Affairs, *Taiwan Industrial Production Statistics Monthly.*

Table A21. Employed Persons by Farm and Nonfarm Households, Korea, 1970 and 1971
(Thousands)

Period	Whole country	Farm households	Nonfarm households
1970 average	9,569	5,024[a]	4,545[b]
March	8,840	4,309	4,513
June	10,859	6,353	4,506
September	10,484	5,906	4,578
December	8,121	3,538	4,583
1971 average	9,708	4,846[c]	4,862[d]
March	8,998	4,437	4,561
June	11,060	6,060	5,000
September	10,598	5,409	5,189
December	8,175	3,478	4,697

Source: Obtained by the author from Economic Planning Board, Korea.
a. 52.5 percent of employed persons.
b. 47.5 percent of employed persons.
c. 49.9 percent of employed persons.
d. 50.1 percent of employed persons.

Table A22. Growth of Employment, Taiwan, 1953–70
(Percent)

Sector	1953–61[a]	1961–70[a]	1953–70[b]
Total employment	2.62 (100.0)	3.66 (100.0)	3.17 (100.0)
Agricultural sector[c]	0.66 (60.2)	0.26 (51.6)	0.45 (38.2)
Manufacturing	6.95 (10.0)	9.31 (13.9)	8.20 (22.3)
Construction	11.36 (2.6)	5.16 (4.9)	8.08 (5.6)
Services	3.90 (12.2)	5.47 (13.2)	4.73 (15.4)
Commerce	2.84 (8.9)	6.59 (9.0)	4.83 (11.6)
Transport and communications	5.01 (3.5)	4.93 (4.2)	4.97 (4.6)
Mining	4.73 (2.3)	−1.03 (2.7)	1.68 (1.8)
Total nonagricultural	5.17 (39.8)	6.52 (48.4)	5.89 (61.8)

Source: Data assembled for the author by CIECD, Taiwan.
a. Numbers in parentheses refer to percent of total employed at start of period.
b. Numbers in parentheses refer to percent of total employed in 1970.
c. Includes forestry and fishing.

Table A23. *Labor Mobility by Industry, Taiwan, 1967–72*
(Number in thousands)

Sector	Total		Primary		Secondary		Tertiary		Inflow into labor market by sector destination (1967–72)	
	Number	Percent	Number	Percent	Number	Percent	Number	Percent	Number	Percent
1967 total	3,984	100.00	1,669	100.00	908	100.00	1,407	100.00	1,231	100.00
1972										
Primary	1,559	32.05	1,367	81.91	12	1.32	20	1.42	160	19.53
Secondary	1,558	32.02	89	5.23	762	83.92	98	6.87	609	45.76
Tertiary	1,748	35.93	62	3.71	57	6.28	1,168	83.01	462	34.71
Total	4,865	100.00								
Outflow from labor market (1967–72)	349	6.55	151	9.05	77	8.48	121	8.60	—	—

Source: Manpower Development Committee, CIECD, *Survey Report on Labor Mobility in Taiwan*, 1972.
— Not applicable.

Table A24. *Labor Mobility, Taiwan, 1967–72*
(Number in thousands)

Sector	Labor force in 1967		Labor force in 1972		Percent increase 1967–72	Intersectoral flow to:[a]				Percent intersectoral inflow to 1967 labor force[b]		
	Number	Percent	Number	Percent		Primary	Secondary	Tertiary	Total	(a)	(b)	(c)
Primary	1,669	41.9	1,559	32.1	-6.4	—	12	20	32	1.9	2.1	1.9
Secondary	908	22.8	1,558	32.0	71.6	89	—	98	187	20.6	22.5	13.0
Tertiary	1,407	35.3	1,748	35.9	35.9	62	57	—	119	8.5	8.6	6.4
Total	3,984	100.0	4,865	100.0	22.1	151	69	118	338	8.5	9.0	6.8

Source: Computed by the author from table A23.
—Not applicable.
a. From the sectors listed in the first column of the table.
b. Column (a) is the ratio of transfers into the sector to original 1967 labor force. Column (b) is the ratio of transfers into the sector to 1967 labor force less those leaving the labor force during the period. Column (c) is the ratio of transfers into the sector to 1967 labor force as adjusted in (b) plus new entrants during the period.

Table A25. Average Monthly Rate of Accession and Separation of Labor by Industry, Korea, 1970 and 1971

	Accession rate			Separation rate		
Year	Mining	Manufac-turing	Construc-tion	Mining	Manufac-turing	Construc-tion
1970	4.7	5.4	3.4	6.2	6.0	3.0
1971	3.9	4.5	2.9	6.6	5.4	2.3
January	4.6	4.8	4.2	9.6	6.7	3.6
February	4.2	5.2	2.2	2.5	4.8	2.2
March	4.6	5.0	4.1	2.7	5.4	1.9
April	4.5	5.5	1.8	5.8	6.1	8.6
May	3.5	4.2	2.5	2.7	4.8	1.1
June	3.2	3.8	1.2	2.8	5.0	0.9
July	5.4	6.1	8.6	3.9	6.9	1.8
August	4.8	5.4	4.7	6.4	5.8	0.5
September	3.0	3.8	1.0	5.5	4.3	0.7
October	3.7	4.3	2.4	4.6	5.4	3.7
November	2.7	3.2	1.0	6.0	5.4	1.4
December	2.6	3.0	1.1	2.6	4.6	1.4

Source: Yearbook of Labor Statistics, Korea, 1972.

Table A26. Indexes of Money and Real Wages, Taiwan, 1968–72
(Percent)

Year	Agriculture		Mining		Manufacturing	
	Money wage	Real wage	Money wage	Real wage	Money wage	Real wage
1968 average	100.00	100.00	100.00	100.00	100.00	100.00
1969 average	118.85	116.43	110.59	104.89	110.78	105.47
1970 average	131.95	124.85	112.21	103.09	125.31	115.18
1971 average	138.89	128.04	126.87	113.41	137.06	122.45
1972 average	153.23	132.67	136.21	116.23	148.90	127.02
January	134.10	122.10	140.34	123.89	150.69	133.06
February	137.01	122.00	101.57	87.84	141.96	122.78
March	140.46	124.57	142.51	123.45	144.16	124.90
April	139.30	122.79	142.89	123.62	146.29	126.53
May	150.44	132.28	132.68	114.28	147.18	126.78
June	156.32	133.36	132.03	112.54	144.82	123.43
July	169.88	145.40	142.02	120.03	146.04	123.43
August	162.66	134.77	124.86	101.85	147.02	119.92
September	148.24	123.73	137.73	112.81	150.53	123.27
October	149.54	127.81	149.13	127.04	155.18	132.16
November	182.39	158.82	146.20	126.06	152.82	131.76
December	168.39	144.48	142.73	121.06	160.24	135.92

Sources: Bureau of Accounting and Statistics, Provincial Government of Taiwan, Monthly Statistics on Price Received and Price Paid by Farmer in Taiwan; Department of Statistics, Ministry of Economic Affairs, Taiwan Industrial Production Statistics Monthly; and Directorate-General of Budget, Accounting and Statistics, Executive Yuan, Commodity-Price Statistics Monthly, Taiwan District.

Table A27. Daily Average Wage for Male Farm Workers, Taiwan, 1972

Month	Wage (Taiwan dollars)
January	68.38
February	69.86
March	71.62
April	71.03
May	76.71
June	79.71
July	86.62
August	82.94
September	75.57
October	76.25
November	93.00
December	85.86
1972 average	78.13

Source: Monthly Statistics on Price Received and Price Paid by Farmer in Taiwan, October 1973.

Table A28. Monthly Average Wage by Sector, Taiwan, July 1972
(Taiwan dollars)

	Labor force		
Sector	Total	Male	Female
Manufacturing	1,792	2,317	1,371
Mining and quarrying	2,253	2,512	844
Water supply and gas	2,800	2,832	1,488
Personal service	2,292	2,659	1,887

Source: Directorate-General, Bureau of Agricultural Statistics, *Labor Statistics Pilot Survey Report,* Taiwan, 1973.

Table A29. Productivity and Wages of Agricultural Labor, Taiwan, 1960–71

| Year | Net output per household (Taiwan dollars) | Man days a year per household | Output per man day | | | Wage (Taiwan dollars a day) | Real wage | |
| | | | Current prices | Constant prices | | | | |
				Amount[a]	Index		Amount[b]	Index
1960	32,573.07	693.21	46.99	48.17	100.0	24.62	25.66	100.0
1961	36,876.07	573.43	64.31	63.89	132.6	33.04	33.49	130.5
1962	32,192.70	571.80	63.30	66.04	137.1	31.13	31.36	122.2
1963	40,097.50	591.69	67.77	65.75	136.5	34.43	33.87	132.0
1964	36,767.70	490.01	75.03	69.09	143.4	33.94	32.44	126.4
1965	38,791.50	518.31	74.84	69.63	144.6	34.81	33.03	128.7
1966	44,214.90	568.56	77.77	70.83	147.0	38.57	35.67	139.0
1967	46,406.90	576.21	80.54	71.55	148.5	38.35	34.23	133.4
1968	51,163.30	585.94	85.85	72.59	150.7	48.44	41.09	160.1
1969	39,580.60	489.53	80.85	70.19	145.7	54.50	45.31	176.6
1970	44,126.40	510.07	86.36	71.70	146.8	60.14	48.85	190.4
1971	50,013.10	462.44	108.15	87.23	181.1	60.74	48.70	189.8

Source: Based on data obtained from the CIECD, Taiwan.
a. Deflated by index of price received by farmer in Taiwan (1961–63 = 100).
b. Deflated by index of price paid by farmer in Taiwan (1961–63 = 100).

Table A30. Labor Productivity, Wages, and Real Wage, Korea, 1960–73
(Earnings and wages in hundreds of won)

	Labor productivity							
Year	Mining (index)	Manufac-turing (index)	Consumer price index	Average monthly earnings	Annual household earnings	Index[a]	Real wage[b]	Real household earnings[c]
1960	75.2	63.9	72.4	73.5	n.a.	n.a.	101.5	n.a.
1961	84.6	71.7	78.4	82.0	n.a.	n.a.	104.6	n.a.
1962	90.9	73.4	83.7	87.5	n.a.	n.a.	105.8	n.a.
1963	91.1	78.2	100.0	100.0	5,540	100	100.0	100
1964	92.9	85.1	127.9	121.5	6,540	118	95.0	92
1965	100.0	100.0	145.4	144.8	7,550	136	99.6	94
1966	100.7	104.0	163.0	170.3	10,370	187	104.5	115
1967	113.1	122.4	180.4	209.0	15,110	273	115.9	151
1968	113.7	146.8	200.6	264.3	17,700	321	131.8	160
1969	108.0	185.5	220.9	325.3	21,000	379	147.3	172
1970	125.1	209.2	249.7	408.5	24,320	439	163.6	176
1971	134.7	224.5	279.6	490.5	28,940	522	175.4	187
1972	n.a.	n.a.	312.6	577.8	n.a.	n.a.	184.8	n.a.
1973	n.a.	n.a.	322.1	n.a.	n.a.	n.a.	n.a.	n.a.

Sources: For consumer price index, International Monetary Fund, International Financial Statistics; other data from Yearbook of Labor Statistics, Korea, 1972.
   n.a.: Not available.
   a. Monthly earnings for wage and salary earning households for all cities in Korea.
   b. Monthly earnings divided by consumer price index.
   c. Index divided by consumer price index.

Table A31. Average Monthly Cash Earnings per Employee by Industry,
Korea, 1970–72
(Won)

Industry	April 1970 earnings	April 1971 Earnings	April 1971 Annual percent increase	April 1972 Earnings	April 1972 Annual percent increase
All industry	18,843	22,163	17.6	24,467	10.6
Mining	18,473	23,546	27.4	27,040	14.8
Manufacturing	15,523	17,737	14.2	19,668	10.9
Electricity, gas, and water	38,016	49,344	29.8	54,387	10.2
Construction	26,320	28,881	9.7	32,817	13.6
Wholesale and retail trade	29,643	33,917	14.4	38,719	14.2
Financing, insurance, real estate, and business services	39,469	45,750	15.9	52,251	14.2
Transport, storage	19,224	21,930	14.1	28,412	29.5
Other services	27,001	31,479	16.5	36,440	15.8

Source: Obtained by the author from the Office of Labor Affairs, Korea.

Table A32. Annual Rates of Growth of Selected Economic Indicators,
Taiwan, 1951–70
(Percent)

Indicator	1951–60	1961–70	1951–70
GDP	7.7	11.0	8.7
Private consumption	7.4	8.0	7.6
Government consumption	6.6	6.1	6.3
Gross capital formation	12.0	15.9	13.8
Exports of goods and services	9.2	22.0	15.4
Imports of goods and services	8.8	17.6	13.9

Source: *Statistical Data Book,* Taiwan, 1971.

Table A33. Indexes of Labor Productivity and Real Wage Rate
for Manufacturing, Taiwan, 1956–69
(1956 = 100)

Year	Labor productivity	Real wage rate
1956	100.0	100.0
1960	119.3	98.3
1965	168.5	128.7
1969	236.4	150.6

Source: *Statistical Data Book,* Taiwan, 1971.

Table A34. Disposition of Annual Average Family Disposable Income,
Taiwan, 1971
(Taiwan dollars)

Income groups	Disposable income	Expenditures	Savings
Under 10,000	8,070	10,644	2,573
10–20,000	15,798	15,296	502
20–30,000	24,424	23,703	721
30–40,000	33,742	32,018	1,724
40–50,000	42,966	39,717	3,249
50–60,000	52,109	47,706	4,403
60–80,000	65,225	59,193	6,032
80–100,000	83,817	72,388	11,429
Over 100,000	120,007	96,364	23,703
Average per family	46,342	42,027	4,315

Source: Report on the Survey of Family Income and Expenditure, Taiwan, 1971.

Table A35. Share of Personal Income Accruing to Different Income Groups,
Taiwan, 1964–70
(Percent)

Income group as percentage of population	1964	1966	1968	1970
Upper 5 percent	16.26	16.23	17.29	14.58
Upper 20 percent	41.05	41.43	41.37	38.36
Upper 40 percent	63.10	63.43	62.74	60.68
Upper 50 percent	79.69	79.62	79.32	78.05
Lowest 40 percent	20.31	20.38	20.68	21.95
Lowest 20 percent	7.74	7.93	8.11	8.55

Source: Prepared for the author by CIECD, Taiwan.

Table A36. Output and Investment per Unit of Labor, Taiwan, 1964–71
(Thousands of Taiwan dollars at current and constant 1963 prices[a])

| Year | Output per unit of labor | | Investment per unit of labor | | Ratio of investment to output (percent) |
	Current prices	1963 prices	Current prices	1963 prices	
1964	25,549	24,944	5,535	5,403	21.7
1965	27,902	27,958	7,260	7,275	26.0
1966	30,184	30,004	7,994	7,946	26.5
1967	30,276	29,799	8,976	8,835	29.6
1968	31,211	20,126	9,967	9,621	47.8
1969	31,338	30,308	10,017	9,688	32.0
1970	34,153	32,159	12,005	11,304	35.1
1971	36,846	34,662	12,842	12,081	34.9

Sources: Taiwan Provincial Labor Force Survey and Research Institute, Quarterly Report on the Labor Force Survey, various issues; and Directorate-General of Budget, Accounting and Statistics, Executive Yuan, National Income of the Republic of China, various issues.
a. Deflated by wholesale price index from International Financial Statistics.

Table A37. Monthly Income and Expenditure per Household, Korea, 1970 and 1971
(Income and expenditures in won)

Item	1970	1971
Persons per household	5.48	5.28
Earners per household	1.33	1.34
Income	31,770	37,660
Earnings	24,320	28,940
Other income	7,450	8,720
Expenditure	30,300	34,810
Food and beverages	11,480	13,460
Housing	5,150	5,950
Fuel and light	1,630	1,810
Clothing	2,980	3,240
Miscellaneous	7,050	8,060
Nonconsumption expenditure	2,010	2,290
Changes in assets	2,950	3,130
Changes in liabilities	390	300
Carry-over from previous period	750	940
Carry-over to next period	690	890
Net monetized consumption total	80	160

Source: Obtained by the author from Economic Planning Board, Korea.

Table A38. Indexes of Number of Employees Required to Produce One Unit of Value Added, Korea and Philippines, 1972
(Average each country = 100)

Product	Korea	Philippines
Consumer goods		
Food	103	96
Beverages	49	44
Textiles	135	200
Furniture and fixtures	192	263
Clothing and footwear	172	286
Intermediate goods		
Wood and products	109	200
Paper and products	83	89
Leather and products	111	263
Rubber and products	167	74
Chemicals other than pharmaceuticals	61	54
Nonmetallic mineral products	106	81
Capital goods		
Basic metals	102	118
Mechanical machinery	143	172
Electrical machinery	145	104
Transport equipment	127	113
Miscellaneous	233	44

Source: Calculated by the author from data furnished by Economic Planning Board, Korea, and Bureau of the Census and Statistics, Philippines.

Table A39. Sectoral Breakdown of Labor Force and GDP, Taiwan, 1953–70

Sector	1953			1961			1970		
	Percent of labor force	Percent of GDP	Percent of GDP/percent of labor force	Percent of labor force	Percent of GDP	Percent of GDP/percent of labor force	Percent of labor force	Percent of GDP	Percent of GDP/percent of labor force
Agriculture	57.0	34.4	60.4	50.0	27.4	54.8	37.0	16.4	44.3
Manufacturing and mining	20.0	16.3	81.5	21.0	23.6	112.4	30.0	31.9	106.3
Other	23.0	49.3	214.3	29.0	49.0	168.9	33.0	51.7	156.7
Total	100.0	100.0		100.0	100.0		100.0	100.0	

Source: The production data are from table A42 and the labor force data are estimated from table A12.

{169}

Table A40. Sectoral Breakdown of Labor Force and GNP, Korea, 1965 and 1973

	1965			1973		
Sector	Percent of labor force	Percent of GNP	Percent GNP/percent of labor force	Percent of labor force[a]	Percent of GNP	Percent GNP/percent of labor force
Agriculture	59.0	39.4	66.8	51.0	22.6	44.3
Manufacturing and mining	10.0	15.5	155.0	14.0	29.5	210.7
Other	31.0	45.1	145.5	35.0	47.9	136.9
Total	100.0	100.0		100.0	100.0	

Source: Production data are from table A43 and labor force data from table A14.
a. 1972.

Table A41. Changes in Relative Productivity of Labor by Sector, Taiwan, 1953–70
(Percent a year)

Sector	1953–61[a]		1961–70[a]		1953–70[b]	
For all sectors	4.36	—	6.20	—	5.33	—
Agriculture	3.62	(57.1)	3.72	(53.1)	3.67	(42.9)
Manufacturing	6.03	(140.5)	4.78	(155.4)	5.43	(137.2)
Construction	−4.41	(157.7)	5.59	(79.6)	0.88	(73.2)
Services	3.46	(169.7)	4.62	(160.6)	4.07	(140.3)
Commerce	1.76	(227.0)	3.76	(186.7)	2.81	(150.9)
Transport and communications	8.26	(100.0)	6.71	(126.2)	7.44	(130.4)
Mining	4.91	(127.8)	6.34	(135.0)	5.67	(138.5)
Total nonagriculture	3.26	(164.8)	5.07	(150.0)	4.21	(135.3)

Source: Calculated by the author.
— Not applicable.
a. Data in parentheses indicate relative productivity of labor by sector at start of period.
b. Data in parentheses indicate relative productivity of labor in 1970.

Table A42.　Rate of Growth of Real Output and Contribution to GDP by
Sector, Taiwan, 1953-70
(Percent a year)

Sector	1953-61		1961-70		1953-70	
GDP[a]	6.98	(100.0)[b]	9.86	(100.0)[b]	8.50	(100.0)[b]
Agriculture[c]	4.28	(34.4)	3.98	(27.4)	4.12	(16.40)
Manufacturing	13.00	(14.5)	14.19	(21.6)	13.63	(30.6)
Construction	6.95	(4.1)	10.75	(3.9)	8.96	(4.1)
Services	7.36	(20.7)	10.09	(21.2)	8.80	(21.6)
Commerce	4.60	(20.2)	10.35	(16.8)	7.64	(17.5)
Transport and communications	13.27	(3.5)	11.64	(5.3)	12.41	(6.0)
Mining	9.64	(1.8)	5.31	(2.0)	7.35	(1.3)
Total nonagriculture	8.43	(65.6)	11.59	(72.6)	10.10	(83.6)

Source: Directorate-General of the Budget, Accounts and Statistics, Executive Yuan, National Income of the Republic of China.
a. GDP is in 1966 prices; but because appropriate deflators were not available, the sectoral output
at 1966 prices was estimated by multiplying GDP at 1966 prices by the proportion of each sectoral
output to GDP both at current prices. This assumes that price changes in each sector were uniform,
and these data therefore contain some margin of error.
b. Numbers outside the parentheses are the percentage of annual increase in the gross product in
each sector, less the percentage of annual increase (or decrease) of the labor force employed in that
sector. Numbers inside the parentheses refer to the percentage of total employment at the start of the
period; data for 1953-70 are for the end of the period.
c. Includes forestry and fishing.

Table A43.　Sectoral Contribution to GNP and Sectoral Rate of Growth,
Korea, 1965-73
(Percent)

Sector	Contribution to GNP		Annual rate of growth 1965-73
	1965	1973	
Agriculture[a]	39.4	22.6	3.6
Manufacturing	13.9	28.4	21.2
Construction	3.3	4.9	16.6
Services	23.9	17.4	6.7
Commerce	13.7	19.0	15.7
Transport and communications	4.2	6.6	18.8
Mining	1.6	1.1	5.6
GNP	100.0	100.0	10.8

Source: Calculated by the author.
a. Excludes forestry and fishing.

Table A44. *Annual Percentage Growth of Labor Force and Contribution to GDP by Sector, Taiwan, 1953–70*

	1953–61			1961–70			1953–70		
Sector	Labor force [a]	GDP	Growth of GDP/growth of labor force	Labor force [b]	GDP	Growth of GDP/growth of labor force	Labor force	GDP	Growth of GDP/growth of labor force
Agriculture	0.75	4.28	5.71	0.12	3.98	33.17	0.35	4.12	11.77
Manufacturing and mining	3.00	12.6	4.20	6.75	13.53	2.00	5.10	13.37	2.62
Other	3.45	6.6	1.91	6.10	10.4	1.70	4.90	8.84	1.80
Total	1.80	6.98	3.88	3.40	9.86	2.90	2.90	8.50	2.93

Source: Calculated by the author.
a. 1953–60.
b. 1960–70.

Table A45. Annual Percentage Growth of Labor Force and Contribution to GNP by Sector, Korea, 1965–72

Sector	1965–68			1968–72			1965–72		
	Labor force	GNP	Growth of GNP/growth of labor force	Labor force	GNP	Growth of GNP/growth of labor force	Labor force	GNP	Growth of GNP/growth of labor force
Agriculture	-0.9	2.5	—ᵃ	1.1	4.1	3.73	0.20	3.4	17.0
Manufacturing and mining	13.5	20.6	1.53	2.3	25.7	11.17	7.1	23.4	3.30
Other	5.5	13.9	2.53	3.1	3.8	1.23	4.1	7.4	1.80
Total	2.75	10.6	3.85	2.0	9.6	4.80	2.25	10.3	4.58

Source: Calculated by the author.

a. Because the increment to the labor force in agriculture was negative between 1965 and 1968, agriculture's incremental contribution to GNP cannot be attributed to incremental labor during this period.

{Statistical Appendix B}

Indonesia and Philippines

Table B1. Population Projections by Age Group, Philippines, 1975 and 1980
(Population in thousands)

Age group	1970 base population		1975 projection[a]		1980 projection[a]	
	Male	Female	Male	Female	Male	Female
0–4	3,451.5	3,313.7	4,019	3,851	4,627	4,417
5–9	2,869.0	2,765.5	3,326	3,199	3,897	3,743
10–14	2,407.8	2,325.3	2,832	2,731	3,290	3,167
15–19	2,016.0	1,945.9	2,376	2,296	2,800	2,703
20–24	1,678.9	1,619.3	1,975	1,906	2,335	2,257
25–29	1,391.1	1,340.1	1,635	1,572	1,932	1,860
30–34	1,150.9	1,109.8	1,350	1,297	1,594	1,530
35–39	949.0	917.2	1,110	1,070	1,309	1,257
40–44	780.4	757.2	910	882	1,071	1,035
45–49	599.6	621.7	743	726	871	851
50–54	473.3	503.6	561	590	700	693
55–59	383.6	400.8	432	469	516	554
60–64	284.9	309.8	336	363	382	429
65–69	200.4	227.5	235	268	281	317
70–74	130.6	152.7	150	181	179	216
75–79	73.0	89.4	85	106	99	128
80–84	45.3	59.6	54	73	64	88
Total	18,885.3	18,459.1	22,129	21,580	25,947	25,245

Source: Bureau of the Census and Statistics, Philippines.
a. Including adjustment for emigration.

Table B2. Population by Age Group and Sex, Indonesia, 1961 and 1971
(Thousands)

	1961[a]			1971[b]		
Age group	Male	Female	Total	Male	Female	Total
0–4	9,152	9,276	18,428	9,653	9,508	19,161
5–9	7,571	7,524	15,095	9,577	9,295	18,872
10–14	4,763	4,417	9,180	7,326	6,902	14,228
15–19	3,567	3,635	7,202	5,673	5,748	11,391
20–24	3,529	4,354	7,883	3,556	4,406	7,961
25–29	3,630	4,543	8,173	4,033	5,009	9,042
30–34	3,555	3,779	7,334	3,664	4,230	7,894
35–39	3,140	2,914	6,054	4,019	4,061	8,080
40–44	2,457	2,310	4,767	3,004	3,026	6,029
45–49	1,923	1,869	3,792	2,399	2,248	4,647
50–54	1,487	1,477	2,964	1,888	1,947	3,835
55–59	1,052	1,040	2,092	1,074	1,061	2,135
60–64	820	812	1,632	1,034	1,189	2,223
65 and over	1,029	1,079	2,108	1,409	1,551	2,960
Total[c]	47,675	49,029	96,704	58,279[d]	60,181[d]	118,460[d]

Source: Central Bureau of Statistics, Indonesia.
   a. Based on 1 percent sample of complete returns.
   b. Preliminary data from advance tabulation, based on 0.3 percent sample of complete returns. Excludes rural Irian Jaya.
   c. Figures may not add to totals because of rounding.
   d. Totals from complete tabulations of 1971 census, including estimate for Irian Jaya, are: male, 59,103; female, 60,129; total, 119,232.

Table B3. Labor Force Participation Rates by Age Group and Sex,
Philippines, 1956–72
(Percent)

Year[a]	Aged 10 and over		Aged 10–24		Aged 25–44		Aged 45–64		Aged 65 and over	
	Male	Female	Male	Female	Male	Female	Male	Female	Male	Female
1956	73.4	41.0	55.1	35.9	95.9	48.6	90.1	47.6	47.4	18.0
1957	74.9	39.7	56.1	35.6	96.9	45.6	92.6	45.8	53.4	18.3
1958[b]	73.8	38.7	53.3	33.1	97.2	45.1	93.5	48.2	51.4	16.6
1959	72.9	38.3	51.2	32.6	97.2	43.6	94.1	48.3	56.8	21.6
1960	71.9	36.0	49.9	30.8	97.1	41.4	93.3	45.4	54.2	18.2
1961	72.1	39.5	49.4	34.1	97.4	45.6	95.1	47.1	54.5	19.6
1962	73.2	41.2	50.8	34.1	97.9	48.9	94.7	50.2	53.2	21.7
1963	71.0	39.1	46.9	33.2	97.9	47.3	95.0	47.3	51.4	18.9
1965	71.3	35.3	47.9	29.2	97.3	42.7	94.9	43.2	56.5	20.9
1966	71.3	38.9	48.0	32.3	97.6	47.4	94.9	45.7	57.3	22.6
1967	69.3	40.1	43.9	31.0	97.6	51.6	95.2	48.1	59.7	20.8
1968	66.1	33.3	40.2	25.8	96.0	43.4	92.3	40.0	55.1	14.2
1971[c]	67.2	32.2	41.1	25.2	96.4	41.7	92.9	38.4	52.4	15.6
1971[b]	68.1	32.7	42.6	25.6	97.3	41.2	93.3	41.0	53.5	17.8
1972[c]	67.8	31.9	42.6	24.2	97.3	41.6	93.3	40.4	57.3	15.4

Source: Bureau of the Census and Statistics, Philippines, Survey of Households for dates shown.
Before July 1, 1958, the survey was known as the Philippine Statistical Survey of Households.
   a. Dates are October unless otherwise noted. Data for 1964, 1969, and 1970 are not available.
   b. November.
   c. August.

Table B4. Seasonal Participation Rates of Urban and Rural Labor Forces by Age Group, Philippines, 1965–72

Year	Aged 10 and over May	Aged 10 and over October	Aged 10–24 May	Aged 10–24 October	Aged 25–44 May	Aged 25–44 October	Aged 45–64 May	Aged 45–64 October	Aged 65 and over May	Aged 65 and over October
Urban
1965	53.3	51.0	39.8	35.7	70.6	70.4	65.8	66.0	29.6	29.1
1966	51.3	50.5	37.9	34.1	68.1	71.1	64.9	67.4	25.0	27.9
1967	54.2	48.4	43.2	30.7	69.0	70.2	66.3	66.0	28.8	31.2
1968	54.6	46.5	40.7	28.7	72.8	69.1	67.9	64.0	30.6	27.2
1969	45.1	47.5[a]	28.9	30.8[a]	65.5	69.4[a]	60.7	61.7[a]	26.5	24.9[a]
1970	48.6	n.a.	33.2	n.a.	63.7	n.a.	63.7	n.a.	32.2	n.a.
1971	48.0	47.9[b]	32.1	30.6[b]	68.0	70.3[b]	62.2	63.4[b]	23.9	24.9[b]
1972	49.7	47.1[c]	34.8	29.7[c]	70.8	70.4[c]	62.2	63.4[c]	21.4	24.2[c]
Rural
1965	59.4	54.1	49.1	39.7	71.4	69.3	70.1	71.0	40.4	43.0
1966	59.4	57.4	49.4	43.3	70.5	72.1	71.9	72.7	39.9	46.6
1967	64.7	57.9	56.5	41.1	73.4	75.6	75.4	74.6	43.6	45.6
1968	64.7	51.2	55.4	35.5	75.2	68.3	75.8	67.5	44.1	38.0
1969	55.6	50.4[a]	44.3	34.2[a]	67.6	67.9[a]	69.1	68.1[a]	41.0	37.8[a]
1970	54.1	n.a.	43.2	n.a.	66.8	n.a.	68.5	n.a.	40.4	n.a.
1971	53.7	51.3[b]	41.9	35.7[b]	66.2	67.5[b]	68.3	69.3[b]	39.0	40.4[b]
1972	54.8	51.0[c]	43.5	35.3[c]	67.9[c]	67.5[c]	67.4	68.6[c]	38.4	42.5[c]

Source: Bureau of the Census and Statistics, Philippines, Survey of Households for the dates shown.
n.a. Not available.
a. August 1971.
b. November 1971.
c. August 1972.

Table B5. Projection of Participation Rates, Population, and Labor Force, Philippines, 1975 and 1980

Date	Aged 10–24		Aged 25–44		Aged 45–64		Aged 65 and over		Total		
	Male	Female	Male	Female	Male	Female	Male	Female	Male	Female	Both sexes
Participation rate (percent)											
1975	46.6	25.7	97.0	41.6	93.4	40.4	53.3	15.4	70.5	32.7	51.7
1980	46.6	25.7	97.0	41.3	93.4	39.1	50.5	15.0	70.5	32.4	51.6
Population (thousands)											
1975	7,183	6,933	5,005	4,821	2,072	2,148	524	628	14,784	14,530	29,314
1980	8,625	8,127	5,906	5,682	2,469	2,527	623	749	17,423	17,085	34,508
Labor force (thousands)											
1975	3,347	1,782	4,855	2,006	1,935	868	279	94	10,416	4,750	15,166
1980	3,926	2,089	5,729	2,347	2,306	988	315	112	12,276	5,536	17,812

Source: Bureau of the Census and Statistics, Philippines.

Table B6. Calculation of Participation Ratio Excluding 10–14 Age Group,
Philippines, 1965–71
(Thousands)

	Aged 10–14		Aged 15 and over		
Year	Population[a]	In labor force	Population	In labor force	Participation ratio
October 1965	3,986	530	17,017	10,234	60.1
October 1966	4,125	652	17,613	11,105	63.1
October 1967	4,269	550	18,229	11,226	61.6
October 1968	4,418	455	18,867	10,916	57.9
October 1969	4,573	503	19,527	11,266	57.7
October 1970	4,733	530	20,210	11,650	57.6
October 1971	4,899	549	20,917	11,739	56.1

Source: Bureau of the Census and Statistics, Philippines.
a. Estimated on basis of 1970 census and 1975 projection.

Table B7. Labor Force and Employment, Philippines, 1965–71
(Population in thousands)

Year	Population aged 10 and over	In the labor force[a]	Employed[b]	Employment rate (percent of labor force)	Unemployment rate (percent of labor force)[c]
October 1965	20,261	10,764	10,101	93.8	6.2
October 1966	21,336	11,757	10,936	93.0	7.0
October 1967	21,524	11,776	10,867	92.3	7.7
October 1968	22,932	11,371	10,471	92.1	7.9
March 1971	25,274	12,288	11,627	94.6	5.4

Source: Bureau of the Census and Statistics, Philippines.
a. Persons ten years old and over who are either employed or unemployed according to footnotes b. and c.
b. Employed persons include unpaid household workers and those not currently working but due to start work within thrity days. Part-time employed workers are those working less than forty hours. Underemployed workers are those wanting additional work.
c. Unemployed workers include all those reported as seeking work on a full-time basis; also those wanting work but not seeking it because of temporary illness, a belief that no work exists, or other factors.

Table B8. *Total Labor Force and Employment, Indonesia, 1971*
(Population in thousands)

Age group	Employed (1)	Seeking work (2)	Total (1) and (2) (3)	Crude unemployment rate (2) of (3) (4)	Ratio of unemployed experienced workers to labor force (7) of (3) (5)	Seeking work first time (6)	Unemployed experienced workers (2) minus (6) (7)	Experienced labor force (3) minus (6) (8)	Unemployment rate among experienced workers (percent) (7) of (8) (9)
Both sexes									
15–19	4,190.6	217.1	4,407.8	4.9	1.6	148.4	68.7	4,259.4	1.6
20–24	3,925.7	196.5	4,122.3	4.8	1.8	122.5	74.0	3,999.8	1.9
25–29	5,251.6	107.3	5,359.0	2.0	1.3	40.3	67.0	5,318.7	1.3
30–34	4,911.7	66.7	4,978.4	1.3	1.1	13.1	53.6	4,965.3	1.1
35–39	5,341.6	67.1	5,408.8	1.2	1.1	8.8	58.3	5,400.0	1.1
40–44	4,035.6	43.3	4,079.0	1.1	0.9	7.1	36.2	4,071.9	0.9
45–49	3,156.8	34.4	3,191.2	1.1	1.0	3.9	30.5	3,187.3	1.0
50–54	2,454.8	31.3	2,486.1	1.3	1.0	7.2	24.1	2,478.9	1.0
55–59	1,313.4	13.7	1,327.2	1.0	0.9	1.4	12.3	1,325.8	0.9
60–64	1,176.7	20.8	1,197.6	1.7	1.2	6.2	14.6	1,191.4	1.2
65 and over	1,187.0	16.2	1,203.2	1.3	0.9	4.9	11.3	1,198.3	0.9
Total[a]	36,951.1	815.0	37,766.2	2.1	1.2	364.3	450.7	37,401.9	1.2

Male

Age									
15–19	2,601.8	159.8	2,761.7	5.8	1.8	111.2	48.6	2,650.5	1.8
20–24	2,565.7	153.9	2,719.6	5.1	2.1	97.6	56.3	2,622.0	2.1
25–29	3,571.6	77.2	3,648.9	2.1	1.3	30.7	46.5	3,618.2	1.3
30–34	3,329.1	49.6	3,378.7	1.4	1.2	9.5	40.1	3,369.2	1.2
35–39	3,724.8	46.1	3,771.0	1.2	1.1	4.7	41.4	3,766.3	1.1
40–44	2,759.7	30.4	2,790.1	1.1	0.9	4.9	25.5	2,785.2	0.9
45–49	2,170.0	28.2	2,198.2	1.3	1.2	2.5	25.7	2,195.7	1.2
50–54	1,637.4	24.3	1,661.8	1.4	1.1	5.2	19.1	1,656.6	1.2
55–59	894.5	10.2	904.7	1.1	1.1	0.7	9.5	904.0	1.1
60–64	792.9	11.7	804.6	1.5	1.1	3.2	8.5	801.4	1.1
65 and over	841.2	9.2	850.4	1.1	0.9	1.6	7.6	848.8	0.9
Total[a]	24,891.7	601.4	25,493.7	2.4	1.3	272.4	329.0	25,221.3	1.3

Female

Age									
15–19	1,588.8	57.2	1,646.0	3.5	1.2	37.1	20.1	1,608.9	1.2
20–24	1,359.9	42.6	1,402.6	3.5	1.2	24.9	17.7	1,377.7	1.3
25–29	1,680.0	30.0	1,710.0	3.0	1.3	9.5	20.5	1,700.5	1.2
30–34	1,582.5	17.0	1,599.6	1.8	1.2	3.5	13.5	1,596.1	0.8
35–39	1,616.7	21.0	1,637.8	1.1	0.8	4.0	17.0	1,633.8	1.0
40–44	1,275.9	12.9	1,288.8	1.3	1.0	2.1	10.8	1,286.7	0.8
45–49	986.7	6.1	992.9	1.0	0.8	1.3	4.8	991.6	0.5
50–54	817.3	6.9	824.2	0.6	0.5	1.9	5.0	822.3	0.6
55–59	418.9	3.5	422.4	0.8	0.6	0.6	2.9	421.8	0.7
60–64	383.7	9.1	392.9	2.3	1.6	3.0	6.1	389.9	1.6
65 and over	345.8	6.9	352.8	2.0	1.0	3.2	3.7	349.6	1.1
Total[a]	12,058.9	213.7	12,272.7	1.7	0.9	91.8	121.9	12,180.9	1.0

Source: 1971 census, Indonesia.

a. Figures may not add to totals because of rounding.

Table B9. *Urban Labor Force and Employment, Indonesia, 1971*
(Population in thousands)

Age group	Employed (1)	Seeking work (2)	Total (1) and (2) (3)	Crude unemployment rate (2) of (3) (4)	Ratio of unemployed experienced workers to labor force (7) of (3) (5)	Seeking work first time (6)	Unemployed experienced workers (2) minus (6) (7)	Experienced labor force (3) minus (6) (8)	Unemployment rate among experienced workers (percent) (7) of (8) (9)
Both sexes									
15–19	531.8	78.2	610.1	12.8	2.7	61.6	16.6	548.5	3.0
20–24	700.5	88.8	789.4	11.2	3.4	61.7	27.1	727.7	3.7
25–29	879.7	33.5	913.3	3.6	1.8	17.4	16.1	895.9	1.8
30–34	830.3	20.0	850.3	2.4	1.6	6.5	13.5	843.8	1.6
35–39	794.0	12.9	806.9	1.6	1.1	3.7	9.2	803.2	1.1
40–44	637.1	10.0	647.2	1.5	1.2	2.5	7.5	644.7	1.2
45–49	458.7	10.6	469.3	2.3	1.8	2.1	8.5	467.2	1.8
50–54	348.6	7.6	356.3	2.1	1.8	1.1	6.5	355.2	1.8
55–59	185.2	4.5	189.8	2.4	1.8	1.0	3.5	188.8	1.9
60–64	118.8	4.0	122.9	3.3	1.9	1.7	2.3	121.2	1.9
65 and over	117.1	3.8	120.9	3.1	2.3	1.0	2.8	119.9	2.3
Total[a]	5,612.6	274.6	5,887.2	4.7	1.9	160.9	113.7	5,726.4	2.0

Male

15–19	345.8	54.9	400.7	13.7	3.3	41.5	13.4	359.2	3.1
20–24	503.5	67.9	571.4	11.9	3.7	46.5	21.4	524.9	4.1
25–29	676.2	27.6	703.9	3.9	2.0	13.5	14.1	690.4	2.0
30–34	638.1	16.6	654.8	2.5	1.8	5.1	11.5	649.7	1.8
35–39	592.1	8.7	600.9	1.4	1.1	1.9	6.8	599.0	1.1
40–44	471.4	6.7	478.2	1.4	1.1	1.5	5.2	476.7	1.1
45–49	343.5	8.9	352.4	2.5	2.2	1.3	7.6	351.1	2.2
50–54	251.5	6.0	257.5	2.3	2.2	0.4	5.6	257.1	2.2
55–59	130.6	4.1	134.8	3.0	2.5	0.7	3.4	134.1	2.5
60–64	80.0	2.8	82.8	3.4	2.3	0.9	1.9	81.9	2.3
65 and over	81.7	3.1	84.9	3.7	3.0	0.5	2.6	84.4	3.1
Total[a]	4,115.1	208.0	4,323.1	4.8	2.2	114.3	93.7	4,208.8	2.2

Female

15–19	186.0	23.2	209.2	11.1	1.5	20.0	3.2	189.2	1.7
20–24	197.0	20.9	217.9	9.6	2.6	15.2	5.7	202.7	2.8
25–29	203.5	5.8	209.3	2.8	0.9	3.9	1.9	205.4	0.9
30–34	192.1	3.4	195.5	1.7	1.0	1.4	2.0	194.1	1.0
35–39	201.9	4.1	206.0	2.0	1.1	1.8	2.3	204.2	1.1
40–44	165.6	3.3	169.0	2.0	1.4	1.0	2.3	168.0	1.4
45–49	115.2	1.6	116.8	1.4	0.7	0.8	0.8	110.0	0.7
50–54	97.1	1.6	98.7	1.6	0.9	0.7	0.9	98.0	0.9
55–59	54.6	0.4	55.0	0.7	0.4	0.2	0.2	54.8	0.3
60–64	38.8	1.2	40.0	3.0	1.8	0.7	0.5	39.3	1.3
65 and over	35.3	0.6	36.0	1.7	1.1	0.4	0.2	35.6	0.6
Total[a]	1,489.5	66.6	1,556.1	4.3	1.3	46.6	20.0	1,509.5	1.3

Source: 1971 census, Indonesia.
a. Figures may not add to totals because of rounding.

Table B10. Rural Labor Force and Employment, Indonesia, 1971
(Population in thousands)

Age group	Employed (1)	Seeking work (2)	Total (1) plus (2) (3)	Crude unemployment rate (2) of (3) (4)	Unemployed seeking work first time (5)	Unemployed experienced workers (2) minus (5) (6)	Employed workers (3) minus (5) (7)	Unemployment rate among experienced workers (6) of (7) (8)
Both sexes								
15–19	3,658.8	138.9	3,797.7	3.6	86.7	52.2	3,711.0	1.4
20–24	3,225.2	107.6	3,332.8	3.2	60.8	46.8	3,272.0	1.4
25–29	4,371.9	73.7	4,445.6	1.7	22.8	50.9	4,422.8	1.2
30–34	4,081.3	46.6	4,128.0	1.1	6.6	40.0	4,121.4	1.0
35–39	4,547.6	54.2	4,601.8	1.2	5.0	49.2	4,596.8	1.1
40–44	3,398.4	33.2	3,431.7	1.0	4.5	28.7	3,427.2	0.8
45–49	2,698.0	23.8	2,721.8	0.9	1.7	22.1	2,720.1	0.8
50–54	2,106.1	23.6	2,129.8	1.1	6.1	17.5	2,123.7	0.8
55–59	1,128.1	9.2	1,137.3	0.8	0.4	8.8	1,136.9	0.8
60–64	1,057.8	16.8	1,074.6	1.6	4.4	12.4	1,070.2	1.2
65 and over	1,069.9	12.3	1,082.2	1.1	3.9	8.4	1,078.3	0.8
Total[a]	33,413.6	595.2	34,008.9	1.8	231.1	364.1	33,777.8	1.1

{184}

Male

Age							
15–19	2,256.0	104.9	4.4	2,360.9	69.7	35.2	2,291.2	1.5
20–24	2,062.2	86.0	4.0	2,148.2	51.0	35.0	2,097.2	1.7
25–29	2,895.4	49.6	1.7	2,495.0	17.1	32.5	2,927.9	1.1
30–34	2,690.9	32.9	1.2	2,723.9	4.4	28.5	2,719.5	1.0
35–39	3,132.7	37.3	1.2	3,170.1	2.7	34.6	3,167.4	1.1
40–44	2,288.2	23.7	1.0	2,311.9	3.4	20.3	2,308.5	0.9
45–49	1,826.5	19.2	1.0	1,845.7	1.2	18.0	1,844.5	1.0
50–54	1,385.9	18.3	1.3	1,404.3	4.8	13.5	1,399.5	1.0
55–59	763.8	6.1	0.8	769.9	0.0	6.1	769.9	0.8
60–64	712.8	8.9	1.2	721.8	2.2	6.7	719.6	0.9
65 and over	759.4	6.0	0.8	765.5	1.0	5.0	764.5	0.7
Total[a]	21,967.1	428.8	1.9	22,396.0	175.8	253.0	22,220.2	1.1

Female

Age							
15–19	1,402.8	33.9	2.4	1,436.7	17.0	16.9	1,419.7	1.2
20–24	1,162.9	21.6	1.8	1,184.6	9.7	11.9	1,174.9	1.0
25–29	1,476.5	24.1	1.6	1,500.6	5.6	18.5	1,495.0	1.2
30–34	1,390.4	13.6	1.0	1,404.1	2.1	11.5	1,402.0	0.8
35–39	1,414.8	16.8	1.2	1,431.7	2.2	14.6	1,429.5	1.0
40–44	1,110.2	9.5	0.8	1,119.8	1.1	8.4	1,118.7	0.8
45–49	871.5	4.5	0.5	876.0	0.5	4.0	875.5	0.5
50–54	720.1	5.3	0.7	725.4	1.2	4.1	724.2	0.6
55–59	364.3	3.1	0.8	367.4	0.4	2.7	367.0	0.7
60–64	344.9	7.8	2.2	352.8	2.2	5.6	350.6	1.6
65 and over	310.4	6.3	2.0	316.7	2.8	3.5	313.9	1.1
Total[a]	11,446.4	166.3	1.4	11,612.8	55.2	111.1	11,557.6	1.0

Source: 1971 census, Indonesia.
a. Figures may not add to totals because of rounding.

Table B11. Experienced Labor Force by Sector and Sex, Philippines, 1972
(Population in thousands)

Sector	Both sexes		Male		Female	
	Number	Percent	Number	Percent	Number	Percent
Agriculture, forestry,						
hunting, and fishing	7,288	53.5	5,776	62.4	1,512	34.8
Mining and quarrying	62	0.5	51	0.6	11	0.2
Manufacturing	1,520	11.2	809	8.7	712	16.4
Construction	502	3.7	498	5.4	4	0.1
Service industries	4,217	31.0	2,113	22.8	2,102	48.3
Electricity, gas, water,						
and sanitary services	41	1.0	37	1.8	3	0.1
Commerce	1,728	41.0	720	34.1	1,008	48.0
Transport, storage,						
and communications	500	11.9	488	23.1	12	0.6
Services	1,948	46.2	868	41.0	1,079	51.3
Industry not reported	25	0.2	16	0.2	9	0.2
Total[a]	13,614	100.0	9,263	100.0	4,351	100.0

Source: Bureau of the Census and Statistics, Philippines, May 1972.
a. Figures may not add to totals because of rounding.

Table B12. Projected Employment by Sector, Philippines, 1973–77
(Thousands)

Sector	1973	1974	1975	1976	1977	Average annual growth rate
Agriculture	7,478.2	7,772.2	8,129.1	8,549.6	8,819.1	4.2
Mining	79.4	86.6	94.2	102.8	112.3	9.0
Manufacturing	1,787.4	1,876.1	1,999.6	2,158.9	2,188.7	5.2
Construction	354.6	380.6	405.0	437.4	631.7	16.5
Transportation	509.6	523.2	544.3	576.4	582.1	3.4
Commerce	1,678.2	1,734.3	1,800.2	1,807.2	1,919.9	3.4
Services	1,850.9	1,892.2	1,937.4	2,042.8	2,045.5	2.5
Total[a]	13,738.3	14,265.2	14,909.8	15,675.1	16,299.3	4.4

Source: Interim Manpower Plan for FY 1974–1977, National Manpower and Youth Council, Philippine Department of Labor. These data were derived by applying the fixed labor coefficient derived from the input-output matrix for 1965 to the growth targets (final demand) for the various sectors in the 1974–77 development plan.
a. Figures may not add to totals because of rounding.

Table B13. Seasonal Change in the Labor Force and in Employment, Philippines, 1965–71
(Population in thousands)

| Year and month | Labor force | Employed | | | Unemployed | |
		Agricultural[a]	Nonagricultural[a]	Total[b]	Number	Percent of labor force
May 1965	11,491	5,813	4,289	10,543	947	8.2
October 1965	10,764	5,563	4,251	10,101	663	6.2
Difference	−727	−310	−38	−492	−284	
May 1966	11,886	6,121	4,510	11,032	854	7.2
October 1966	11,757	6,149	4,514	10,936	821	6.9
Difference	−129	+28	+4	−124	−33	
May 1967	13,274	6,385	4,818	12,186	1,089	8.2
October 1967	11,726	6,153	4,384	10,837	909	7.8
Difference	−1,502	−232	−434	−1,349	−180	
May 1968	13,534	7,078	4,956	12,481	1,053	7.8
October 1968	11,371	5,481	4,713	10,470	900	7.9
Difference	−2,163	−1,597	−243	−2,011	−153	
May 1971	13,220	6,282	5,751	12,585	636	4.8
March 1971	12,288	5,488	5,885	11,628	661	5.4
Difference	−932	−794	+134	−957	+25	

Source: Bureau of the Census and Statistics, Philippines, Survey of Households.
a. Excludes those with a job but not at work.
b. Includes those with a job but not at work.

{187}

Table B14. Labor Force by Industry, Indonesia, 1971
(Population in thousands)

Industry	Both sexes				Male				Female			
	Total	Employed	Seeking work	Percentage ratio of those seeking work to those employed[a]	Total	Employed	Seeking work	Percentage ratio of those seeking work to those employed[a]	Total	Employed	Seeking work	Percentage ratio of those seeking work to those employed[a]
Agriculture[b]	24,946	24,772	174	0.7	17,001	16,876	125	0.7	7,945	7,896	49	0.6
Manufacturing[c]	3,045	3,022	23	0.8	1,616	1,599	17	1.1	1,429	1,423	6	0.4
Commerce[d]	4,152	4,113	39	0.9	2,353	2,331	22	0.9	1,800	1,783	17	0.9
Construction[e]	750	737	13	1.7	739	727	12	1.6	11	10	1	0.9
Public Utilities[e]	38	38	0.3	0.8	36	36	0.3	0.8	2	2	0	0.0
Transport[e]	932	916	16	1.7	914	898	16	1.8	18	18	0	0.0
Services	3,980	3,923	57	1.4	2,904	2,863	41	1.4	1,076	1,060	16	1.5
Finance[f]	98	95	3	3.1	81	79	2	2.4	17	16	1	0.6
Other[g]	1,749	1,593	156	8.9	886	773	113	12.8	863	820	43	0.5
Subtotal	39,690	39,210	480	1.2	26,530	26,182	347	1.3	13,160	13,028	133	1.0
Seeking work for first time	408		408		300		300		108		108	
Total	40,098	39,210	888	2.2	26,830	26,182	647		13,268	13,028	241	

Source: 1971 census, Indonesia.
a. Excluding those seeking work for first time.
b. Includes hunting, forestry, and fishing.
c. Includes mining and quarrying.
d. Includes restaurants and hotels.
e. Includes storage and communications.
f. Includes real estate and business services.
g. Activities not adequately defined.

Table B15. *Employment by Category of Worker, Indonesia, 1971*
(Population in thousands)

Category of worker	Both sexes				Male				Female			
	Employed	Seeking work	Total	Percent of total	Employed	Seeking work	Total	Percent of total[a]	Employed	Seeking work	Total	Percent of total[a]
Professional and technical	870	14	884	2.2	598	12	610	2.3	273	2	275	2.1
Administrative and managerial	1,359	15	1,374	3.5	1,096	11	1,107	4.2	263	3	266	2.0
Clerical	1,244	18	1,262	3.2	1,106	14	1,120	4.2	138	4	142	1.1
Sales	4,019	37	4,056	10.2	2,256	21	2,277	8.6	1,763	16	1,779	13.5
Services	1,486	26	1,512	3.8	851	14	865	3.3	635	12	647	4.9
Farmers	23,722	164	23,886	60.2	16,052	118	16,170	60.9	7,669	46	7,715	58.6
Other production[b]	4,682	51	4,733	11.9	3,204	44	3,248	12.2	1,478	7	1,485	11.3
Others	1,828	157	1,985	5.0	1,019	114	1,133	4.3	808	43	851	6.5
Subtotal	39,210	482	39,692	100.0	26,184	349	26,533	100.0	13,026	133	13,160	100.0
Seeking work for first time		408	408			300	300			108	108	
Total	39,210	890	40,100		26,184	649	26,833		13,026	241	13,268	

Source: 1971 census, Indonesia.
a. Percent of the total male or female employed and seeking work, but excluding those seeking work for the first time.
b. Includes transportation and equipment operators.

{189}

Table B16. Percentage Distribution of Family Income by Main Source, Philippines, 1971, 1965, and 1961

	Philippines		
Source of income	1971	1965	1961
Total annual family income (thousands of pesos)	23,714,334	13,023,610 (19,926,233)[a]	7,931,666 (5,070,165)[a]
Wages and salaries			
Agricultural[b]	6.3	7.2	6.1
Nonagricultural	38.0	35.7	35.7
Subtotal	44.3	43.0	41.9
Entrepreneurial activities			
Trading	7.7	7.8	9.8
Manufacturing	3.1	2.9	3.1
Transport	1.6	1.2	1.4
Other enterprises	1.4	1.2	2.5
Profession or trade	1.6	1.8	0.1
Agriculture	21.5	24.2	24.4
Subtotal	36.8	39.1	41.3
Other sources			
Share of crops, livestock, and poultry raised by others	2.5	2.8	2.8
Rent received for lands, buildings, or rooms and for other properties	1.7	1.5	1.4
Rental value of owner-occupied house	7.0	7.9	6.4
Pension or retirement benefits	2.1	1.6	1.7
Gifts, support, assistance, and relief	3.6	2.1	2.0
All others	1.9	2.1	2.5
Subtotal	18.8	18.0	16.8
Total percentage[c]	100.0	100.0	100.0

Sources: Bureau of the Census and Statistics, Philippines, *Survey of Households* and *Family Income and Expenditure Survey* for the years shown.
n.a.: Not available.

	Rural		
Source of income	1971	1965	1961
Total annual family income (thousands of pesos)	12,493,416	6,327,716 (9,694,061)[a]	3,512,793 (6,663,768)[a]
Wages and salaries			
Agricultural[b]	10.6	12.6	n.a.
Nonagricultural	24.5	18.1	n.a.
Subtotal	35.1	30.7	26.0
Entrepreneurial activities			
Trading	5.5	6.2	4.1
Manufacturing	2.8	3.4	1.6
Transport	2.0	1.0	0.8
Other enterprises	0.6	0.5	n.a.
Profession or trade	0.7	0.3	n.a.
Agriculture	37.2	44.6	61.7
Subtotal	48.9	55.9	68.7
Other sources			
Share of crops, livestock, and poultry raised by others	2.6	3.6	n.a.
Rent received for lands, buildings, or rooms and for other properties	0.5	0.5	n.a.
Rental value of owner-occupied house	6.6	5.5	n.a.
Pension or retirement benefits	1.6	0.3	n.a.
Gifts, support, assistance, and relief	2.5	1.7	n.a.
All others	2.2	1.8	n.a.
Subtotal	16.0	13.4	5.3
Total percentage[c]	100.0	100.0	100.0

a. Data in parentheses are at 1971 prices, derived by inflating data at current prices by cost of living index of *International Financial Statistics*.
b. Includes fishing, forestry, and hunting.
c. Figures may not add to totals because of rounding.

(Table continues on following page.)

Table B16 (continued)

Source of income	Total urban		
	1971	1965	1961
Total annual family income (thousands of pesos)	11,220,868	6,695,894 (10,258,109)[a]	7,981,766 (8,477,642)[a]
Wages and salaries			
Agricultural[b]	1.6	2.2	n.a.
Nonagricultural	53.0	52.4	n.a.
Subtotal	54.6	54.5	55.5
Entrepreneurial activities			
Trading	10.1	9.3	10.3
Manufacturing	3.4	2.5	2.8
Transport	1.2	1.4	2.1
Other enterprises	2.2	2.0 ⎫	3.1
Profession or trade	2.6	3.1 ⎭	
Agriculture	4.0	4.9	19.0
Subtotal	23.4	23.2	37.3
Other sources			
Share of crops, livestock, and poultry raised by others	2.3	2.0	n.a.
Rent received for lands, buildings, or rooms and for other properties	3.0	2.4	n.a.
Rental value of owner-occupied house	7.5	10.1	n.a.
Pension or retirement benefits	2.6	2.7	n.a.
Gifts, support, assistance, and relief	4.8	2.6	n.a.
All others	1.8	2.4	n.a.
Subtotal	22.0	22.2	7.2
Total percentage[c]	100.0	100.0	100.0

Sources: Bureau of the Census and Statistics, Philippines, *Survey of Households* and *Family Income and Expenditure Survey* for the years shown.
    n.a.: Not available.

	Manila and suburbs		
Source of income	1971	1965	1961
Total annual family income (thousands of pesos)	4,085,629	3,016,318 (4,620,000)[a]	1,728,429 (3,278,830)[a]
Wages and Salaries			
Agricultural[b]	0.2	0.2	n.a.
Nonagricultural	55.7	57.6	n.a.
Subtotal	55.9	57.7	78.0
Entrepreneurial activities			
Trading	8.6	6.4	8.6
Manufacturing	2.8	1.8	1.9
Transport	1.2	1.2	2.0
Other enterprises	1.8	1.8⎫	3.3
Profession or trade	4.1	4.8⎭	
Agriculture	0.3	0.4	1.4
Subtotal	18.8	16.3	17.2
Other sources			
Share of crops, livestock, and poultry raised by others	2.7	0.2	n.a.
Rent received for lands, buildings, or rooms and for other properties	5.5	4.5	n.a.
Rental value of owner-occupied house	6.8	13.0	n.a.
Pension or retirement benefits	3.3	1.6	n.a.
Gifts, support, assistance, and relief	6.4	3.9	n.a.
All others	0.6	2.8	n.a.
Subtotal	25.3	25.8	4.8
Total percentage[c]	100.0	100.0	100.0

a. Data in parentheses are at 1971 prices, derived by inflating data at current prices by cost of living index of *International Financial Statistics.*

b. Includes fishing, forestry, and hunting.

c. Figures may not add to totals because of rounding.

Table B17. Percentage Distribution of Annual Family Income by Amount and Main Source, Philippines, 1971, 1965, and 1961

	Total families					
	1971		1965		1961	
Source of income	Thousand	Percent	Thousand	Percent	Thousand	Percent
Wages and salaries[b]	2,727	43.0	1,996	38.9	1,598	36.0
Entrepreneurial activities						
Trading	392	6.2	317	6.2	274	6.2
Manufacturing	199	3.1	192	3.7	88	2.0
Transport	83	1.3	59	1.2	53	1.2
Others (including practice of profession or trade)	106	1.7	80	1.6	62	1.4
Agriculture[c]	2,455	38.7	2,229	43.5	2,090	47.2
Subtotal[d]	3,235	51.0	2,877	56.1	2,567	58.0
Other sources						
Landowner's share of crops	107	1.7	103	2.0	71	1.6
Rents[e]	17	0.3	13	0.3	9	0.2
Pensions and retirement benefits	60	0.9	37	0.7	49	1.1
Gifts, support assistance, and relief	160	2.5	86	1.7	97	2.2
All others	41	0.6	14	0.3	35	0.8
Subtotal[d]	384	6.0	253	4.9	261	5.9
Total[d]	6,347	100.0	5,126	100.0	4,426	100.0

Source: Bureau of the Census and Statistics, Philippines, Survey of Households and Family Income and Expenditure Survey for the years shown.

n.a.: Not available.

a. Inflated by the cost of living index from International Financial Statistics.

Annual income (1971 prices)[a]											
Below 3,000 pesos			3,000 to 5,999 pesos			6,000 to 9,999 pesos			Over 10,000 pesos		
1971	1965	1961	1971	1965	1961	1971	1965	1961	1971	1965	1961
43.5	41.7	47.3	33.8	35.5	31.1	14.5	13.0	12.4	8.2	9.8	9.2
49.3	47.9	41.6	29.4	32.3	37.2	11.6	9.4	7.2	9.5	10.4	14.0
61.8	61.5	62.5	23.8	29.4	20.4	7.4	6.8	8.4	7.0	2.3	8.7
45.8	56.3	34.3	34.9	33.9	43.3	11.2	4.6	11.7	8.3	5.2	10.7
38.1	43.2	38.7	19.6	22.2	27.4	22.1	10.2	17.7	20.1	24.4	23.7
78.8	77.7	86.2	15.9	17.9	11.2	3.8	3.3	1.8	1.4	1.1	0.8
72.1	72.2	78.4	15.3	20.4	15.3	9.2	4.5	3.5	3.5	2.9	2.8
70.9	63.0	67.6	16.2	26.9	12.7	7.1	2.8	11.8	5.8	7.3	7.8
31.9	45.4	35.5	15.9	4.5	14.9	42.0	23.8	14.4	10.1	26.3	35.2
24.9	24.7	40.8	15.5	24.6	28.5	22.0	16.2	14.8	38.4	34.5	14.5
67.9	70.5	85.5	14.6	15.4	11.3	9.2	10.8	3.8	8.3	3.3	n.a.
52.3	n.a.	n.a.	24.6	n.a.	n.a.	10.4	n.a.	n.a.	12.7	n.a.	n.a.
58.7	56.3	67.7	16.1	21.6	18.0	12.2	10.0	8.4	12.9	12.1	8.9
59.0	59.5	66.4	25.0	26.4	21.2	10.0	8.0	7.0	6.1	6.1	5.3

b. Agricultural and nonagricultural.
c. Includes fishing, forestry, and hunting.
d. Figures may not add to totals because of rounding.
e. Includes rental value of owner-occupied housing and land rents.

Table B18. Percentage Distribution of Families by Income and Region, Philippines, 1965 and 1971.

Annual family income (pesos at current prices)	Philippines (total) 1965	Philippines (total) 1971	Manila and suburbs 1965	Manila and suburbs 1971	Ilocos and Mountain Province 1965	Ilocos and Mountain Province 1971	Cayagan Valley and Bataan 1965	Cayagan Valley and Bataan 1971	Central Luzon 1965	Central Luzon 1971
Under 500	11.6	5.2	0.8	0.2	15.2	5.5	23.3	5.6	6.6	4.2
500–999	17.7	12.1	2.4	0.9	28.5	18.7	28.1	15.4	15.9	8.9
1,000–1,499	16.7	12.2	5.3	1.7	20.2	18.5	20.4	23.6	15.4	9.1
1,500–1,999	13.5	11.8	9.0	4.0	13.9	11.6	15.0	17.6	12.4	8.0
2,000–2,499	9.9	9.6	11.9	6.9	5.7	7.9	3.1	9.8	11.4	9.9
2,500–2,999	7.6	8.1	9.9	8.6	4.0	4.7	4.5	6.7	9.9	8.1
3,000–3,999	8.9	12.5	14.8	15.3	5.5	9.4	0.7	8.2	10.7	15.0
4,000–4,999	4.6	7.5	10.3	10.9	3.6	6.6	1.8	4.7	7.2	10.6
5,000–5,999	2.8	5.0	7.3	7.6	1.0	4.7	2.0	1.8	3.3	7.2
6,000–7,999	2.5	6.4	7.7	13.3	1.1	5.3	0.7	3.5	3.3	8.0
8,000–9,999	1.5	3.6	6.3	9.1	0.2	1.2	0.3	0.8	1.6	4.7
10,000 and over	2.6	6.1	14.3	21.4	1.1	5.8	0.3	2.1	2.3	6.2
Total percentage[a]	100.0	100.0	100.0	100.0	100.0	100.0	100.0	100.0	100.0	100.0
Median family income	1,648	2,454	3,720	5,202	1,555	1,814	975	1,652	1,984	3,118
Percent increase[b]		49		40		17		69		57
Average family income	2,541	3,736	6,590	7,785	1,633	3,299	1,322	2,390	2,595	4,127
Percent increase		47		18		102		81		59
Number of families (thousands)	5,126	6,347	458	525	302	346	175	260	739	855

{196}

Annual family income (pesos at current prices)	Southern Luzon and Islands 1965	Southern Luzon and Islands 1971	Bicol 1965	Bicol 1971	Western Visayas 1965	Western Visayas 1971	Eastern Visayas 1965	Eastern Visayas 1971	Northern Mindanao 1965	Northern Mindanao 1971	Southern Mindanao 1965	Southern Mindanao 1971
Under 500	6.9	3.9	11.6	3.5	9.7	3.4	21.0	13.7	10.0	4.3	14.9	3.2
500–999	10.3	8.6	19.5	18.1	20.1	8.7	22.8	18.9	19.9	14.6	18.9	11.8
1,000–1,499	12.6	11.2	22.3	18.0	22.0	13.8	18.8	13.1	15.8	14.1	17.3	9.6
1,500–1,999	16.2	10.1	13.2	13.8	15.0	14.8	13.4	14.1	12.6	12.8	14.4	13.6
2,000–2,499	14.4	8.6	7.6	9.5	9.2	13.8	7.4	7.7	10.0	11.1	11.6	10.9
2,500–2,999	9.9	8.2	8.1	7.9	7.7	10.9	5.9	6.8	7.8	8.2	5.0	9.2
3,000–3,999	12.7	14.6	8.1	11.0	8.4	12.5	5.4	8.7	9.9	13.5	8.0	13.5
4,000–4,999	6.3	8.3	3.3	5.4	2.3	6.6	1.5	4.4	4.3	7.5	4.0	8.0
5,000–5,999	2.9	5.1	4.2	3.3	2.0	4.3	1.5	3.4	2.7	4.8	1.5	5.5
6,000–7,999	2.5	8.8	0.6	1.2	1.5	4.7	0.9	4.5	2.9	4.9	3.2	6.5
8,000–9,999	1.5	4.3	0.6	3.6	1.2	2.9	0.7	1.7	2.9	1.6	0.4	3.8
10,000 and over	3.9	8.2	1.0	4.6	0.8	3.4	0.7	2.9	1.3	2.5	0.9	4.4
Total percentage[a]	100.0	100.0	100.0	100.0	100.0	100.0	100.0	100.0	100.0	100.0	100.0	100.0
Median family income	2,139	2,960	1,422	1,874	1,458	2,332	1,167	1,652	1,670	2,186	1,468	2,549
Percent increase[b]		38		32		60		42		31		74
Average family income	3,025	4,332	2,024	2,784	1,990	3,206	1,622	2,548	2,342	3,062	2,004	3,577
Percent increase		43		38		61		57		31		78
Number of families (thousands)	640	869	407	496	570	670	859	980	361	522	615	825

Source: Bureau of the Census and Statistics, Philippines.

Note: When the percentage increase in the median family income exceeds that of the mean, as in Manila, this can be considered evidence of a more even distribution of income. A substantially greater increase in the mean than in the median—as in Ilocos, the Mountain Province, and to a lesser extent in the Cagayan Valley—indicates a less even income distribution. For the country as a whole, little change occurred in income distribution by this test. Since the consumer price index (*International Financial Statistics*) increased by 53 percent between 1965 and 1971, it appears that the median increase fell by about 8 percent and the average increase fell by 11 percent for the country as a whole.

a. Figures may not add to totals because of rounding.
b. From 1965 to 1971.

{197}

Table B19. Distribution of Total Family Income by Deciles of Urban and Rural Families, Philippines, 1971

Decile of families from lowest to highest income	Share of total family income (thousands of pesos)	Percent of total income	Deviation from 10 percent	Cumulative percentage share	Average income within group (pesos)
Urban and rural					
First	295,445	1.2	−8.8	1.2	466
Second	576,792	2.4	−7.6	3.7	909
Third	836,272	3.5	−6.5	7.2	1,318
Fourth	1,096,446	4.6	−5.4	11.8	1,728
Fifth	1,390,774	5.9	−4.1	17.7	2,191
Sixth	1,743,929	7.4	−2.6	25.0	2,748
Seventh	2,168,039	9.1	−0.9	34.2	3,416
Eighth	2,813,178	11.9	1.9	46.1	4,432
Ninth	4,002,833	16.9	6.9	62.9	6,307
Tenth	8,790,577	37.1	27.1	100.0	13,850
Total[a]	23,714,284	100.0	71.8		3,736
Urban					
First	167,452	1.5	−8.5	1.5	876
Second	343,319	3.1	−6.9	4.6	1,795
Third	463,777	4.1	−5.9	8.7	2,425
Fourth	569,058	5.1	−4.9	13.8	2,975
Fifth	686,203	6.1	−3.9	19.9	3,588
Sixth	847,662	7.5	−2.5	27.4	4,432
Seventh	1,064,636	9.5	−0.5	36.9	5,566
Eighth	1,371,521	12.2	2.2	49.1	7,171
Ninth	1,869,798	16.7	6.7	65.8	9,776
Tenth	3,837,443	34.2	24.2	100.0	20,064
Total[a]	11,220,868	100.0	66.2		5,867
Rural					
First	183,685	1.5	−8.5	1.5	414
Second	343,434	2.7	−7.3	4.2	775
Third	481,008	3.9	−6.1	8.1	1,085
Fourth	629,742	5.0	−5.0	13.1	1,420
Fifth	780,020	6.2	−3.8	19.3	1,759
Sixth	963,134	7.7	−2.3	27.0	2,172
Seventh	1,207,877	9.7	−0.3	36.7	2,724
Eighth	1,525,835	12.2	2.2	48.9	3,441
Ninth	2,072,737	16.6	6.6	65.5	4,674
Tenth	4,305,944	34.5	24.5	100.0	9,711
Total[a]	12,493,146	100.0	66.6		2,818

Sources: Bureau of the Census and Statistics, Philippines, *Survey of Households* and *Family Income and Expenditure Survey,* May 1971.
a. Figures may not add to totals because of rounding.

Table B20. *Percentage Distribution of Family Expenditures by Location, Philippines, 1961, 1965, and 1971*

Expenditure	Total Philippines			Rural			Total urban			Manila and suburbs		
	1961	1965	1971	1961	1965	1971	1961	1965	1971	1961	1965	1971
Food	53.8	53.8	53.7	59.5	60.6	59.3	48.4	46.1	47.1	42.3	40.4	41.5
Housing	8.3	9.1	9.4	5.6	5.0	6.8	10.9	13.7	12.5	15.4	20.1	18.0
Wearing apparel	7.0	6.5	6.2	7.7	7.0	6.2	6.4	6.0	6.3	5.8	4.8	5.9
Health, education, and transportation	7.1	7.8	8.4	5.6	6.2	6.8	8.8	9.7	10.4	9.3	10.0	11.1
Miscellaneous	23.8	22.9	22.3	21.6	21.2	20.9	25.5	24.5	23.7	27.2	24.7	23.5
Total[a]	100.0	100.0	100.0	100.0	100.0	100.0	100.0	100.0	100.0	100.0	100.0	100.0

Sources: Bureau of the Census and Statistics, Philippines, *Survey of Households and Family Income and Expenditure Survey* for the years shown.
a. Figures may not add to totals because of rounding.

Table B21. Percentage Distribution of Population by Monthly per Capita Expenditure, Indonesia, 1969–70

Expenditure group (rupiah)	Urban and rural		Urban		Rural	
	Indonesia	Java	Indonesia	Java	Indonesia	Java
Up to 300	1.45	1.81	0.43	0.56	1.64	2.06
301–500	7.25	9.09	2.16	2.59	8.19	10.39
501–750	16.41	20.54	9.05	10.75	17.76	22.51
751–1,000	17.72	20.28	11.73	12.89	18.81	21.76
1,001–1,250	14.21	14.65	13.56	14.39	14.43	14.70
1,251–1,500	11.01	10.15	12.02	12.44	10.83	9.69
1,501–2,000	13.92	11.58	18.79	17.67	13.03	10.36
2,001–2,500	7.58	5.51	11.45	10.72	6.88	4.47
2,501–3,000	3.87	2.56	7.70	6.53	3.17	1.78
Over 3,001	6.57	3.83	13.11	11.47	5.37	2.30
Total[a]	100.0	100.0	100.0	100.0	100.0	100.0

Source: Survey Social Ekonomi Nasional (October 1969–April 1970), Biro Pusat Statistik, Jakarta, Indonesia.
a. Figures may not add to totals because of rounding.

Table B22. Daily Wage Paid on Estates, Indonesia, 1970 and 1972
(Rupiah)

Crop	January–December 1970			January–June 1972		
	Harvesting	Processing	Average	Harvesting	Processing	Average
Rubber	109.04	99.55	106.74	145.34	141.54	144.86
Tea	76.73	99.84	93.74	120.74	129.70	120.80
Coffee	76.66	68.17	76.81	96.00	91.15	93.85
Cinchona	62.91	50.18	42.60	127.23	101.14	112.91
Sugar cane	193.36	155.81	178.30	204.07	206.66	204.86
Palm oil	179.82	173.29	177.32	236.16	245.92	237.56
Tobacco	99.10	78.21	100.56	165.24	118.59	140.74
Chocolate	70.26	45.10	61.55	77.61	88.69	77.91
Hard fibers	166.15	75.59	136.05	146.80	132.05	136.47
Average wage	114.74	119.62	115.04	148.61	166.23	150.23

Source: Biro Pusat Statistik, Jakarta, Indonesia.

Bibliography

Bibliography

Books

Berg, Elliot J. "Wage Structures in Less Developed Countries" in A. D. Smith (ed.), *Wage Policy Issues in Economic Development*. Ann Arbor: University of Michigan Press, 1968.

Beyer, John. *An Economic Framework for Project Analysis in India: Some Preliminary Estimates*. New Delhi: Ford Foundation, December 1972.

Clive, W. R. *Potential Effects of Income Redistribution on Economic Growth*. New York: Praeger, 1972.

Dasgupta, Partha, Amartya Sen, and Stephen Marglin. *Guidelines for Project Evaluation*. New York: United Nations Industrial Development Organization, 1972.

Fisher, Malcolm R. *The Economic Analysis of Labour*. New York: St. Martin's Press, 1971.

Ginsberg, Eli. *Manpower for Development*. New York: Praeger, 1971.

Harbison, Frederick H. "Possible Solutions to the Problems of Unemployment in Newly Developed Countries" in *Manpower and Employment in Lower Income Countries*. Washington, D.C.: Agency for International Development, February 1971.

Little, I. M. D., and J. A. Mirrlees. *Manual of Industrial Project Analysis in Developing Countries*, vol. 2, *Social Cost-Benefit Analysis*. Paris: OECD, 1969.

Little, I. M. D., and J. A. Mirrlees. *Project Appraisal and Planning for Developing Countries*. New York: Basic Books, 1974.

Little, I. M. D., Tibor Scitovsky, and M. Scott. *Industry and Trade in Some Developing Countries*. Paris: OECD, 1970.

Mandani, Mahood. *The Myth of Population Control*. New York: Review Press, 1972.

Squire, Lyn, and Herman G. van der Tak. *Economic Analysis of Projects*. Baltimore: Johns Hopkins University Press, 1975.

Tinbergen, Jan. *The Design of Development*. Washington, D.C.: World Bank, 1958.

Turner, H. A. *Wage Trends, Wage Policies and Collective Bargaining: The Problems of*

Under-developed Countries. Cambridge, England: Cambridge University Press, 1966.

Turnham, David, and Ingelis Jaiger. *The Employment Problem in Less Developed Countries.* Paris: OECD, June 1970.

Articles

Arrow, Kenneth, Hollis Chenery, Bagicha Minhas, and Robert Solow. "Capital Labor Substitution and Economic Efficiency." *Review of Economics and Statistics,* vol. 43, no. 3 (August 1961), pp. 230–40.

Azzi, Corry F., and James C. Cox. "Shadow Prices in Public Program Evaluation Models." *Quarterly Journal of Economics,* vol. 88, no. 1 (February 1974), pp. 158–65.

Baghwat, Avinash. "The Main Features of the Employment Problems in Developing Countries." International Monetary Fund Staff Papers, March 1973.

Berry, R. A. "Factor Proportions and Urban Employment in Developing Countries." *International Labour Review,* vol. 109, no. 3 (March 1974), p. 223.

Bruno, Michael. "Estimation of Factor Contribution to Growth under Structural Disequilibrium." *International Economic Review,* vol. 9, no. 1 (February 1968), pp. 49–62.

Bruton, Henry J. "Economic Development and Labor Use: A Review." *World Development,* vol. 1, no. 12 (1973), pp. 50–55.

Chang, K. "Measurement of Employment and Unemployment in Taiwan." *Industry of Free China,* vol. 22, no. 5 (November 1964).

Crisostomo, C., and R. Barker. "Growth Rates of Philippine Agriculture, 1948–1969." *Philippine Economic Journal,* vol. 11, no. 1 (First Semester 1972), pp. 88–148.

De Wilde, John C. "Manpower and Employment Aspects of Selected Experiences in Agricultural Development in Tropical Africa." *International Labour Review,* vol. 104, no. 5 (November 1971), pp. 367–85.

Dixit, Avinash, and Nicholas Stern. "Determinants of Shadow Prices in Open Dual Economies." *Oxford Economic Papers,* vol. 26, no. 1 (March 1974), pp. 42–53.

Dunlop, John T., and Melvin Rothbaum. "International Comparisons of Wage Structures." *International Labour Review,* vol. 71, no. 4 (April 1955), pp. 347–63.

Frank, Charles R. "Urban Unemployment and Economic Growth in Africa." *Oxford Economic Papers,* vol. 20, no. 2 (July 1968), pp. 250–74.

Friedman, Milton, and others. "Determinants of Wages (Real and Money) and Prices." *Journal of Political Economy,* vol. 80, no. 3 (September/October 1972), pp. 10–20.

Harberger, Arnold C. "On Measuring the Social Opportunity Cost of Labor." *International Labour Review,* vol. 103, no. 6 (June 1971), pp. 559–80.

Harris, J., and M. P. Todaro. "Migration, Unemployment and Development." *American Economic Review*, vol. 60, no. 1 (March 1970), pp. 126–42.

Harris, J., and M. P. Todaro. "Wages, Industrial Employment and Labor Productivity: The Kenyan Experience." *East African Economic Review*, vol. 1, no. 1 (June 1969), pp. 1–15.

Hughes, Helen. "Scope of Labor-Capital Substitution in the Development Economies of Southeast and East Asia." World Bank Economic Staff Working Paper no. 140. Washington, D.C.: January 1973.

Jackson, Dudley, and H. A. Turner. "How to Provide More Employment in a Labour Surplus Economy." *International Labour Review*, vol. 107, no. 4 (April 1973), pp. 315–38.

Knight, J. B. "Wages and Employment in Developed and Underdeveloped Economies." *Oxford Economic Papers*, vol. 23, no. 1 (1971), pp. 42–58.

Krishna, Raj. "Unemployment in India." *Economic and Political Weekly* (March 3, 1973), pp. 475–77.

Lal, Deepak. "Disutility of Effort, Migration and Shadow Wage Rate." *Oxford Economic Papers*, vol. 25, no. 1 (March 1973), pp. 112–16.

Lewis, W. Arthur. "Economic Development with Unlimited Supplies of Labour." *Manchester School of Economic and Social Studies*, vol. 22, no. 2 (May 1954), pp. 139–91.

Lewis, W. Arthur. "Unlimited Labour: Further Notes." *Manchester School of Economic and Social Studies*, vol. 26, no. 1 (January 1958), pp. 1ff.

Lewis, John. "Designing the Public Works Mode of Antipoverty Policy." Princeton-Brookings Study of Developing Countries Income Distribution, September 1974 (drafted), pp. 8–9.

Mazumdar, D. "Underemployment in Agriculture and the Industrial Wage Rate." *Economica*, vol. 26, no. 104 (November 1959), pp. 328–41.

Miller, Richard U. "The Relevance of Surplus Labour Theory to the Urban Labour Markets of Latin America." *International Institute of Labour Studies Bulletin*, no. 8 (1971), pp. 220–45.

Oshima, H. T. "Labor Force Explosion and Labor Intensive Sector in Asian Growth." *Economic Development and Cultural Change*, vol. 19, no. 2 (January 1971), pp. 161–83.

Ranis, Gustav. "Industrial Sector Labor Absorption." Economic Growth Center, Yale University. Discussion Paper 116. New Haven: July 1971, pp. 30–32.

Reynolds, L. G. "Economic Development with Surplus Labour: Some Complications." *Oxford Economic Papers*, vol. 21, no. 1 (March 1969), pp. 15–55.

Reynolds, L. G. "Wages and Employment in the Labor Surplus Economy." *American Economic Review*, vol. 55, no. 1 (March 1965), pp. 19–39.

Ruprecht, T. "Labor Absorption Problems and Economic Development in the Philippines." *Philippine Economic Journal*, vol. 5, no. 2 (Second Semester 1966), pp. 289–312.

Solow, Robert M. "Technical Change and Aggregate Production Function." *Review of Economics and Statistics*, vol. 39, no. 3 (August 1957), pp. 312–20.

Stewart, Frances, and Paul Streeten. "Conflicts between Output and Employment Objectives in Developing Countries." *Oxford Economic Papers*, vol. 23, no. 2 (July 1971), pp. 150–60.

Stiglitz, Joseph E. "Alternative Theories of Wage Determination and Unemployment in LDCs: The Labor Turnover Model." *Quarterly Journal of Economics*, vol. 88 (May 1974), pp. 194–227.

Streeten, Paul. "Technology Gaps between Rich and Poor Countries." *Scottish Journal of Political Economy*, vol. 19, no. 3 (November 1972), pp. 213–30.

Todaro, Michael P. "A Model of Labor Migration and Urban Unemployment in Less Developed Countries." *American Economic Review*, vol. 59, no. 1 (March 1969), pp. 138–48.

Watanabe, T. "Improvement of Labor Quality and Economic Growth: Japan's Postwar Experience." *Economic Development and Cultural Change*, vol. 21, no. 1 (October 1972), pp. 33–53.

Wellisz, Stanislaw. "A Reconsideration of Shadow Pricing of Labor in Dual Economies." Paper published by the Institute of International Economic Studies, University of Stockholm, 1973.

Williamson, J. G. "Capital Accumulation, Labor Saving and Labor Absorption Once More." *Quarterly Journal of Economics*, vol. 85, no. 1 (February 1971), pp. 40–65.